W9-COL-584

"In a choice reminiscent of Kay Redfield Jamison in *An Unquiet Mind*, Shapiro writes about his own responses to Dr. Amelia's revelation. . . . Each season, book after book rolls toward the public pregnant with ruin. Here is a rare story about healing that seems earned." —*The Plain Dealer*

"Honest and perceptive. . . . A very sensitive and engrossing medical memoir." —*Publishers Weekly*

"[Shapiro] preserves an important message: Doctors are human beings who falter sometimes and must find solace before they resume their lives."
—*The Arizona Republic*

"A fascinating view of the interactions between a psychologist and his patient during the therapeutic process. . . . A revealing narrative of self-discovery."
—*Kirkus Reviews*

DAN SHAPIRO

Delivering Doctor Amelia

Dan Shapiro is an assistant professor of clinical psychiatry at the University of Arizona, and the author of *Mom's Marijuana*. An expert on physician self-care and physician-patient relationships, he has been featured in *The New York Times*, the *Chicago Tribune*, *Salon*, and on ABCNews.com. He lives in Tucson.

For more information, visit Dr. Shapiro's Web site at www.danshapiro.org.

Delivering Doctor Amelia

The Story of a Gifted Young Obstetrician's Error

and the Psychologist Who Helped Her

Dan Shapiro

VINTAGE BOOKS

A DIVISION OF RANDOM HOUSE, INC.

NEW YORK

To my brother, David,
who will always be *10-Boy* to me

Acknowledgments

I owe.

　　Most of all I owe my patients, who honor me by allowing me into their lives.

　　I owe the people who have trained under me: the psychology interns, psychiatry residents, and integrative medicine fellows at the University of Arizona, from whom I have learned so much.

　　I owe my former clinical supervisors: Harry Grater, Hugh Davis, Jacque Goldman, and Steve Boggs, at the University of Florida. I owe Arthur Klein, Bill Pollack, Walker Shields, and Joe Shay at McLean Hospital. I owe my mentor, Gerry Koocher, at Harvard. I owe Irv Yalom, Viktor Frankl, Elvin Semrad, Carl Rogers, Milton Erikson, and George Kelly, whose writings on the complexities of the human character and clinical practice have profoundly impacted me, and the legion of clinical researchers toiling away to separate science from lore.

　　The following people helped me by discussing or reading early versions of the manuscript: Ann Jones, Bennet Davis, Siquan "Ae" Todsen, Hugh Miller, Ken Fox, Kathy Fox, Charles "Chuckles" Brodsky, C. Eric Schulman, Joshua Sokol, Linda Salas, Gretta Brodsky, and Nicole Schulman.

　　I owe Deborah "Babbie" Tussing, Scott Freeman, Ron Wright, and the distance learning associate fellows in the Program in Integrative Medicine at the University of Arizona, who welcomed me into their professional lives.

I owe folks at the Iowa Summer Writers festival, including my teachers, Cecile Goding, Wayne Johnson, and all of the participants.

I am indebted to my writer's group, where I have found kindred spirits and terrific writers and thinkers: Diane Senechal, Charlotte Lowe-Bailey, Joanna Dane, and especially Jennifer Lee Carroll.

I owe my friends who read the book when it was nearing completion and who were particularly encouraging: Lois Bursik, Jonas Bromberg, Betsey Bromberg, Lynn Goolsby Coppola, and Audrey Schulman.

Two readers did close, critical reads and were enormously helpful. They are Rochelle "Ro" Bagatell and Patty Weiss Gelenberg.

I owe Andy Weil, a friend, writer, and brilliant mind, who has been enormously encouraging. I owe Alan Gelenberg, my boss at the University of Arizona, who continued to support me even after I made his life harder by sneaking off the tenure track to see patients and write books.

I owe Shaye Areheart, my editor, whose consistent confidence in my writing has been one of life's staggering surprises. Thanks also go to the Crown Publishing Group and Jenny Frost, Tina Constable, Sara Kippur, Teryn Johnson, Jean Lynch, Jason Gordon, Fearn Cutler de Vicq, and my independent publicist, Tammy Richards-LeSure. I especially owe Whitney Cookman, who designed the beautiful book jacket.

I owe Judith Riven, my agent, who is editor, advocate, and literary mother.

I owe my parents, Ann and Mark Shapiro, and my children, Alexandra and Abigail Shapiro, for always reminding me of the importance of creativity.

David Shapiro, my brother, has remained my most dedicated reader, having been through the manuscript countless times. He helped with my first book as well, and was particularly skilled at getting me to give up passages that I loved, but that had no business occupying space in the book. For example, during the writing of my first book, *Mom's Marijuana,* I wrote a lovely passage about the Northern Lights and the first people who crossed the Bering Strait. In retrospect, it was horrible stuff. David gently told me I had to get rid of it. During the rewriting of this book we discovered the "track changes" tool in Microsoft Word. Using track changes, we could e-mail the document back and forth, and I could see, in red, text David thought I should change or edit. During one particularly dark period of editing, when I felt the book was hopeless, I found that David had reinserted the Northern Lights passage in a uniquely bad spot, perhaps to remind me of how far I've come, or perhaps to torture me in the way that only a brother can. Despite that, I love him and am deeply grateful.

And above all, I owe Terry, who supported me writing at all hours of the day. And who read in the car and in bed late at night, and who put up with me interrupting her to ask questions or to make her read a paragraph, and who drove around during the last twenty minutes of our babysitter's time on a cool Tucson night in October and helped title the book. I love her with all my heart.

What shall we think of a well-adjusted slave?

—Abraham Maslow

Only the wounded doctor can heal.

—Carl Jung

One becomes a therapist because of his own desperation.

—Elvin Semrad

Author's Note

While writing this book my love of narrative nonfiction has collided with my professional obligation to protect my patient's confidentiality. I have tried to be loyal to both professions. I have rendered my patient unrecognizable by disguising details and in a few places have combined the experiences of two patients. In all of my decisions I have labored to preserve my patient's core and fundamental issues, as well as the pace, tone, and outcome of our work. My patient is aware of this book and has read early versions; she is satisfied that her confidentiality has been protected and that the story matches important parts of her experience. As a result, I consider most of this work narrative nonfiction, but there are sections that have been fabricated to protect her identity.

The sentiment I'm trying to convey was better described by Mark Twain in the opening of *The Adventures of Huckleberry Finn*: "There was things he stretched, but mainly he told the truth."

Prelude: Lauren

I sat behind Lauren Riley in seventh-grade English. Like me, Lauren was a camouflaged soul, invisible to peers. She was bright and always had some precocious book in her bag like Richard Bach's *Jonathan Livingston Seagull* or J. D. Salinger's *Franny and Zooey*. The protagonists were always smart and sensitive and misunderstood.

In the race toward puberty Lauren was behind most. She was a little heavy around the middle, as if the extra stores of toddlerhood had never burned off. Breasts, which had a magical power over me, were starting to make their first appearance among our most advanced female classmates, but Lauren remained flat. She had long, straight brown hair and split ends. Her clothing was always conservative and never quite fit. She usually dressed in dark colors and some of her dresses were homemade, the stitching obvious. Our lockers adjoined. The inside of her locker door was covered with newspaper articles about famous women pilots and politicians and a carefully written list of countries she wanted to travel to in alphabetical order—1) Canada, 2) Denmark, all the way down to 10) USSR—with only Canada checked off at the top.

In seventh grade, notebooks were our vanity plates. At the time, heavy blue canvas three-ring binders were the most common. Using one of them, I could keep all of my subject notes in one place, making organization easy. Most students scrawled across the fronts of them. JESSE AND RACHEL, TRUE LOVE

FOREVER. Or the names of rock bands: BLUE OYSTER CULT and AC/DC. Or sports teams: RED SOX, PATRIOTS, or CELTICS RULE. Lauren carried separate notebooks for each class and had the names of famous women written on her binders. For science, she had MADAME CURIE written in neat cursive on the front of the notebook, and HARRIET TUBMAN for history.

She redefined quiet. In English, if Ms. Pearlman asked an open question such as, "There are four points of extra credit toward your next test grade to anyone who can answer this very special question, a very challenging question," Lauren would sit as still as an oak and drop her head toward her desk.

"Who can tell me why Holden lied so often?" Ms. Pearlman asked us once. We'd been reading *The Catcher in the Rye.* I thought it was funny that he lied so much but I had no idea why. There was silence in the room as Ms. Pearlman slowly walked down our aisle. Paul Croteau and I figured it out once, that she paced a few miles every day up and down the aisles. Ms. Pearlman could wait for an answer. She was as patient as a stalker.

Ms. Pearlman arrived at Lauren's desk and smiled gently at her. "Lauren."

And Lauren said, without moving even a hair, "Maybe Holden lied to shield himself so that people would never really get to know him?," her soft voice disappearing into her desk. Ms. Pearlman smiled and repeated Lauren, as if she were translating for the rest of us, "That's right. Holden lied to shield himself," and then Lauren and Ms. Pearlman stared at one another, Lauren's eyes wide open like a scared rabbit, afraid of a follow-up question. Then Ms. Pearlman turned and continued up the aisle and Lauren exhaled softly into her hand.

Ms. Pearlman often tried to get Lauren to repeat whatever she'd said. When she asked us to explain why the man in "The Tell-Tale Heart" heard the pounding under the floor, four of us had provided answers like "Killing people makes your senses intense" or "The guy had, like, come back to life, man." Lauren said flatly, "He felt guilty." Ms. Pearlman prodded Lauren a few times to repeat herself until her voice was loud enough to be heard beyond her own desk, and then Ms. Pearlman stopped pacing. She smiled directly at Lauren, as if they had shared a private confidence. We all looked from one to the other, as if we were at a tennis match, before Ms. Pearlman went back to her pacing.

I teased Lauren every now and then. Her hair was so long that it occasionally covered my desk when she sat down, long brown strands fanning out across the surface like a peacock's tail. A few times I'd kneeled on my chair and put my head under her hair and asked David Roth to look at me.

"Check me out, I'm Lauren's twin brother." Lauren would spin quickly, a frown at first, and then a slight smile, and she'd gather her hair together and hold it to her chest. She never said anything, but I knew she wasn't angry.

One morning before English, I went to sit in my seat behind Lauren and found a note on my chair. It was folded in the "note" style, an elaborate origami square with triangular folds that made the note small and tight. Across it was my name written in neat cursive. I fought to open it and then stared at Lauren's careful handwriting. *I need to tell you something . . .* it read.

I said, "What's up?" but Lauren was turned away from me in her chair, her head down, and she didn't turn around. I waited. No response. I wrote a question mark below her writing on the note and tried to fold it back up in the right style but I couldn't get the final flap to fit. I gave up and dropped it back over her shoulder.

She opened it. While she wrote I considered the note and perked up. Recently I'd started to identify new feelings. One of them was for Lauren's best friend, a girl named Debbie. Notes were a common way to share romantic information because a friend could act as an ambassador and keep the evidence of everything said on both sides. The rules of adolescent diplomacy were elaborate and serious.

The note landed back on my desk. Folded perfectly as before. I struggled and then unwrapped it. *You can't tell a soul.* Standard procedure. I studied the letters. They were perfectly formed, the *Y* written in cursive looped perfectly. I scribbled "OK" and didn't even try to fold the note up properly. I dropped it again over her shoulder. Her head bowed and she scribbled more. Then she turned in her seat and looked back at me squarely and put the note on my desk, unfolded. Beneath my hastily scrawled "OK" was her response.

It's about me and my dad. I don't know what to do.

Not about Debbie. I sank. Lauren spun back around, leaving me staring into her fleshy neck. At the time, marital disputes were an epidemic. A lot of our friends' parents were divorcing. When Cathy Fox had suddenly vanished from math, Roland Cheyney had told me, "Her mother is taking her back to South Dakota where she's from. Man, like, it snows every day and it never gets above twenty degrees there." That night at dinner I'd studied my parents and cleared the dishes without being reminded. Maybe Lauren is going to have to live with her father?

There was some activity in the class and Ms. Pearlman quietly said, "Hush up, now," and then told all of us to turn to page 121 of our readers. Lauren reached under her desk and pulled up her Edgar Allan Poe reader. Then she folded her hands over her book, the ready student.

I wrote another *??* on the note and this time folded it to the best of my ability. When Ms. Pearlman looked down into her book and began to walk, her back to me for a moment, I slid the note around, onto Lauren's lap. She let it sit there. I pulled up my book, quickly found page 121, and waited. I felt eyes on me and looked at Ms. Pearlman, but she was opening her book and said, "The Raven." Looking to my left, I saw David Roth looking at me. He put his eyes toward Lauren, nodding slightly and then toward me, as if asking if we were "going out."

I gave him the finger, hiding it behind my other hand.

Ms. Pearlman told Michael Almonte to read. He was in the dreaded first spot in the front of the room in the corner. Michael was a bright kid who hated to read aloud but after a brief complaint, he complied and started with a slow pace, his voice carrying the slightest Italian accent.

Once upon a midnight dreary, while I pondered, weak and weary,
Over many a quaint and curious volume of forgotten lore . . .

I'd met Lauren's dad once when he came to pick her up because Lauren's mother was sick. She was sick quite a bit. Mr. Riley was a short, slight man with a lot of hair. He wore black glasses that were too big for his face and had a chain on his belt that disappeared into his pocket. His pants were always baggy, as if he'd lost fifty pounds but had never bought new clothing.

The note landed back on my desk, again folded fastidiously. I used my pencil to pry it open. Ms. Pearlman asked Wallace Crenshaw, sitting next to Michael, to read next. Wallace barked out each word as if doing the play-by-play at a baseball game. Whenever he tripped over a word he started the entire sentence over.

I looked at Ms. Pearlman. She mouthed the words, as if she could magically help Wally read the lines accurately. I looked down into the note.

My father touches me.

Suddenly my mouth was dry and my whole body went stiff. Wallace Crenshaw's staccato rendition of "The Raven" screamed in my ears.

"'Tis some visitor," I muttered, "tapping at my chamber door;
Only this, and nothing more."

And there it was. It descended on me like a curtain. A divide between childhood and adulthood, Lauren perched on one side, her plump childlike body holding out her hand to me, and I still on the other. My face felt hot.

I wrote, *Tell your mom?* and handed it around her into her lap.

She wrote for a few moments and I listened to Wallace pound out Poe's poem. Lauren's note landed back on my lap. *No way.* <u>*Would kill her.*</u> Ms. Pearlman called on someone else and I sat listening, my pencil hovering over the note. A fantasy brewed of me waiting with three friends for Lauren's father outside of Connecticut General, where he worked as an actuary. All of us wearing masks and carrying baseball bats. It would be dark. "Working late, Mr. Riley?" I'd ask him. Then we'd surround him and he'd ask who we were and what we wanted. I'd beat the bat in my hands a few times, like in the union movie, just to show we were serious, and his eyes would open wide. Maybe he'd pull out his wallet and offer it. "We don't want your fucking money," one of us would say. Then I'd say, "If you touch your daughter again, we'll kill you." My voice would be deep and powerful, like Paul Robeson's or Darth Vader's. I felt a rush of adrenaline and my head felt clearer.

She needed to be rescued. *Call the cops,* I wrote. I handed it over and Lauren read it and shook her head while she carefully wrote a response. What was wrong with calling the cops?

I looked up and Leo Gerome was reading.

And the silken sad uncertain rustling of each purple curtain
Thrilled me—filled me with fantastic terrors never felt before. . . . .

Lauren handed the note back. I opened it.

Won't work. Don't want foster care. They could take me and my little brother away. If the police didn't believe me, I'd be stuck with my father, and he'd know I'd told on him, then what?

I didn't have a response. I sat in the chair feeling restless. There had to be an answer. A good answer. There's always a solution. Isn't there? Lauren spun in her chair, grabbed the note, folded it up, and the exchange was over.

That evening, at home, I got down the yellow pages and looked up the number of an anonymous help line in Hartford. Then I called Lauren; her family's number was in the book. An adult male voice answered the phone and said, "Who is this again?" after I had already told him. When Lauren came on I asked how she was.

"Fine," she said, curtly. I heard his voice in the background asking who the hell it was. I realized it was probably the first time Lauren had been called by a boy.

I said, "I got the number of a hotline, for people in . . . you know . . . the same situation. Uh, it's . . ." and I read off the number quickly, but I could tell she wasn't writing it down. Then she said, matter-of-factly, "I have to go." And she clicked off.

I stood for a moment listening to the dial tone. It hadn't gone at all as I'd expected. On the bus, on the way home, I'd imagined us talking for an hour, and me eventually giving her the number. Of course, in my fantasy she didn't really need it anymore, because I'd been so helpful and, somehow, telling me had solved everything. I fantasized about her telling all of our friends, and especially Debbie, what a decent guy I was, how mature.

Then I began to worry. Maybe I shouldn't have given her so much advice? Maybe I should tell my parents? But that would probably make things worse; they'd call the cops, or the school principal, or reporters. Lack of assertiveness was never one of their shortcomings. I hung up and went down to my room, turned on a comedy show, and tried to forget it.

Lauren and I never spoke about it again. I didn't have the courage to ask her what had happened. Or even how she was. I stopped teasing her. I think I stopped talking to her altogether. When I saw her in the halls she usually had her head down, her notebooks pulled to her chest. When I saw her at her locker I waited for her to leave and then went to my locker.

Two years later, when we were in ninth grade, Lauren suddenly disappeared. She just didn't show up for school one day.

There were rumors about her being pregnant, or a secret pot-head, or that she was involuntarily put into a hospital up in Boston.

I never saw her again.

It's been twenty-two years since I last spoke with Lauren. I'm a clinical psychologist now. I can't say what impact she had on my choice of career, only that she's never far from my mind when I'm doing therapy. I'm still terrified that someone will keep something hidden from me for a long time, and when they do tell me the truth, I'll be useless. When they finally beg me to throw something into the frothy water to save them I'll scurry along the banks, frantic, unable to find anything that will help.

Session One

Dr. Amelia Sorvino's reputation preceded her. She was an obstetrician on our faculty, a rising star and a favorite physician with pregnant moms in the community. When I said her name in the waiting room she smiled at me, a warm open smile, and stood up. She had full lips and dimples, light gray eyes, and wore no makeup. A beautiful woman. I guessed that she was my age, in her mid-thirties.

Once in my office we sat down and I explained the rules of therapy. I told her about confidentiality, and how we keep charts that are distinct from her medical record, and how long we'd most likely be together. I had her sign a form indicating that she understood. Then, as I always do, I asked her what had brought her in.

She said she didn't know. Maybe she shouldn't have come. Then she smiled at me again, warmly.

Treating physicians has become one of my specialties, though it wasn't my intent. I joined the psychiatry faculty at the University of Arizona in Tucson in 1995 with an expertise in counseling people through major medical crises. At the time, I had just finished a clinical postdoc at Harvard focused on counseling people through medical challenges. By then, I'd also survived a five-year bout with cancer myself, including a bone marrow transplant and more chemotherapy and radiation than one person should be allowed to enjoy. I felt well prepared for that work; I understood it from both sides of the bed. But after

I'd been on the faculty eight months, and had treated the patients of one of our surgeons, he decided to come see me himself.

I was surprised. Surgeons have a reputation for thinking that they are "above the fray." He turned out to be sensitive and insightful. We worked on his relationship with his family, his conflicts with his brothers, and his flirtation with alcoholism. Before our treatment was complete he'd referred a few of his friends to me, also physicians. Soon about a third of my patients were doctors. I liked the work. Probably because they're passionate, articulate, and motivated, but maybe it's also because I enjoy the tables being turned.

In the beginning, the art of therapy is hearing the patient accurately. When I was in training an older supervisor shared that therapy is like frogs on lily pads. Frogs won't move unless their lily pads sink, and one frog can balance perfectly on a lily pad. When two frogs get on a pad together, the lily pad will start to sink and at least one must hop to another. The art is showing the patient that you're on the lily pad with them, that you get where they are. If they don't feel that you get it, then they won't go anywhere.

The way therapy starts is critical. If the therapist starts with questions, a pattern is established that suggests that through answering questions, healing occurs. In my experience patients know which lily pads to hop on better than I do, and my questions don't usually lead to healing. So I waited for Amelia to begin. Eventually she spoke.

"I'm a competent person; I trained at some of the best institutions in the country. I was at Wesleyan for undergrad and Penn for medical school and then I came here for residency. I was asked to join the faculty as soon as I was done. I should feel competent. I did until recently. But I've lost that. Maybe I'm just being silly; I'm sure you have people to see who are really ill. I'm not really ill. I'm fine."

Changing the topic, she said, "This is a comfortable room." I thanked her and waited. My office is small and windowless, but pleasant. There's a slate water fountain, a gift from my wife, and a leather love seat my patients sit on. I sit a few feet away on a comfortable office chair. The walls are decorated with framed diplomas from Vassar, the University of Florida, and Harvard, a print of a snow leopard and another of a lighthouse triptych with the ocean gathering around it, salt spray and fury. The silence expanded.

Eventually, she spoke.

I don't know where to start. Does it matter? I've had this feeling of lost competence before, just not recently. It's so familiar. I remember the last time I felt like this. It happened when I was a second-year resident and rotated through a hospital in Douglas, Arizona. No one else in the residency wanted to go out there. As you know, it's a border town and it's incredibly poor. Many of the patients are Mexicans, some are illegals, and they often don't get as much prenatal care as they need. But that's the kind of work I've always liked, when I'm most needed. So I leapt at the chance.

I'd only just finished my internship and, though I'd delivered a handful of babies, I was always under the close supervision of an attending physician and other residents. It was an exciting time for me; I was starting to feel like a physician.

Well, on the fourth day of the rotation I drove out there. I liked the drive. You pass the Rincon Mountains and go through Bisbee. I love the high Sonoran Desert and until you get into Douglas it's pretty. Douglas is not pretty. If you've been out there, and traveled at all, you know that Douglas is like the Third World. There are houses on dirt roads and many of them are just plywood slapped together. There are dogs everywhere. And skinny kids. It's got that same sadness as Nogales or El Paso. I read somewhere that in border towns everyone lives in the shadow of the American dream.

Anyway, the morning started badly. After I got to the clinic a nurse told me that the attending physician had had car trouble on I-10 outside of Dragoon and hadn't made it in yet. It was just me and the chief resident, Mike. He was a good guy, and he told me not to worry, the rotation was reasonable; it never got all that heavy and he'd help me through anything that came up.

The first patient had been there since the previous night. She was going to deliver twins. He introduced me to her; she was already on the monitor. He explained that she had diabetes, and told me I was lucky to be there because the birth could be tricky. Isn't that horrible, during training we enjoy someone else's complication? But that's how it is. Anyway, the mom was coming along slowly.

About an hour later another patient came in. The chief told me to go evaluate her; "Just don't do anything important," he told me. So I went. She said she was Mexican born, and nineteen. She had short, jet black hair. Her hands were tough, like leather. I never asked what she did for a living but it had to be outdoors. She had spots of blood on the hem of her dress and down the back.

She spoke English well, she said she was only twenty-three weeks along and that she hadn't felt the baby kick lately. A full-term baby is forty weeks, so twenty-three weeks is very early. The mom had been getting good prenatal care; she'd been into the clinic a few times during the last month. That was rare out there. I did an ultrasound. The machine was old and I wasn't great with it but it looked to me like the baby was measuring only twenty weeks or so, and the baby's heart rate was low. At least the mother had stopped spotting.

Her husband was there, a sweet guy, beaming, even though he was a little worried; it was like he was putting on a smile for her. He didn't speak as much English and she translated for him. She said her husband was a painter, he painted houses when he could get the work. He reminded me of Jay, my husband. Anyway, he was painting a house about ten miles away when she started spotting. She had no idea how to get ahold of him—they didn't have cell phones or pagers—so she went out walking, looking for him. There were only a few places he could be, she thought. He wasn't at the first couple of houses and by the time she found him it had been four hours.

After the ultrasound I asked her to wait a moment. I left her room *and went back and ran her case by Mike. He asked me some questions and then said that we should watch her overnight. He told me to put her on a monitor, have her follow strict bed rest, and depending on how the baby was doing, we might try to transport her to Tucson. He said he'd take a look when he could get away.*

I talked to the staff and they arranged for her to be admitted and I went back and tried to be helpful for Mike. The first twin was crowning when one of the nurses came back and told me my patient's baby was having some strange heart readings. Mike said it was probably just the monitor, all the equipment sucked, and so I went back to her, thinking we'd just need to move the monitor, they fall off all the time, even the best ones.

But when I got there my patient was in labor. She'd started having contractions about two minutes apart. It was too early for her to deliver and I gave her terbutaline but it didn't stop the labor. That baby was coming. I ran back to ask Mike to come help me, but when I walked into the room it was obvious that he couldn't. He had just done an episiotomy and he was about to deliver the first twin; the mom was screaming and pushing. He had to yell over her. He told me to stall as long as I could, to deliver her if I had to, and he'd be there as soon as he could.

I ran back and I remember the hallways were quiet. I felt like I was in high school after everyone else had gone home. Before I got to her room another nurse showed up and told me we had two more women in labor who'd just come in. It was going to be a long morning.

When I got back it was obvious that she was in active labor, trying not to push. She had a desperate look, like an animal. Her baby was crowning, he was coming. I tried to remember how early a baby could be born and still survive. Twenty-three weeks? Maybe we could get him to the Neonatal Intensive Care Unit, the NICU in Tucson, where the most ill babies and preemies go. The whole thing happened much faster than I thought it would. She delivered fast and the next thing I remember, I was holding her baby. I could tell right away that he wasn't okay. He was blue and purple. He looked puny too, the tiniest creature you'd ever seen. I tried to resuscitate him, turning my back to his parents and pressing my finger into his chest, but he was gone. He had these purple-colored fingers with the tiniest nails. I stood there holding him and his mom asked what was happening, is he okay? I didn't know what to do.

I carried him across the room and into the bathroom and stood, staring at him, not knowing what to do. There were diapers in a pile. I held him with one hand and cleaned him, I washed his little face with the corner of a washcloth and tried to put a diaper on him. It was huge and it didn't fit. Then I put one of those little blue hats on him. It was too big for him. I realized I was trembling. I stood in there a long time. Then, finally, I carried him back out and was standing there when one of the older nurses, a big Mexican woman, put a hand on my shoulder. She took the baby, gently pulled the hat off of him, and brought him over to the mother and gave him to her, and she held my hand and the mom's hand and was looking at all of us. I remember every word she said. "Chica, your little baby boy wasn't ready to come into the world and he didn't live. But you look at him. See, he has perfect lips, and perfect ears, and a perfect chin. Girl, you can have a healthy baby. You all name him, and stay with him as long as you like. When you're ready you let us know." She left the little baby on Mom's chest. The mom and dad didn't make a sound. The room was silent.

Then the nurse, her name was Leslie, gently pulled me into the bathroom and closed the door behind us. I was still holding the little blue hat in my hand. She took the hat and got a cloth and washed my face. She stroked my hair as if she were my mom and she said, "And you, mira, *you look at me. You did everything you could have. Don't think for a moment that you could have been the cavalry and saved that baby. Some babies aren't meant for this world and I've seen a lot of babies and that one wasn't ready. You forget everything they taught you in Tucson about saving twenty-two-weekers, you did everything you could.* Comprendes?"

She hugged me for a long time and I started crying and apologized, I felt so unprofessional, and then she said, "I see a lot of you come and go. You took the time to find this silly blue cap and put it on him. You're different. You care. You're going to be a good doctor." And I swear to God I've never wept so much in my life. Just hearing those words. It was the first time anyone in the field had ever said that to me. Not one of the residents or faculty ever said much that was encouraging. They never really said it to anyone, but she did, and she held me and brushed the hair from my eyes and then patted me on the butt and said, "We've got a long day ahead, you go back out there and deliver some healthy babies." So I did.

Amelia looked at me for the first time. She spoke slowly.

"That's why I'm here. It's not what happened back then that's important, it's that I feel that way again. Just like I did in that bathroom. Lost. The world swirling by while I stand frozen in place. I've been secretly hoping you'd be that fat Hispanic woman. I want someone to envelop me in her arms and tell me I'm going to be all right. That I'm going to find my way out of this. But she isn't here. And I don't think anyone can help me."

She sat back and looked at the walls and my bookcase. She took a tissue and dabbed her eyes, though I couldn't see any tears.

"This feeling of being lost, of incompetence, do you know where it's coming from?" I asked.

"I might. I think I do. But I'm not ready to talk about that, is that okay? Do you mind? I know it must seem silly to come to a psychologist and then not want to talk about it." She laughed. When she smiled her face opened. It reminded me of someone, but I couldn't remember whom. My first instinct was to press her a little, she seemed strong enough, but then I thought of the advice of an old supervisor, Arthur Klein. "If you give her time, she'll give you time."

"Would you mind if I asked you about symptoms?" I asked. How's your sleep? Fine. How many hours do you get? Seven. Do you wake too early or have trouble falling asleep? No. Tell me about your energy, concentration, and libido. Okay. Medications? None. Illnesses? Appendectomy; and then, as I always do, I asked, "Are you having any thoughts of hurting yourself?"

She shrugged, scratched her arm, and didn't say anything. It was an unusual response. Most of my patients immediately answer the question, eager to reassure me. For a moment I felt as if I were on a riverbank in the mist and something looming, something scaled and dangerous, was rising in the fog just beyond my vision. Then she said quietly, "No. No suicidal thoughts. No plan. No intent." She broke the spell, and I felt silly. She was fine.

"I'm sure you're wondering why I'm here. I am too. I don't completely know how to do this. How to use this time. Do I just tell you the things I've been thinking about?"

"Therapy is like a long winter drive. You'll know where we need to go better than I, so you'll take the wheel and I'll sit in the passenger seat. While driving, you'll have your eyes on the road. From my vantage I may notice landscapes you haven't studied before, and together, we'll find our way to warmer climes."

She smiled at me again. "I like the way that sounds."

"I'll give you a little hint, it doesn't matter which direction we go. Just start the car. We've got time. We'll find our way," I offered.

The silence was more comfortable this time.

"Okay. Here's something I've been thinking about. Do you ever get a song lodged in your head? I have this Talking Heads song in my head. I don't even like the tune. There's one line that goes, 'This is not my beautiful house, this is not my beautiful wife.' That's me. I've awakened in a strange life and I want to know how I got here. Maybe that will help me get home, you know?"

"That's good, keep driving."

"I haven't worked for seven months. I'm not a doctor anymore and I'm not sure I care. I feel numb. I've been trying to think back to the first time I wanted to be a physician. It seems like it's what I've always wanted, but I think it actually goes back to the death of my grandfather."

"Your grandfather was a physician?"

She laughed.

No. My grandfather was a bear. He was six foot three and must have weighed three hundred pounds. Massive. He'd worked as a butcher his entire life in the Italian Market in South Philly. After my grand-mother died, when I was two, he moved in with us. Our bedrooms were next door to each other and right outside the kitchen.

When my father and his brothers were growing up, they say Grandpa was a fierce disciplinarian with a temper and elaborate rules. The man I knew was nothing like that. Maybe because I was his first grandchild. Or maybe he changed when Grandma died. Anyway, the man I remember was a giant with a billowing laugh and stubble. I don't know how it started, but by the time I was nine, we were locked in a battle of pranks.

We had a basement that was unfinished. It was dark, cold, and, in my imagination, infested with insects and monsters. The water heater was at the foot of the stairs, a huge white cylinder with pipes coming in and out of it like arms. It made terrifying knocking sounds. The wash-ing machine and dryer were also down there. One afternoon—I must have been eight—Mom told me to go down and get my nice shirt out of the dryer. I was taking piano lessons down the street and Mom made me dress up for the lessons. I walked down the creaking wooden stairs, around the water heater, and then finally found the string for the light-bulb. Before I could pull it, I heard a soft growling sound. Then it broke into a roar, and I could swear that I saw a saber-toothed tiger crouched behind the water heater. I screamed and ran up the stairs, stumbling over the bottom steps. I hadn't even reached the top when I heard him behind me, laughing and snorting. I stood in the doorway screaming, "That wasn't funny! That wasn't funny!" But it only made him snort louder. I told him I hoped he choked. He was alternatively howling and gasping for breath as he made his way up the stairs.

I think that's when I stole all of his underwear. I hid it under my mattress. He came out into the kitchen for breakfast the next morning in his bathrobe. Mom asked him if he was feeling okay. He said, "I feel great." And he kept staring at me as he made his way around the kitchen getting his bowl and the milk. I was eating at the table, trying to be casual. My little sister Cora kept saying, What? What's so funny? and then I couldn't take it anymore and I laughed so hard that Cheerios almost came out my nose.

Now we were seriously engaged. He short-sheeted my bed, nailed my backpack to the floor, and turned off the hot water when I was in the middle of a shower. Once he put pillows under his blankets and one of my grandmother's wigs so that when I went in to wake him up I thought something had happened to him. I was standing there saying, "Grandpa, wake up, Grandpa, wake up," when I felt cold water on my forehead. The old bastard was hiding behind the door with a water pistol. "You're so immature!" I yelled at him and he howled.

In fairness, I cut the buttons off his favorite shirt, replaced his shampoo with rubbing alcohol, and took apart his bed once. Mom and Dad tried to stop us, but Grandpa was above the law of the house, and as long as I was just responding, I couldn't get in trouble. "I can't just let him torture me!" I argued to my parents, who looked the other way. Grandpa'd nod soberly when they told him to quit, that it was hard enough having three girls in the house without him making things worse. He agreed over and over again but never changed.

I think, if we'd had the time, we would have eventually destroyed all of each other's possessions.

He wasn't all practical jokes. I remember running to him when Melissa O'Donnell made fun of me at school. He was the one person I wanted to see. It felt like no matter how big I got, Grandpa would always be able to protect me. That day he rubbed my hair and sang me children's songs in Italian.

Grandpa could be a pain in the ass, too, but usually he took that out on my father. They fought most often in the kitchen. Grandpa liked his food a certain way, and those ways died with Grandma. That's when he missed her the most, and it came out in rage. Once he threw a tray of lasagna at the wall. "So you finally show yourself, you damned cretino," my father screamed at him.

And then, a few weeks before my tenth birthday I went into the bathroom and found Grandpa on the floor, his fleshy legs white on the red linoleum. His face was pressed against the tub and he kept opening and closing his mouth but didn't say anything. I thought it was one of his jokes but then I saw a gash on his forehead from where he'd fallen, deep crimson, and I ran to get Mom. The ambulance came and four big men carried Grandpa out on a stretcher. He was still opening and closing his mouth.

We visited him in the hospital. I was excited, because I'd never been to a hospital. I didn't get the gravity of the situation. My parents were serious, but when it came to Grandpa, he never followed their rules. When we got there, it wasn't what I'd expected. I thought the hospital would be clean and white like in Marcus Welby on television. Marcus Welby's hospital was well organized and people spoke quietly. But when we walked into University Hospital I smelled piss. There were people everywhere: in the hallways, in wheelchairs, on gurneys, and even in the stairwells. They were yelling and moaning. It was chaos. My parents were lost for a while, we couldn't find Grandpa's room. There were different wings. Mom was carrying Brenda and she got frustrated because Brenda was complaining. Then we found him. He was sharing a room with two shriveled old men who looked like they were already dead. The place smelled like a locker room.

The shades were open and the room was stuffy and bright. Grandpa moaned and moaned and Dad mashed the call button but no one came for a long time. I went and stood next to Grandpa and tried to talk to him. I expected him to tell me everything was okay. Stop worrying, Picolina. But he didn't hear me. Finally a nurse appeared and Dad begged her to bring something for Grandpa. I'd never seen him beg. She brought back a doctor and I thought, "Finally, now everything will be okay." The doctor injected some medication and Grandpa stopped moaning.

The image that's sharp in my memory is of me standing alone in the corner of the room, looking through the sunbeams and floating dust motes at the doctor huddled over Grandpa, listening to his chest with the stethoscope. The doctor squinted. The skin under his jaw was unshaven and his hair was long; he didn't look like a doctor.

I don't remember how long Grandpa was in the hospital, but I do remember the cemetery. It was one of those early spring days, the first warm day in a long time. It was raining and the grass had just been cut. It smelled like spring. I couldn't believe Grandpa was gone. When they started lowering his casket into the ground, Dad began fidgeting; he put his hands in and out of his pockets. He was wearing this ridiculous suit; it was missing a button and had a tear in the back. His hair had little beads of rain on it. I was old enough to be embarrassed for him. When the casket reached the ground and they pulled the ropes up, Dad dropped into the grave.

He didn't say a word; he stepped forward and dropped in like a lead weight dropping into water. I rushed forward, but Mom grabbed me and pulled me back and both of my uncles yelled and pulled him out. It was awkward, the grass was wet, and it took them a few minutes.

When Dad came out he had red mud on his knees, his tie, and the back of his hands.

That was the first time I thought about being a doctor. I could have saved Grandpa. I could have stopped him from dying. I could have saved Daddy.

After Amelia was gone her voice lingered. I love voices and accents. I learn as much from the cadence, pitch, and energy of a voice as I do from the content. I'm often reminded of similar voices. When talking with someone I might suddenly remember the gravel in the butcher's voice at Copaco meatpackers, where I worked when I was sixteen. Or the syrupy thickness of Arthur Klein's voice, my supervisor at McLean when I was finishing my training. Or the low whisper of Terry's voice on Sunday mornings before we had Alexandra, when the days were ours. I have a terrible memory for names, but I never forget a voice. Voices are a soul's signature.

When people talk about meaningful parts of their lives, their voices change. A voice that bounces along may suddenly go steady and smooth, or a tenor that fills the room with volume may drop low and quiet.

Amelia's voice was brittle and tight. When emotional her voice rose and then disappeared, as if all of her energy were devoted to *not* giving voice to her truths. She reminded me of an older woman I treated in Boston who went blind rather than face her husband's obvious abuse.

I started my chart note. I wrote down what I knew about her family and drew a family tree with circles representing women, squares for the men. Next to each shape I recorded what I knew about that relative. Then I wrote down her presenting complaint, the symptoms she told me. The next part of the note is mental status but I stopped writing. In this section I record suicidal and homicidal ideation, intent, and plan.

I realized I was attracted to her. This isn't unusual. I'm attracted to a lot of patients, a lot of people. But some, both men and women, charm me quickly, leave me more fascinated than functional. She was like that. I felt that I could sit and listen to her for hours. I love long narratives. Not all patients reveal themselves in that way, but I'm usually enchanted when they do. I like peeking behind the walls of other people's lives.

The danger when I'm fascinated is that I'm more likely to miss something. The most dangerous thing to miss is a patient's suicidality. Almost 70 percent of people who try to kill themselves visit a health professional in the month prior to the attempt. I don't want to be one of those professionals. I know that some anguish is lethal, but even now, after fourteen years of practice including my training, I'm terrified that a patient will kill himself when I could have prevented it. I've seen firsthand what happened to a psychologist when his patient killed herself.

It was 1994 and as part of my training, I did a yearlong clinical internship at McLean Hospital, a psychiatric hospital affiliated with Harvard. By then I'd already done four years of therapy training at the University of Florida, but this internship was total immersion in clinical work and McLean had a great reputation. For every hour of outpatient therapy I did, I received one corresponding hour of face-to-face supervision with an experienced supervisor who listened to tapes of my sessions and reviewed every therapeutic choice I made, one by one. Of all the places I interviewed, McLean had the greatest variety of patients. There were separate units for every flavor of human suffering: a mood disorders unit, a psychotic disorders unit, and several units for people struggling to overcome personality disorders.

In its wealthier years, McLean was a psychiatric hospital for the well-off. Covering over two hundred hilly, rural New England acres just west of Boston, the hospital was a therapeutic sanctuary run by some of the best-trained clinicians in the world. Clients typically spent months to years on the campus, and a few had their original homes copied and duplicated on the grounds. This explains the architectural chaos; there's a massive Tudor, a few Victorians, and even some postmodern structures. The center of the campus, though, is a series of six impressive four-story brick buildings that roar legitimacy.

One afternoon about eight months into the internship, I was walking from Waverly House, one of the personality disorder units, to the cafeteria, when I came on a girl who'd hanged herself from the lowest level of the fire escape on one of the four-story buildings. I'd been trying to catch up to three guys I worked with when one of them, Mac, pointed to her with authority. I froze. They were twenty yards ahead of me and I couldn't hear what they said, but John and Lee, the other two guys, frantically opened a door and disappeared into the building. *They'll save her,* I thought.

I recognized her—Rachel. She was wearing red jeans, a T-shirt, and a floppy white sailor's cap. The sheet, wrapped around the lowest rail on the fire escape, was white and spotless, twisted and taut. She dangled a few feet below the thick knot, ten feet off the ground. She was already stiff, one hand curled awkwardly. Her T-shirt was pulled up, exposing a bone-colored navel. Standing there, I had a crazy thought that she was only sleeping. Her head drooped forward and her cheeks still had color, as if she'd just been running and was resting now. I took a few urgent steps forward. Mac turned around and stopped me, saying, "Slow down, Doc. She's already gone. John and Lee will try to get her down before the other patients spot her. It's contagious."

I felt my legs flexing. One of her sneakers was untied and a long black lace drifted beneath her foot like a severed anchor line. Mac stood under the fire escape and tried to light a cigarette. He flicked a silver lighter a few times and turned away, out of the breeze. Smoke twirled up around him, crossed in front of her, and disappeared.

The next day I was in the chart room in Waverly House when Rachel's therapist came in. I knew Dr. Epstein from his lectures to the interns. He was a good presenter in those seminars. Organized and always in a tweed jacket, he looked the part of the careful professor. But that morning his salt-and-pepper hair stuck out in all directions like Medusa's snakes. He grunted a hello, grabbed Rachel's chart and sat down, still wearing his down coat, and flipped through the pages. The coat was massive with a fur lining and big pockets. But it was a beautiful Boston morning, probably in the high 60s. There was a film of sweat on his neck.

He must have found what he was looking for because he hunched over the chart and began to read. He started clicking a pen open and closed. I'd just made some tea, so I offered him some, thinking it might settle his nerves. He looked at me, puzzled for a moment. I repeated my offer.

"Tea? Now? No. No," he said. As if I'd interrupted an opera.

Rachel had been living at Waverly House, the personality disorders unit where I was assigned. It was a three-story Victorian, the kind I love, with nooks and crannies, oak banisters, and careful woodwork on every door. The unit functioned like a large household. The doors were unlocked; the patients cooked each other meals and did all the household chores. The milieu was supposed to be therapeutic. According to theory, personality disorders are born in our earliest family interactions. On the unit, patients had the opportunity to reenact family conflicts in an

environment in which therapists could observe and use the interactions to engender insight.

Some patients thrived on the unit, but not Rachel. She was
withdrawn and chronically suicidal. She quietly did her assigned
chores and kept to herself. No one would blame Dr. Epstein, I
thought, for Rachel's death. But then again, I didn't know what
he'd done behind closed doors. Supervisors and master clinicians
rarely allow themselves to be seen working with patients. In
most cases, only therapists and their patients know what is said
during therapy. It's one of the more frustrating aspects of our
business. There is no other profession where experts teach by
describing what they do instead of *showing* it. I can't imagine
learning to shoe a horse or perform surgery or guide an airliner
safely to the runway without getting to watch someone do
it well. And yet, throughout my entire training, I saw a supervisor work directly with patients in therapy on only a handful of
occasions.

Three days after Rachel hanged herself I was waiting for one
of my supervisors, Arthur Klein, to appear in his office for our
weekly supervision when Dr. Epstein walked past carrying a box
of books and hurried down the stairs. His office door was open
and I walked over and looked in. Books were on the floor and
piled precariously on his desk, typewritten pages were scattered
everywhere and his phone dangled off the hook. A plant in
the corner had been knocked over and a mound of dirt sat in
front of it.

He brusquely walked by me, back into the office.

"Dr. Epstein. You're leaving?" I asked him.

"What the fuck does it look like I'm doing?"

"Because of Rachel?" I asked. He grabbed another box and
walked past me, his shoulder almost plowing into mine.

Later, during our supervision, I asked Arthur about Dr.
Epstein. He told me that Sydney Epstein had been at McLean for
twelve years. He had interned there, just as I was doing, and had

been offered a faculty spot. They were coveted jobs; the perks included a faculty appointment at Harvard Medical School. He took the job and he'd never worked anywhere else. Now he was giving up psychology completely. He'd told Arthur that he had money saved and he was going to try something different. After supervision as I was leaving the building I saw a pile of boxes at the foot of the stairs and Epstein ahead of me carrying two boxes toward the parking lot, the flap of his shirt hanging out in the back.

Session Two

I was startled when I went to get Amelia from the waiting room for our second session a week later. I always study what my patients wear; it's usually a transmitter of how they feel, or want others to think they feel. She was in a summer dress, its fabric thin and clingy. She'd washed her hair and it was down. She looked younger. The carefree young woman.

She settled into the leather love seat and started.

"I almost didn't come back. I still don't think you're going to help me, but there was something about the way you sat there last week, curled up in your chair, that felt safe. You didn't pressure me. I feel like I told you a lot more than I wanted to. And, even though I don't think you're going to help, I don't think you're going to hurt me either, so I'm back. On the way here I was thinking about what I should talk about and I still don't know where to start."

"Remember the driving metaphor? Just put the key in the

ignition. My guess is that most roads will lead us to where we need to go."

"I want to talk about how I became an obstetrician. It's the most important part of my life; let's talk about that."

"That would be fine," I said.

I was a medical student in my third year at Penn when I saw my first birth. At the time I'd been thinking about dropping out. Medicine and I weren't hitting it off yet. I'd rotated through surgery and internal medicine and I did fine—my residents and patients liked me, but the surgeons seemed like glorified plumbers and the medicine docs spent their lives with patients who had chronic illnesses they'd never cure.

I hadn't found my place yet. I was getting good grades and the medical school was very supportive but I felt pretty lonely. The medical school profs downplayed the competition but it was there. We competed with one another because good grades meant good residencies. In the third year I had one dreadful rotation after another. Then I did obstetrics and was assigned to a resident, a doctor finishing her training, who asked me to call her Sally. On only my second day on the service Sally told me I could help her deliver a baby.

I remember it was raining and cool, just pouring outside, when I got to the hospital. It'd been hot for weeks before that. The air had that after-thunderstorm crispness. I was in a good mood, my first in weeks. Sally met me in the morning and told me that if I got the scut work done first, I could assist her in a birth in the afternoon. So I rounded on all the deliveries from the day before. All the moms were sleeping or with their newborns. Sally taught me how to do the charting and then took me to Labor and Delivery.

She introduced me to this couple in one of the rooms and told me that I could stay there with them. The mom-to-be was named Amy and she was in her fifteenth hour of labor. It felt anticlimactic. She was just lying there, sleeping between contractions, and the dad was reading a parenting magazine.

Amy and I started talking. We were just about the same age. We liked the same music. Then she started to look uncomfortable. She kept fidgeting and moving around. She had a contraction and groaned, and then just a minute later another one. I didn't know what to do. I shot out of the room and pleaded with one of the nurses, who told me to relax. "There's still plenty of time." She paged Sally but she didn't show up. The nurse didn't look worried, so I tried not to panic, though I did have this fear that no one else would show up and I'd have to deliver the baby myself.

Amy's contractions were getting more intense, and closer together, only fifty seconds apart. Finally, Sally waltzed into the room. She seemed so calm. I exhaled for the first time in an hour. She said, "Having fun?" to me, and then showed me how to check for dilation. It was the first time I touched another woman like that, and I felt nervous, but Sally was so natural about it. She said to Amy, "That doesn't hurt, does it?" to prove to me that it was painless. Amy was almost fully dilated and then the contractions came on again, powerfully this time, and I saw the head coming through, this hairy little scalp pressing through the birth canal.

I hadn't realized a woman could open like that. Her vagina looked like a flower in one of those time-lapse photography documentaries. It was so primal and real. Amy screamed as she pushed and the baby's huge head came out, followed by the rest of him. There was blood and fluid everywhere. New life. I just stood there in shock. I felt like the room had suddenly grown larger and I was a speck.

Sally smiled at Amy and said, "You did it!" and she lifted up this skinny baby boy. Sally took a towel and scrubbed him down. He had mucus in his mouth and nose. I thought the baby would be fragile, but she held him firmly while she cleaned him and suctioned his nose and mouth. She didn't cut the cord right away. She tenderly put the baby boy on Amy's chest and let mom and baby stay attached for a little while. Anthony, the baby—I still remember his name—didn't cry. His eyes were open like he already knew his mother. Then Sally helped the dad cut the cord.

Amy and her husband wept. And I realized that I was crying too. Sally put an arm around my shoulder and whispered in my ear, "What's up with you? In a few moments we're gonna deliver the placenta and you need to be more functional." Then she elbowed me in the ribs and smiled. "This never gets old."

We had a quick lunch together after the delivery. Sally had grown up in a tiny town in Alabama; she saw her first birth when she was still little. One of her neighbors delivered right in her house. Her mother wasn't a real midwife but she helped out at births. Then when Sally was older she helped her mom and the doctor with a few of the local births. For her it was a natural occupational choice; she knew what she wanted to do from the start. Not me. But that day, seeing that woman open up and release that child . . . To be part of that . . . How real it was. How important. For the first time in my entire life I felt like I had found true north. Now I've lost that. I'm directionless. All these months, it's been six or seven . . . too long.

We sat in silence. For the first time I understood the magnitude of the loss she was suffering from not delivering babies.

In my life I've had a handful of moments that were awesome and scary, moments when I've felt painfully small, fully alive, connected to nature and the rest of humanity. Once when I swam naked in the ocean, surrounded by phosphorescence, bright green speckles of life that rolled and glittered in the surf. Or the time up on Wassum Peak in the Tucson mountains, when Terry and I climbed up at sunset in time to watch the sun set and a full moon rise at the same time, the sky streaked with violet and pink.

The power of those moments always surprises me, like an old friend unexpectedly tapping me on the shoulder in a faraway city. But Amelia had these moments at work every day, whenever she helped a new life into the world. I couldn't imagine having that many. Or trying to come to terms with losing them.

Eventually, she broke the silence.

That same autumn when I saw my first delivery, I was dating a guy from Iowa. He was everything the boys I dated in high school weren't. He was all-American and beefy, a general surgery resident. He seemed clean-cut until you realized how much he drank. Anyway, I went to his house for Thanksgiving. His family lived in a tiny town twenty miles north of Iowa City. Flying in, Iowa looked brown. Big ugly squares of brown. Tom told me we were in soybean and corn country. Then he said that things were different at his house. I asked what he meant and he said, "It'll be a little more conservative than you're used to." And he said it with pride. As if he wasn't the one who got drunk at every opportunity.

We landed at the tiny airport and right away I felt out of place. In the Philadelphia airport you see all walks of life, from the working-class baggage handlers to Wall Street types, Italian, Jamaican, Puerto Rican, Asian. It's all there. But this was different. It felt like I'd jetted back in time. Everyone was white. Tom recognized two guys at a car-for-hire booth. He stopped to talk to them. I could tell he couldn't remember their names but he bullshitted along. Then his parents appeared. Tom's dad was a family doc, a big man. He shook my hand and I had this feeling that he didn't approve of me. Tom's mom was wearing a diamond-studded cross around her neck. I took one look at it and knew my skirt was too short.

On the drive to their house Tom's dad asked about my last name and if I was Italian. Only he said it, "I-talian." I told him I was half Italian. Then he told me he liked Italian food. Tom's mom was sitting next to me in the backseat. She agreed, saying, "Baked ziti is his favorite." Then she nodded vigorously. Tom's dad asked what my father did for a living and I don't know why, but I said, "He's in the mob." Tom laughed so hard that he snorted. He had a great laugh. His parents didn't laugh at all. And then I said, "He's a legitimate business-man"—I think it's a line from The Godfather.

"Of course he is," Tom's dad said. It was downhill from there. The Thanksgiving meal was dreadful. The food was good and plentiful, but we didn't get to eat it for a long time because the praying before the meal went on for weeks. I'm spiritual, but not into organized religion. I'm assuming you're Jewish. This could have been the Passover meal for the length of time it took us to get to the point where we could lift our forks. Everyone had their own opportunity to add something to the prayer and when they got to me I just said, "Thank God for food." The kids started giggling and I caught one of the cousins shooting a glance at Tom's dad.

Of course they had us sleep in different rooms. I had Tom's old bed-room and he slept on the couch in the living room. I thought he might sneak in for a little taboo sex, but he didn't. And the house was hot. They kept it hovering around 90 degrees. I couldn't sleep. You'd think conservative people would conserve heat.

On the Friday after Thanksgiving I got up early—in time to see Tom's dad arriving back at the house from work. It was 5 A.M. and he looked a mess. He was in wrinkled sweatpants and he looked like he'd just stepped off an eighteen-hour flight from China. He didn't look happy to see me. He was probably still smarting from the Thanksgiving meal; I'm sure I seemed rude to him. But when we met in the kitchen I asked if I could make him a cup of coffee and he said, "I'd be grateful." So I started to make some. I think I realized that I missed times like this, with an older man. By then my father was already in the middle stages of Alzheimer's. While we waited for the coffee to brew, he asked which branch of medicine I was heading into.

I told him I was thinking of general surgery and asked him if he was glad he did family practice.

"I've tended the families here for all but the years I was in Korea. It's the only life I know. And I never much liked operating rooms. I was just out at the Wikle house. The little ones have the flu something terrible. Hannah had a fever of about one hundred four and Kylie, her little sister, was close behind."

He told me that he'd taken care of Hannah and Kylie's mom for pneumonia when she was their age. That he'd even treated their grandmother before her, though she was already nearing the end when he started practicing. He didn't go to people's houses much anymore, he was getting too old for midnight house calls, but he still enjoyed the ones he did. Then he stopped and put down his coffee and looked away from me. He said, "My son thinks his checkbook balance is the most important thing in his life, but it isn't. I've had something better. At the end of the day I know I've done something worthwhile. If you don't mind my saying so, I suspect you'll find that's important as you get on, too."

That afternoon Tom volunteered us for a visit to his grandmother who was in a nursing home nearby, and on the way he stopped at a cemetery and got a blanket out of the car. He pinched me on the ass and winked.

"You've obviously done this before," I said to him.

"I neither acknowledge nor deny . . ." And he carried the blanket deep into the cemetery and put it down between these headstones in a far corner. It was late afternoon and the place was deserted. It was cold but fun. It just felt good to be out of that broiling house, and Tom's body was his best feature. I liked being pressed against him.

When we were done Tom picked up the blanket and wanted to leave but I was in no rush to get to the nursing home. I started reading the headstones. I walked the rows reading them out loud. It didn't take long to realize that most of the graves were infants. There were graves for babies who lived only a few days, and mothers who died in childbirth buried next to them. Rows and rows of them. Old moms. Young moms. Boys, girls, twins. Some of the babies weren't even named.

Then I sat next to one of those little stones, a baby named Emma who had died the day she was born, in 1912. The letters had green moss growing in the granite. "Lent to her parents, returned to God," was all the stone said.

Sitting there, next to Emma, I understood the stakes.

Therapists like to pretend that they're never distracted in therapy. That they don't think about their own lives. But for six years now, I've been supervising psychiatrists and psychologists in training. As our patients find the vein of truth about their lives it often reminds us of ours. As Amelia discussed finding her profession and the stakes, I thought of my choice. The seeds that grew into my professional direction were planted when I was very young.

I remember playing outside on the stoop, at six years old, hidden by the bottom part of the screen door. I was pushing Matchbox cars, running them across the bumpy concrete of the stoop, not paying attention to my parents, who were inside, in the kitchen, talking. In my memory their voices mingled with the percussion of glasses and silverware being put away. Then I heard something my mother said in the middle of the conversation.

"I just hope she went fast."

"I dunno," said my father. "It takes four minutes, doesn't it? For the oxygen?"

"How could this happen? She was so young. Just a girl, still. Really. Thirty is just a girl."

I stopped pushing the cars and listened. A revelation. Suddenly things made sense. Lately our home had been confused. I wasn't great with time yet, but recently my younger two cousins had come to live with us. Girls. I'd met them before but we'd never spent that much time together. Andrea was the older of the two, a little younger than me, and Ellen was eighteen months. My parents carried my brother's old crib down from the attic for Ellen and put down a mattress for Andrea. Girl stuff covered the oak desk and bookcases in Dad's study: puppets, dresses, art supplies, and a few boxes full of toys. Even though they were girls, they did have a few cool things. A Lite Brite with hundreds of brightly colored pegs, an Etch A Sketch, and a Spirograph. They didn't play with any of it.

Ellen was silent. Andrea was quiet too, until we had meals. Then she turned into a kitchen hurricane. She'd howl and run her hand along the table, upending bottles of milk and bowls of Cheerios. Dad or Mom would hustle her upstairs and then she'd be back a while later, holding on to their necks, doing the post-cry gasp, cheeks wet and raw.

Kneeling on that back stoop I understood why Andrea and Ellen lived with us. Their mother, my aunt Gwen, must have died. When Mom said, "I hope she went fast," I got it. I knew that death was a place you go. Like the bakery or Connecticut. Only your body didn't go with you. Details were confusing, but the fact of Aunt Gwen's death was not.

A few days later I got up the nerve to ask how she died. Mom was walking me to school and she made me repeat the question. Then she stopped walking and said, "Don't miss much, do you?" I asked her again. Mom's eyes became little slits of intense concentration. She said slowly, "Aunt Gwen died of a blood clot."

I must have made a face because she said, "Don't worry, it's not the kind of thing that will happen to me or to you or Dad or anyone else you know." Then she held out her hand to me. End of conversation. I didn't enjoy holding her hand when we walked: I was grown up, in first grade already, but this time I took it.

Andrea and Ellen lived with us for six months. When we had baths together, David and I would play with our boats and make monsters out of the sponge toys, but Andrea and Ellen just got in quietly, soaped up and rinsed off their sleek bodies, and then held up their hands to get out. They were all business. While David and I ran our cars along the lumpy roots in our little patch of grass in the backyard, Andrea and Ellen sat quietly on the patio like little statues.

I knew what was wrong. I knew that Andrea would play with us if we gave her our mom, but I didn't want to. And whenever I thought about it I felt scared. I found myself hovering around the living room and kitchen where Mom spent most of her time, being good, or "less energetic" as Mom called it, hoping that she wouldn't leave with Andrea and Ellen to go live with Uncle Rick.

Months passed. Routines developed. Mom put down the girls at night, Dad the boys. Mom dressed the girls, Dad the boys. Then one day Uncle Rick appeared at the front door. He showed me his new digital calculator. It had long rectangular black lines that made up the numbers. He gave me a silver dollar, winked at me, and told me not to tell Mom. Then he carried Andrea and Ellen out to his Buick, slammed the trunk, and they were gone.

In the autumn of my senior year of high school I learned how Gwen really died. I was driving Mom down Woodland Avenue toward the middle of town. The sun was setting, bathing the leafless branches of oak and sycamore in purple light. We were driving to Park Avenue Pizza to pick up a night-before-Thanksgiving dinner and chatting about a friend of the family who was going to have brain surgery.

"You know Ma, I pay attention when people have operations on veins, arteries, or capillaries, on account of what happened to Aunt Gwen."

"Why Gwen?" Mom asked.

"You know, her dying from that blood clot, and everything."

"What are you talking about?"

"The blood clot."

"Gwen didn't die of a blood clot."

With adolescent sureness, I said, "Yeah she did." And then, "She didn't?"

Mom looked out the passenger window and said, "We never told you?"

Gwen was thirty when she died. She was stunning. The kind of woman that men stop to look at. "She was the kind of woman that women stopped to look at too," Mom added. Gwen was Jewish, dark-skinned, with big brown eyes. She walked with her chin up, like a queen. When my mother's brother, Rick, married her, the family was impressed that he could land such a beauty.

The year after Rick and Gwen were married, her father killed himself and something in Gwen changed. She'd had a tumultuous relationship with her father. "Gwen's father was not a happy man," Mom told me.

Rick didn't know what to do to help her. He threw himself into his work. His job as a safety engineer required that he spend weeks at a time at plants around the country. Back at home, Gwen took care of Andrea and Ellen. It was summer in New England, the season of family trips, Fourth of July celebrations, but without Rick maybe she grew isolated and lonely. She shopped. She took trips to the local boutiques in West Hartford and bought fancy dresses and shoes and coats. But as the summer wore on the clothing hung in the closets.

"We don't really know why she did it, of course," Mom said. "Maybe she had a serious depression, or maybe she was manic-depressive, or maybe it had something to do with her father. We don't know. She did it at Nana's house, in the basement. Rick and Nana were out running a few errands. She put the girls to sleep, went down the stairs, and used a rope. The heating pipes are exposed in the basement. Nana and Uncle Rick found her a few hours later. That's why the girls came to live with us, to give Uncle Rick a little time to get himself together."

The next day, over Thanksgiving dinner, I watched my cousin Andrea. She's beautiful, with curly black hair and brown eyes. She's curvy and funny. And for the first time it occurred to me that everyone else at the table was part of a couple, except for her and Nana. Andrea had never had a serious boyfriend, or girlfriend. No long-term relationships. She didn't joke about a future family like her little sister. And it would be that way for years.

She's afraid to do to children or a lover what was done to her, I thought. Afraid of being vulnerable to anyone again, and maybe afraid of hurting them. She's suffering from her mother's relationship with her own father.

It was a revelation. That loss and trauma pass down through families like batons in relays, one to the next and then the next. And I wondered what it would be like to intercept that baton. Stop the runners.

Session Three

Amelia was late to our third session. She bustled into the office, dropped her backpack, and settled into the couch. She had run up the stairs and it took her a little while to catch her breath. After she'd calmed, and we'd exchanged pleasantries, she said, "Since we started meeting I've been thinking a lot about my family. I don't know why. I'm supposed to blame my mother for everything, right? But I haven't thought about her at all. I've been thinking about my aunt."

"Tell me."

"Does everyone do this? Am I supposed to think about her?"

I sat quietly. I didn't need to tell her that there weren't rules.

"You're no help," she teased.

"Your aunt?"

Aunt Susan stayed with us for a month when I was twelve. She was my mom's older sister. She showed up one day with a bright orange suitcase; she was taking trains across the country and had started in Oregon; she'd just left a commune that my dad called a hippie cult. I'd met her before, but I must have been very young. I answered the door and there she was. She wore a summer dress and had the longest hair I'd ever seen, it went all the way down her backside. She was tall and had strong, tanned arms. She could have been an Amazon. When I opened the door she took a photograph of me. The flash was startling.

"Gotcha! Ah, you must be the one they call Amelia! Take me to your leader!" She glided right by me into the house and yelled out my mother's name. My sisters and I had been playing; they were both behind me and she took photos of each of us. Brenda was terrified and ran to go get Mom. I was transfixed.

Mom wasn't as glad to see her sister as I thought she'd be. She was somber and said something like, "What do you need?"

And Aunt Susan said, "I'm good, how are you?"

"What do you need?" Mom said again.

"Just a place to crash for a few, I won't be a bother." And then she started tickling Cora and Mom cracked a tiny smile.

"Paolo's not going to like it."

"Sweet-talk him. I promise not to be a bother."

That night, Susan went through our pantry and threw out a lot of our food before Dad got home. Everything we had in cans and boxes went into the trash. Mom caught Aunt Susan walking out to the garbage with a big garbage bag of food.

"What the hell are you doing?"

"This stuff will kill you. They suck the vitamins right out of these things. It's soulless food, it comes from machines instead of the ground. I'm saving your lives."

"Thanks, but let us kill ourselves slowly like we'd planned, please." And Mom snatched the bag.

By then I'd moved into Grandpa's old room, just off the kitchen. Mom told me I had to move back in with my sisters Brenda and Cora to make space for Aunt Susan, but Susan told me I could come back and visit my room and even sleep with her if I wanted. At the commune she slept in a common area with nine other people, she could sleep anywhere, she said.

So we slept in the same bed. Her body was amazing, she was so strong and lean, I thought she was the most beautiful woman I'd ever seen. She didn't cover up her body like everyone else in my family. She walked around my room naked. Her eyes were the brightest blue and there was this calm about everything she did. The first night she stood in my room buck naked, going through my books. She was the first person to study them carefully.

"Nancy Drew is crap. James Herriot is crap." Then she looked at me. "Kafka said, 'A book should serve as the ax for the frozen sea within us.' Ain't that right? I bet you're frozen. I'd be frozen living here. You don't need this shit anymore. You need to be reading the big girls. I'm getting you some poetry, you need to be reading Sylvia Plath and Anne Sexton." And while I wouldn't have known it before, the minute she said it I realized that I did feel frozen.

On weekends and after school she took me everywhere with her. She liked to drive with the windows rolled down, no matter how cold it was. Once we went to a café bookstore down on South Street. She called it her bohemian homeland. We found a table and she bought us a sprout sandwich and we split it. It was terrible, but I wanted desperately to like it. I could tell that she belonged there. People dressed like her, ponytails, earrings, Rastafarian hair. They were playing James Taylor and the music surrounded us.

I remember this one moment vividly; there was a guy there, older than me, probably seventeen, with muscular arms. He had a ladder and he was putting books away on a top shelf. He must have been a good fifteen years younger than she was, but she said, "Check him out. Look at that ass. And did you see his eyes?" It was the first time an adult confided sexual feelings to me. I'd seen the assistant principal at school watching some of the older girls, but that was disgusting. This was different. I didn't feel anything looking at his ass, but I wanted to.

She said, "Do you want to meet him? I'll get him to come over here. Most men love younger women."

I said, "No!" But I kind of hoped she'd bring him over anyway. When he got down off the ladder she caught his eyes and smiled. Susan beckoned him over. He came up to us and Susan said, "Meet Amelia."

He smiled at me and shook my hand. "It's great to meet you," he said. And then, "I gotta go back." It was a great moment for me. I didn't giggle or act like a little girl. I met his eyes and Susan said to me, once he was out of earshot, "You're going to be dangerous."

She'd only been with us for a few weeks when I overheard my mother and Susan fighting. My room was next to the kitchen, where they were arguing. They were trying to whisper, but that's what caught my attention. I pressed my ear to the door. Mom said she'd found it. Susan said she didn't know what she was talking about. Mom said she wouldn't have her children exposed to that. Susan told her to back off. That the fucking bottle wasn't hers. I didn't get what they were talking about and I didn't understand why my mother would harass her own sister. It wasn't fair. In those days it felt like my parents tried to ruin anything good that happened for me.

Susan was incredibly smart. She said that she'd been an A student in high school and that I should study hard and listen to my parents about schoolwork. She'd gotten into Penn but only lasted a semester before she left. The way she described it, she'd had a burning to see the world and knew that after she'd traveled she'd go back to the university, she just hadn't wanted to yet. She'd lived in California, in Colorado, in Texas, and was planning on going to Alaska when she put together the money. I was sure I'd do the same thing.

Then one afternoon I came home from school and walked into the bathroom and found Susan sitting naked on the toilet, with a bottle of rum in her hand and a magazine on her lap. She looked at me and said quietly, "Doesn't anybody fucking knock?" She seemed zoned. I pretended that I just needed my hairbrush; I grabbed it and got out of there.

Afterward, I pretended that nothing had happened. A few days later, on Saturday morning, Dad knocked and knocked at our door, and then burst into our bedroom and told Susan she had to leave. I was still half asleep. "Paolo, you're so tense," Susan said. "You need to meditate, it would clear you out. I'm teaching Amelia, she's awesome." And she put a hand on my belly. Dad tried to be calm in front of me, but I could tell he was already angry. His shoulders crept up to his ears when he was mad, but she didn't know how to read him. He said, "You're leaving."

I said, "Why does she have to leave?" but Dad said, "She knows why."

Susan said, "Paolo, you're a paranoid. What are you so afraid of?"

I remember seeing the veins in my dad's forehead and the tips of his teeth behind his lips. He kept repeating himself: "You're getting out of my house." And she kept asking why. Finally he came around the bed and told me I had to leave the room so they could talk. I tried to protest but he grabbed my upper arm. I was in a huge T-shirt and panties; he didn't usually come into my room when I wasn't dressed but he didn't seem to care this time. I was furious. "You ruin everything good that happens for me!" I got up and stormed out. Mom was in the kitchen and she closed the door behind them.

The next morning Susan left. We were having breakfast when she announced to us girls that it was time for her to leave. Then she said to my youngest sister, who was about six then, "So Brenda, you're going to be the pretty one, and Cora, you're the athletic one, and you, dear Amelia, you're the smart one."

I was devastated to see her go. She was the only person I knew with a magical adolescent to adult dictionary—she was generationally bilingual.

Every year around my birthday Aunt Susan mailed me a letter with a list of books I should be reading. Some were great. When I turned *thirteen she wrote that I should read* Romeo and Juliet *because I was Juliet's age and it was important that I learn about passion. When I turned sixteen she wrote that I should read* War and Peace *so I could learn about household politics. In one of the letters she said that she was in Anchorage working in the fisheries, another one came from Toronto, and in one she wrote that she was in Italy studying at a university.*

A few years later—by then I was in college—I was cleaning out my room and came across the letters again. I'd saved them in their original envelopes. That's when I realized that the letter she'd written from Italy was postmarked from Buffalo. All the letters, from Alaska and Toronto and San Diego, were mailed from Buffalo. Susan still lives up there. She has an on again, off again thing with an older guy. I think she waitresses mostly. I haven't seen her in years.

Amelia held one hand on her forehead; with the other she scratched her scalp. She closed her eyes, still back in those years.

I asked, "What brings her to your mind now?"

"I don't know."

"Any themes in what you've just told me that stand out?"

"Uh . . . I don't know." She shrugged and I waited. "I've been pretty bad at keeping in touch with people, I haven't spoken to her in a few years. I wish I was better about that. Maybe I'm thinking about her because I'd like to be better at connecting with people. Who knows. I've been thinking about her constantly, in the shower, on the drive over here, I even talked to Jay about her. We looked for her number but couldn't find it. Then I realized I didn't want to talk to her anyway."

I wanted to keep talking about Aunt Susan, she sounded important to me, but Amelia changed the subject. I asked her about Susan again but she just shrugged. She wasn't ready to tell me what brought her into therapy and I continued my wait. Instead, she filled the remainder of the hour with her frustrations with the work she was doing, called quality assurance, or QA.

The physicians in her clinic had been audited by a state

agency and cited for sloppy recordkeeping. Everyone knew her records were always impeccable. "I'm a bit of a perfectionist," she admitted. Her department was paying her to read the charts at home and make recommendations. It was boring work but it paid the mortgage, she said. I couldn't follow all of the bureaucratic details but it resonated with me when she said that the charts got more physician care than the patients and that the regulations for charting were getting severe. Then time was up and she left. I felt a lingering dissatisfaction with the session; I worried that we weren't getting anywhere, but I had another patient to see.

The Saturday morning after our session I went hiking with Terry, my wife, and Alexandra, our two-year-old, up Seven Falls out of Bear Canyon in the Catalina Mountains. Covering 200 square miles and rising to 9,100 feet, the Santa Catalinas have five distinct vegetation zones. From the saguaros in the foothills where we live to the towering Douglas firs up at 6,000 feet and higher, the mountains are craggy and dramatic, especially for me, a New England native, whose only exposure to towering mountains was a car trip to the Rockies when I was eleven. Now, from our house, we can drive thirty minutes into the Catalinas and enjoy a temperature drop of thirty to forty degrees and a view all the way into Mexico.

Hiking felt like a good way to burn off Saturday-morning energy so we packed up nibbles and diapers and hit the road. We drove to Sabino Canyon State Park, caught the open-air tram to the trailhead, and started walking. We zigzagged through Bear Canyon, along and across a cold stream, before switchbacking up to the falls, a series of dramatic cliffs that draw visitors from all over the world. I had Alexandra in the infant carrier on my back and we walked the gradual incline to the falls.

On the way up, Alexandra was in full babble, talking to the

trees and prickly pear cacti, but on the way back her head dropped onto my neck as she fell into deep slumber. Terry and I had a nice pace and enjoyed a comfortable silence. The mountain and desert reminded me of Mr. Venezia, my earth science teacher in eighth grade. I hated earth science, but not because of the topic. It was interesting to learn how you could tell the age of a river from how much it curved, or why it hails in the summer, or what attracts lightning. Our textbook was fantastic. I considered it the bible of the natural world and taped its broken cover and erased as many of the former students' marks as I could. I liked my classmates, too. They were honors students.

It was Mr. Venezia who made the class unbearable.

Mr. Venezia was Italian. He frequently reminded us of his background. Whenever he was upset, which was often, he'd grumble, "Don't get my Italian up." And he'd wave his hand in the air as if an earthquake might commence at any moment if we weren't vigilant. He was a little man, maybe five foot six, and he had a bald spot with a single mole, dead center. It looked like a bull's-eye. His most impressive physical characteristic, though, was his mouth. He had an unusually large jaw. When he talked he opened his mouth wider than necessary and would occasionally leave it agape, mid-sentence, as if he didn't quite have the muscular strength to close it after a tiring string of words.

When I was in eighth grade, our school experimented with new seating arrangements. Instead of the traditional classroom-style seating we pushed our desks together into little squares, four to a group. We still did all of our work alone, but the squares presented an illusion of cooperation and group learning.

Jennifer Wells, Nerissa Edwards, and Paul DeCrasantis sat in my square. Paul was short and slight, and, like Mr. Venezia, Italian. He was a funny kid who pretended that he didn't care about his schoolwork, but he worked hard. Jennifer was quiet, preppy, and tall. Nerissa was a born leader and also very funny. During class she'd whisper about where she'd like to land some lightning if she could, or how she bet she could hit the mole with one shot if given a spitball and a straw, and then once, when Mr. Venezia's mouth appeared to be frozen open, she suggested that he might, in reality, be a Muppet.

One morning I walked into earth science before the bell and found that my square mates were already there. Paul and Jennifer were talking. Nerissa stood up. She handed me a small card that looked like a bingo sheet and then gave similar sheets to Paul and Jennifer. Across the top, where the word *Bingo* might have been, was *Squid.*

"Good, you're all here early." And then she turned to me and said, "You got a buck?"

"What for?" I asked, skeptical.

"Don't get your panties in a wad," she said. "You can keep your buck if you want, but you aren't going to want to. Today we're playing squid bingo. You probably haven't played squid bingo before, have you, Danny?"

I shook my head.

"I bet none of you have. Well, your friend Nerissa is going to educate you. Write the names of all the people in the class on your card in a random order, fill in all the little boxes with names, leave the middle open for Mr. Venezia. That's the free space. Now, whenever someone says something moronic you get to mark the square. To declare bingo you gotta raise your hand and ask Mr. Venezia a question with the word *squid* in it. First person to get squid bingo wins everyone's buck. Get it?"

"You're a genius," I said and pulled out my lunch money.

"Finally, someone who understands me," she said. Paul and Jennifer produced dollars and handed them to Nerissa. Then we all wrote the names of our classmates on our cards.

Paul asked, "Why is Mr. Venezia the free space?"

Nerissa looked at him.

"Okay. I get it."

Mr. Venezia came in a few minutes later. He told kids to get off the radiator and ordered David Roth to give back Seth's jacket and then he started, his voice a few decibels louder than necessary, "Find your seats, you don't want to get my Italian up today." And he waved his little hand in the air. Ray Romero and Brad Murray got off of the radiator and sat down. A few kids came in late and Venezia glared at them. Then class started. We were learning about photosynthesis. Venezia turned and wrote *oxygen* and *carbon dioxide* on the board and Nerissa whispered, "Let the games begin."

Using colored chalk, Mr. Venezia drew a sun in one corner and then he drew a plant—actually, it was an incredible likeness of a juniper. He was a talented artist, but we all knew better than to compliment him. Then he drew lines from the sun to the plant, and used arrows to show carbon dioxide going into the plant and oxygen emerging. Just as he was finishing, Norman Rakins asked, "Hey, Mr. Venezia, is carbon dioxide the same stuff that comes out of mufflers?" I looked at my square mates. They were searching their cards for Norman's name. Paul checked off a box.

In fairness, my classmates weren't idiots. If we followed Nerissa's rules it would have taken us months to fill our cards. Everyone seemed to know that Venezia was in one of his moods, and they didn't want to risk speaking. Class participation was sporadic and we started checking off the names of anyone who spoke. Toward the end of class I only needed Andrew Arnold or Seth Kursman to say something and I'd have squid. I had a good chance. Seth talked all the time.

Then David Roth raised his hand and asked a question about what was going to be on the test. Paul looked up and smiled. As Mr. Venezia's answer wound down, Paul's hand shot up.

"Mr. Venezia," he yelled, urgently. Mr. Venezia looked startled for a second and then called on him. Paul said, "Man. Okay. Let's say you had this massive plant, like huge. And it didn't get much light 'cause it was under water." And he looked at me and then at Nerissa. "You know, down there with the squids and stuff." And he smiled and nodded and Nerissa and Jennifer started laughing. And I started laughing.

Nothing happened. Then Venezia made a slight movement with his hand; it quivered in midair as if signaling us to stop, and his mouth hung open, frozen. Then everything sped up. Venezia shot forward, his arms outstretched as if he might tackle Paul. Both of Venezia's hands wrapped around one of Paul's arms and he yanked.

"Yo, Mr. V!" Paul protested as he was snapped out of his chair, off his feet and dragged by an arm out into the hall. Paul kicked his legs, trying to get them under him while Venezia screamed, "You little shit, you've never had respect, you're a no-good son of a bitch, that's what you are!" and he paused for a second, trying to open the door while he held the struggling Paul in his other hand like a huge angry salmon. A few of us stood, unsure of what to do. Paul was hanging by his arm, the pressure on his shoulder looked enormous, and then Mr. Venezia pulled him out of the door and shut it behind him. We could hear Venezia continuing, "What kind of little rat mother . . ." For a moment Paul was visible through the glass, terror in his face. Some of us were still standing. Ray Romero rushed toward the door but it flew back open and Venezia leaned back into the room and choked out, "Ray Romero, you find your seat now!" Paul squealed on the other side.

"Mr. Venezia, man . . ." Ray said.

"NOW," said Mr. Venezia, a finger pointing toward the chairs, and his chin quivered.

Then the door shut and they were both gone. There was silence. Nerissa got up and walked to the door, opened it slowly, and peeked out.

"They're gone," she said, and shrugged at all of us. We were quieter than usual. Steve Kessler said, "That asshole. Someone should tell someone about that asshole." But we didn't do anything. We sat there.

Eventually Mr. Venezia came back, opened the door, and walked up to the board. He whispered, "Now, where were we?"

When I got home I told my parents. My mom called Ms. Arnold, who was on the PTA. She already knew about it. It was a favorite topic in homeroom and at lunch. Over the next weeks there were meetings. Even the superintendent got involved. Paul was switched to a new class. He told me in gym that Venezia was reprimanded by the principal and had to write a letter of apology to him and his parents. Back in Venezia's class all the squares got broken up and we had to put our desks in columns and rows like our other classes and the year crawled on.

The thing that stayed with me, though, was how Venezia reacted to Paul. There were lots of other kids in the class who deserved a wallop more than Paul. Mike Flagg liked to make sucking sounds with his teeth when Venezia's back was turned. Ray Romero sometimes threw wadded-up pieces of paper at the trash can all the way across the room in the middle of one of Venezia's lectures, and Nerissa could back-talk better than George Carlin.

Paul was a good student. He got his homework in on time and got B's on the pop quizzes. He was polite and may have been the only kid in the class who'd never said an unpleasant thing about Mr. V. The squid bingo was rude but not far beyond the culture of a central Connecticut public school heading downward. After all, there were about thirty-five of us in there.

Then, a few weeks after it happened, we were running in gym and I passed Paul at the water fountain, his mouth agape, waiting for the thin stream of water. As I jogged by I realized he reminded me of someone. And then it came to me. He looked like a young Mr. Venezia. He was short, had the same square jaw, the same dark features and tired eyes, and I could imagine Paul standing up in front of the class, one hand on the desk, the other hanging in midair. It was a noxious thought, but when I looked back at Paul it was undeniable. I stopped jogging and watched

Paul drink the water. His jaw looked big. They could have been brothers, or the same person at different ages.

Then what happened made sense. Paul reminded Mr. Venezia of someone else. Probably himself. Maybe a brother or cousin or friend. Someone who'd hurt or disappointed him. So he lashed out at Paul.

Walking along the trail, I started thinking about Amelia's recollection of Aunt Susan. I still didn't know why she'd told me that story. In therapy, people often express themselves indirectly, through urgently told narratives that seem, on the surface, to have no connection to anything we'd been discussing. But when I examine these stories carefully, they often give birth to their true content.

I made the connection. Something about Susan reminded Amelia of herself.

Session Four

When Amelia came in for her fourth session she sat down wearily and told me she'd just run into a colleague in the elevator who didn't realize she'd been out for seven months, and she hadn't told him the truth. The colleague had gotten off the elevator on the seventh floor also, and expected her to walk down the hall to the nursery with him, but instead, Amelia had come into the double doors marked PSYCHIATRY. The friend had coughed and waved good-bye, confused. I acknowledged how challenging that must have been, and then said, "I've been thinking about your aunt Susan."

She said, "You too? See, it's contagious." She laughed.

"I think there's something about Susan that reminds you of yourself."

"Huh," she said. "Hey, what happened to me doing the driving in here?"

"I noticed something along the road," I said. "Are you afraid that what happened to Susan will happen to you?"

She chewed the inside of her cheek. "No. Aunt Susan and I aren't alike. She was always passionate. Too passionate. She drank to calm herself. I'm not passionate. I'm empty. I'm numb. I don't feel anything."

"How much are you drinking?"

"Not much. A glass of wine with dinner a few nights a week."

When I want to know the truth from a patient, I ask the same question three different ways, at three different times. This would be my second time inquiring about her self-destructive tendencies. "Are you having thoughts about hurting yourself?"

"No. Honestly, I'm not. You can stop looking so worried."

"I'll tell you why I've asked. To me, most health care professionals who work on the front line are like ocean liners: by the time anyone can see that we're sinking, we've taken on too much water and it's too late. We've been trained to appear unaffected by stress, which helps keep medical teams and patients calm, but it also prevents anyone from noticing that we're struggling." I stopped for a second. We stared at one another. "I wonder if you've had Aunt Susan on your mind because she was the first person from your life who looked good on the outside, but was struggling desperately on the inside?"

She scratched the back of one of her hands. Sighed.

"Okay, you're on target about the ships. Maybe I haven't been completely honest. That doesn't mean I'm going to run off and kill myself."

"Not completely honest?" I asked.

"Right. I told you my sleep was fine; I misled you a little."

She leaned forward as if we were about to close a business deal. "Okay, look. If I tell you the truth you have to promise not to worry about me. I can't stand looking at you when you look worried. Your forehead gets those little lines on it and I feel like I'm sitting in the principal's office after smoking in the girls' room or something." She smiled at me again. That wide-open smile that says "Nothing bad can happen." Wait a minute. Focus. That smile is a warning flare.

Most of the time I'm fine. I promise. I really am. . . . But sometimes, when I lie down, a simple thought, anything, might start me off, it could be about the weather woman on the news who said it was unseasonably warm. I'll think, what an unusual job she has. I bet she works late, tracking hurricanes and tornadoes, and then I'll think about hurricanes, children clinging together, and wind whipping open screen doors and dust and what do crippled kids think during hurricanes? Do they watch their mother's eyes to understand what's happening? Then I'll think, this is a stupid thing to think about. It's unseasonably warm. Is the air-conditioner working? What the hell is that weather woman doing at work when her crippled kids need her at home?

Every thought moves back to children. Scared kids, vulnerable kids, screaming kids. You know what? Right now I hate kids. I wish we were all hatched unaided at eighteen years old, just laid in a nest and left to fend for ourselves like turtles. I can't stand children right now.

My dreams are horrible and please don't ask. I'm not ready to talk about them. When I awaken in the morning I can tell I'm not done sleeping, but I can't cycle through shallow sleep after 4 A.M. without waking up entirely and when I do I'm relieved to be up. Usually my jaw hurts from grinding my teeth and my shoulders are tight. I didn't used to drink coffee until I got to the hospital but now I hit the pot even before my shower. I used to be a one-cupper but I'm up to four mugs a day.

It's not only my sleep. It's awkward to tell a man this, but you're a shrink, right. I just finished my period. I used to embrace them. I never felt that they were disgusting like some of my friends. Don't get me wrong, they can be a nuisance, but I was proud when I first had a period. They've always represented my femininity. They remind me of my connection to the rest of nature. I have my own tide cycle like the ocean and I'm no different from any other female on the planet, a tigress or blue whale or even a water beetle. It helps that during my luteal phase, when I'm premenstrual, I've never been bitchy. I get sentimental. No, that's wrong, sentimental sounds like it's not genuine emotion. I get more in touch with how deeply I feel about things. My own passions awaken once a month. Like clockwork. At least they used to.

But for the first time in my adulthood my cycle is off kilter. It used to be every thirty days. Clockwork. Now it's twenty-one days or thirty-five. This month I bled for two days, last month for nine. I hate it now. I don't know why. I resent it. The intrusion. The reminder. It feels like my body is rejecting my reproductive system. And I'm tired of bleeding.

It's impacting our intimacy too. Jay doesn't know what to do. Our sex is sterile. It's more like a negotiation than a fucking. For the first time in my life I want to feel how desperately he loves me, how desperately he wants to be in me. I want him to be willing to shed every other part of his life and take me. Before all this happened I cared about foreplay but not anymore. Now I want loving carnage. I'm so hungry to know I exist, that someone else has noticed me. I know you'll tell me that I should let him know what I'm thinking but it's not the same. I don't want him to act like it. I want him to be it. To hunger for me so completely that he can't keep his hands off me.

Jay's a good man who just wants his old wife back. I want her back too.

I felt like I was holding a fragile glass; a wrong move and all would be shard and sliver. The mist was clearing but something important was still missing.

"I know that you and Susan are different in important ways. But is one of the similarities that you both look strong to the people around you, even when you're not?"

"She seemed so together. She was such a ball buster."

"How do you calm yourself? You don't drink?"

"No. Honestly, no. I don't drink. My bane is food. I eat to cope." Amelia is a thin woman. "Before you ask," she continued, "I don't purge. I've never used laxatives or thrown up on purpose. But I do binge. Sometimes when I can't sleep I raid the fridge, I turn off my brain and attack. I'll devour whatever's there. Leftover pasta and cheese and pickles and anything. I'm a serial leftover annihilator. Jay can always tell when I've been into the fridge at night because I become vicious. I can't believe I'm telling you all of this."

I felt a nagging from something she'd said earlier and then remembered it. "Before, when you were talking about your sleep, you mentioned not liking children. I didn't understand that part." She paused, seeming on the verge of telling me something, and then stopped.

"Please. Just give me time," she said.

Session Six

In therapy, people often take two steps forward and one step back. When supervising I often tell the residents that therapy is a negotiation of depths and shallows. In the fifth session Amelia had focused on her parents again and talked about strained friendships. Despite the potential depth of the topics, she tread only in the shallow end. I let her. By the end of the session I realized I'd been transfixed, but hadn't really learned anything new.

Amelia carried her backpack into our sixth session. She had deep circles beneath her eyes and her cheeks looked puffy. She dropped her backpack on the floor next to the love seat, and note cards spilled out of it onto the carpet. There were about thirty of them.

"Oh, sorry," she said. She leaned over and started picking them up. "These are actually related to you. These cards got me in here." She collected them into a neat stack and carefully zipped them into the backpack. "You know, I'm getting used to seeing you. I even looked forward to coming in today. Not that you're helping me at all. But there's something comforting about this office. You have to promise not to rearrange the room at all. Maybe it has feng shui or something."

I nodded. Waited. Then she cleared her throat and said, "I've been so angry at Jay lately. For little things. Not getting the trash out. Wiping the toothpaste on the towels. Existing, I think. I'm so much neater than he is. I have fantasies about what life would be like without him. A little apartment. Simple."

When patients talk about their spouses with anger I often ask them how they met. When people are truly preparing to split up they revise their romantic history. Descriptions of candlelight, broad shoulders, and electric first touches are replaced with words like *accidental* and *convenience*. Instead of sharing the time they were caught in the rain and pressed against one another for warmth, the patient will say, "He was a ticket that helped me get away from my parents," or "She turned into a whiner the minute we were alone, but I stayed anyway."

I met Jay at an art show in Philadelphia. The gallery was once a bar and it had old wooden floors that sagged when you walked. I'd just finished the first rotation of my internship at the University of Arizona and I had a long weekend so I flew home to visit my mother and little sister. In those days, my little sister was studying art at Penn and she took me to the opening. When we walked in I was so happy—everyone looked so not medical. So not like Tom. All the guys had long hair or dreadlocks or earrings or tattoos.

It was crazy crowded. There was great blues playing in the background and artsy teenagers carrying platters of hors d'oeuvres. My sister and I held hands and started looking at the art. Eventually, we came on this lanky guy with hair halfway down his back. He was wearing overalls and a Greek fisherman's cap. He looked scruffy and confused; he was checking out this massive painting of a blue spoon that looked like it was floating. The sun was reflected in the spoon and there were clouds too. The funky guy looked at us and said, "This is swill, eh?" and I told him I kind of liked it.

"What do you know about art?" I said I didn't know anything but I knew what I liked and I liked it. He spoke like a bully.

He said, "Okay. Why do you like it?" And I told him I liked how my attention was drawn to the sun's reflection, and I liked the depth of the color and the soft curves of the handle, like a woman's body. He shook his head a few times and just walked away. Rude bastard. My sister goes, "You realize that he's the one who painted it. He's a grad student a few years ahead of me. He's hot for you. Did you see how he played with his hair while he talked to you?"

So I went to find him. He was by himself, gulping down a cream cheese puff and looking at a sculpture made of plastic milk jugs. I told him I was impressed with his painting and he chewed a few times and he smiled. He had a nice smile and I thought he was going to say something nice but he coughed out, "So what."

It was funny and different from the guys in med school who were so eager for you to tell them how bright or interesting they were. Then he got right in my face, still smiling, and said, "Am I supposed to find solace in your opinion? I paint because I love to paint. Because I have to paint. If I wait for you to come find me and tell me you love the spoon, or hate the spoon, then I lose that fragile thread that stretches from me to the canvas."

That was all I needed to hear. I said, "You had me at 'So what.'" And I smiled at him and kissed him on the cheek, spun, and walked away.

About a half hour later I was leaving with my sister and he stopped us outside. He'd obviously been waiting for me because he grabbed my arm and gave me a piece of newspaper with his name and number scrawled on it. Before I could respond he was gone.

I was only in town for a few days so I called him the next morning. That evening he picked me up from Mom's in a white and orange Ford pickup. He pulled into the driveway and Mom opened the curtain and peeked out at him and grimaced.

"Your father would've never let an automobile fall into such disrepair!" I hushed her but she was right. The muffler sounded like a jet engine and the blinker plastic was cracked. There were holes in the seats and even the fabric on the roof was falling down. He took me back to his apartment and we ordered Chinese take-out and talked about art and fascism and medicine. He was completely unimpressed by physicians. He asked me if I talked to my patients, if I really got to know them. He wanted to know what it was like to watch a birth. And I wanted to know how he felt when he painted. If he painted with his eyes or with his heart. He told me everything I asked. That's what I liked about him. There was no superficial chatter. He'd find a topic and bore into me about it. I felt naked around him, he saw everything.

We didn't sleep together that night. We just lay on his bed together. He said he didn't want to have sex. Wasn't ready for that. It was probably a line but I was so taken with him. I felt so different around him, free to rethink things. If he'd wanted it, I would have given him my body, I would have given him anything. I really did love him from "So what."

The next morning I flew back to Tucson. I fully expected never to hear from him again. We said we'd write each other but I knew it wouldn't happen. He didn't seem like a writer and he said that phones were "alienation tools." I left and jumped right back into the thick of internship.

A month later I came home after a long day; I'd been on call the night before, and an orange and white pickup truck was in my driveway. I was totally exhausted and it didn't register. I just went into my little house and thought maybe my roommate had a friend over. But then I remembered the broken blinker.

I went out and looked in the passenger window. There he was, slumped against the door of the truck, asleep. It must have been 90 degrees, maybe even hotter in the truck. I woke him up and said, "You drove all the way here?"

He said, "So what?" And smiled at me. He had the best smile. He looks so gruff and angry until he smiles and then you just want to squeeze him.

He got out of the pickup, stretched, and jumped into the bed of the truck. He was wearing overalls without a shirt, and I could see his navel. He was so lean in those days. He untied something in the back, and carried his painting of spoons into my little house.

"I had to drop this off," he said. It was the sweetest thing anyone has ever done for me.

We sat quietly. She looked up and behind me, lost in the memory.

Lately I've been so angry at him, and I don't know why.

I came home from grocery shopping, this must have been a few weeks before I started seeing you, and the house was covered with little note cards. We live in a mud adobe. It's a nice house with Saltillo tile and high wood-beamed ceilings. The first card was on the door leading into the kitchen from the garage. It said, "Selling Babe Ruth to the Yankees." At first I didn't get it. I opened the door and came into the kitchen and there was one on the fridge. It said, "Accepting the gift of the Trojan Horse." On the stove there was another: "Forming the band Air Supply."

When Jay heard me puttering in the kitchen he came in. He wanted me to look all over the house with him but I needed to get the groceries in, so that's what I did first. When I'd gotten in all the cold stuff he followed me around. They were affixed everywhere. In the sink and on the cabinets, in the hallway and on the bed and in the bathrooms and closets and even a few on the ceiling fixtures. "Agreeing to a convertible drive near the grassy knoll," "Y2K hysteria," "Sending 'advisors' to Vietnam," "Shirley Temple not taking the role of Dorothy in The Wizard of Oz," *"Jimi Hendrix trying heroin."*

I found some on the front door and there was one down on the mailbox. "Putting Michelangelo's David within reach of anyone." "Agreeing to stay behind as a weather reporter when they evacuated for Hurricane Andrew." "Deciding to be a weather reporter in the first place." "France agreeing to the Louisiana Purchase."

There were personal ones, too. "Purchasing and wearing the Elton John sunglasses you wore at Lynn's wedding." "Not having sex with me behind P. F. Chang's last week." By then, of course, I got it. They were all mistakes. The last card was under my pillow. It said, "To err is human."

It was cute. And funny. And it cheered me up a little. But that wasn't good enough for Jay. He expected an epiphany, violins building to a tearful catharsis. He would've been happy if I'd fallen into his arms and swooned. I just wasn't in the mood. I know that error is human.

Anyway. I smiled and hugged him and then went back to finishing the groceries. It was sweet. He followed me back to the kitchen and said, "That's it?" He had his hurt little boy face on. He puckers his cheeks and he covers his lower lip with his upper. It's the face he puts on when I don't want to have sex or I don't feel like talking to his parents on the phone.

I said, "What's up with you?"

"Do you get it? You don't seem to get it." I was tired already. I'd just spent two hours buying groceries. I hadn't been sleeping. It was just the wrong time.

"Do I get what? That error is human? Of course. Thanks for the reminder."

"But you don't seem any different," said Jay.

"What do you expect? I'm just going to shake off what I did to that child, to those people?"

"Did you know that the only difference between the productive artist and fifty other people is that the productive ones learn from their mistakes and keep working?"

I couldn't believe he said that. I felt this rage boiling up in me.

"I didn't spill some paint, Jay. Back off. Leave it be."

"No. We can't go on like this. You moping around the house, crying to Lynn on the phone all day and looking like this."

"Like what, Jay?"

"You look tortured."

"You're a landscape architect, Jay. If you mess up, someone's yard doesn't get watered. When I fuck up, a family is never the same. Don't fucking talk to me about moping."

He had the sense not to say anything for a few minutes and then he said, "We can't go on like this." And he rubbed his hands together like his job was finished. He does that when it's time for us to stop talking. Like he's got my grime on his hands and he can't quite rub it off. "You need to see someone, Ames. Before it rips us farther apart." Then he went around the house pulling all the cards off, and I went out back and tried to cry. I felt like I needed one of those exhausting sobbings but I didn't have the energy. I could only muster some pathetic sighing.

Later, that night, I saw the note cards in the trash and fished them out. I put them in my backpack. It was sweet, what he did. I don't know why it didn't reach me. But I realized he was right. I was sinking. Soon I'd dip under and be gone.

I know from the scientific literature that people who have intimate relationships live longer. In towns in which a sense of community is emphasized, there is less heart disease. Like storm cellars, social connection and intimacy keep us safe when tornadoes come.

Unfortunately, many of us push people away when we are in crisis—usually the people we need the most. I've seen it over and over, and did it myself when I battled cancer. When I was frustrated with relapses and the relentless chemotherapy, at times I freely vented my anger on those least deserving it. The people I needed the most. My mother. My wife.

Now I worried that Amelia was doing the same to Jay.

"It sounds like he's trying pretty hard to reach you," I said.

"Yeah. I guess he is. I just wish he'd do it a little better. He really sucks at understanding lately."

"You remind me of someone on a mountain hike in unfamiliar country. You're up there in the snow when you start to hear wolves. And they get louder and louder and the sun is going down. You're scared and you begin to run. And you're carrying a heavy pack and running as hard as you can and the wolves notice you and start coming for you just as you find a line of trees. You come to a small hut and you bang on the door just as the wolves arrive. Finally the door opens and there's Jay. There with you. Willing to do anything to help. But he doesn't know how to get rid of the wolves. And he's never carried a pack like yours. And so you get angry at him. The wolves aren't his fault. His inability to understand the burden of responsibility you've carried on your back isn't his fault."

"I've been hard on him?"

"Sometimes when we most need to connect we alienate the people important to us because they don't reach out to us in exactly the way we want."

"Maybe. That's fair. But he does say some moronic things."

"I think you've reacted in a natural but not helpful way to his attempts to reach out to you."

She nodded slowly, agreeing with me, but I also thought she bristled. She rubbed her cheek and her voice was halting. It was the first feedback I'd given that was critical of her. I wondered how she'd respond. She was quieter than usual for the remainder of the session.

"Thank you," she said when our time was up. "See you next week." And she was gone.

When I was in training I had supervisors who advised us never to offer opinions to our patients. It was our job to stay out of the patient's way as long as they were safe and making any progress. But then Arthur Klein, my supervisor at McLean, said to me, "If you came to me in therapy, and in the course of our work you said you thought the sun rises in the north, what would you want me to say?"

"I'd want you to tell me the truth, that it rises in the east."

"Just don't forget how crappy it feels when you've been waiting for the sun to rise in the wrong place for twenty years and some scrub tells you to look over your shoulder."

Session Seven

A melia canceled her next session. Her tenuous voice said into my voice mail, "Uh, I have to meet with some people. Sorry to call at the last minute, but I can't make it. Um. Same time next week. Thanks. Sorry." I wondered if my feedback about her husband during the previous session had hurt her. If meeting people was an excuse.

A week later, when I opened the double doors into the waiting room, Amelia looked different. Her hair had been styled; it was just as long but now it had a wave to it; and had it been colored? She smiled and followed me down the hall to my office. She sat down and said, "Sorry about last week. I had an offer I couldn't refuse. I feel great now, though. I took Ambien last night for the first time. Sleeping pills. Damn miracle. I slept for ten hours straight and if I had nightmares, I don't remember them. It's good to see you, Doctor Dan. You know, I like this little office. It's homey. Comfortable." Then she looked at me. "You look tired. I think today we should focus on you. You look like you could use some time over here. I bet this couch is more comfortable than your office chair. We could switch places for an hour. No one'll know. They loved me on my psych rotation. Tell Doctor Amelia your problems."

I smiled at her. When we're at our best, the most energized and happiest, we are most able to think clearly about the hardest parts of our lives. I said, "Are you ready to tell me what really brings you in here?"

"You're no fun. I knew you'd ask that. And I'm in such a good mood today. You sure we can't talk about you? That would be more interesting." I waited. And waited. Eventually she leaned back on the couch and looked up at the ceiling.

Stacy was my patient. I met her in February when she was ten weeks pregnant. She was a paralegal at a local firm and her husband used to work in the copper mines south of Tucson. When the mines went under they moved up here. He was doing odd jobs when we met. She is a petite little thing, about five feet tall or so. And sweet as she could be. She had that rosy glow that some pregnant women get. That's what I remember about her, she had freckles and rosy cheeks. She was a giggler, too. Every time I touched her she giggled.

She came in for her first visit with her husband. You'd have thought they were going to have the baby that day from how excited they were. They hung on every word I said, as if I were the baby oracle. I like treating people like them. Sometimes we get moms who don't care that they're pregnant. They're numb through the whole thing. Not them.

Her prenatal visits were routine. She was already doing everything right, eating well, exercising, she'd cut back at work to avoid the stress. I think we talked about caffeine; her husband didn't want her to drink coffee at all. I told her I didn't think it was a big deal if she had a cup a day, but then she decided not to. That was the level of our conversations. I liked her from the start.

I also remember their first ultrasound. When they saw the fetus and its little heart pounding away, they cried. That happens frequently: the baby isn't real to new parents until they see and hear it. Sometimes I turn up the volume so that the baby's heartbeat fills the room. Ba-boom. Ba-boom. Ba-boom. It's the first time they feel the new life intertwined with theirs.

I remember one visit when she came in alone. She asked about sex during pregnancy. She said that since she'd gotten pregnant she was "hot to trot." She worried the baby could sense what was happening during sex. I told her not to worry, that sex was fine. I felt like I was her older sister.

She sailed through her pregnancy. She had a few bouts with nausea but gained a reasonable amount of weight. Her pressure was fine. I think the worst thing we dealt with was a little ankle swelling. I didn't see her husband again until we started to get close, at about thirty-four weeks or so. By then she'd stopped working.

It's fun to be with the new mothers when they're excited. It's one of the only parts of medicine where you work with happy people on joyous occasions. At that visit she came in and showed me Polaroids of the baby's new room as if she needed my blessing. She asked about the height of changing tables, what I knew about car seats, bottles, and breast pumps. She was practically manic.

They were going to Lamaze together. They'd decided they wanted as natural a childbirth as possible. She still wanted to deliver in the hospital, but she didn't want an epidural or other pain meds. She wanted to experience the birth completely. I ask all my moms to fill out questionnaires about the birth; it helps me understand what they want, and then we talk. It gives me an opportunity to explore the implications of their plans with them. That's when I warn all my moms about the possibility of C-sections. I have the same conversation with all my new mothers, just so we're on the same page.

So we had the questionnaire conversation, and she giggled through it. She didn't hear a word I said. After I talk about C-sections and other possible complications, most moms are sober, but she just said, "It's really going to happen, isn't it? I'm really going to be someone's mommy! Thank you so much." I told her I hadn't done anything yet, but she hugged me and left.

I don't remember the next visits. I saw her a few more times but her antepartum was uncomplicated. I looked forward to delivering her.

She was late. She got to her due date and nothing happened. Three days, four days. It's completely normal, of course. About a week later her labor finally started. She came into the hospital saying that she was in labor, but when I checked she hadn't dilated at all. I sent her back home. Her contractions weren't regular, still averaging twenty minutes apart.

"But I'm in labor!" she told me.

"You're just starting. Go home and rest." She seemed devastated when I sent her home. She came back the next morning in real labor. She was a few centimeters dilated but still wasn't having regular contractions. It would have been cruel to send her home again.

We brought her into a labor room. They're beautifully decorated. They have fancy wallpaper and large beds with window views of the Catalina Mountains. She settled in, playing the CD from The Big Chill and fiddling with a new video recorder, one of those digital gizmos you can fit in your palm.

I'm encouraged when moms dilate to four centimeters because it means that they're in the active phase of labor. Most moms dilate one more centimeter an hour until they're completed at ten centimeters. So four centimeters is a sign that the show is starting. The other nice aspect of active labor is that we can help things along if mom gets exhausted. We can give IV Pitocin to stimulate contractions. Stacy and her husband wanted as natural a childbirth as possible, so that was out.

Stacy dilated slower than most. Late that afternoon she was still only at three centimeters but her contractions were getting more regular. I expected her to go active at any time so I stayed in the hospital that night. I slept some but not well—I used to be able to sleep anywhere. These days it's home or nothing. Anyway, every few hours I looked in on her. She was sleeping sporadically, pretty exhausted. Her husband had some back problems and he was completely sleep deprived. At one point the alarms went off in the physicians' pod because the baby's heart had decelerated, and I rushed in, but it turned out that she had just moved in her sleep and the monitors had been pulled off her belly. I put the monitors back and tried to go back to sleep.

At 2 A.M. she was still only a little more than three centimeters dilated. Finally at about 5 A.M. she got to four centimeters. I told her she was now officially in active labor. At this point I was doing all right. I'd had a few hours of sleep during the night and I was excited to help her deliver.

By sunrise, Stacy was a different woman. Even though she'd only been in labor, really, for ten hours, to her it felt like a few days and she looked it. Her husband was bouncing between exuberance and exhaustion. I recognized the sleep-deprivation mood swings. I get like that too. So now she started to dilate, one centimeter an hour, but we had a new problem, prolongation of descent. The cervix was dilating but Stacy's little girl, our passenger, wasn't descending down the birth canal. We were going to have the curtain open but no star. I had this instinct right then that I should do a C-section. It was a feeling, a powerful feeling, that it was the right thing to do. But I knew Stacy didn't want that and the algorithm didn't say it was time. I checked the telemetry strip, the piece of paper coming out of the heart rate monitor.

Stacy's baby was having early decelerations. Her heart rate was dropping to 100 during contractions; in newborns we want their heart up around 120. But this happens all the time during some labors. As long as the decelerations are early, or happen during the contraction, we don't worry, it usually means the child's head is being mildly squeezed a little during the contraction. It happens in most births.

Late decels are different. That's when the fetal heart rate drops after the contraction is over. That usually means the baby isn't getting enough oxygen. Or if the baby's heartbeat doesn't change at all during contractions that can be bad too; it can mean the heart is hungry. The concern, of course, is that the baby's central nervous system isn't getting oxygenated blood. When I checked she wasn't having any late decels and the variability was fine. I had no reason to do a C-section, even though I still wanted to.

I suggested a cesarean to Stacy—that it was an option—but she was adamant. She reminded me that in our country we do more C-sections than anywhere else in the world by far. I think some of her emotion was the sleep deprivation talking, but she was right, too, C-sections are real surgeries. Vaginal births are beautiful. Natural. But I still had that urge to do the cesarean. She told me she wanted to wait just a little longer.

I waited and then checked on the baby again, maybe forty minutes later. She was still higher than we'd like. She wasn't coming down and she was a little twisted too. Nothing bad, but not great either. At about 7 A.M., the new shift of nurses arrived. One of the nurses who had Stacy the morning before came in and said, "You guys are a wreck." She was great. She got the husband to go get some food and walk around a bit. She put Stacy in McRobert's position. In McRobert's the mom sits up and grabs her knees. It can help with descent, but it was still too early. I went and got a cup of coffee and came back.

At this point I felt aggressive about getting the baby out. It's my job to balance my patient's desire for a natural birth against the probability of birth complications. Dad came back and I explained this to both of them. Stacy asked if we could wait just a little longer. She had an edge in her voice. I remember feeling like I'd be failing them if I did the C-section. I said I'd check. When I measured, the baby had dropped down to about +2; we grade descent from −3 to +3. The baby still had a few centimeters to go. We talked about options. I put a probe in her uterus, an IUPC that measures the strength of her contractions. They were fine, which suggested that it could be the size or shape of her pelvis that was the problem. This happens sometimes with tiny moms.

"I can try to bring her down using suction, or forceps." We talked about it and I decided to try the suction but it didn't work. Finally I tried forceps.

Forceps are like metal salad tongs, only they're in the shape of spoons. I laid them on each side of the baby's head and tried to pull her down. It took some work. You have to pull hard. I did but it didn't work either. Anyway, I checked and thought she'd moved a little bit, another centimeter, maybe down to 2.5. Then I looked at the strip again and there wasn't a lot of variability in the fetal heart strip. Her heart was beating at the right rate, but it wasn't changing at all. Even with contractions. I must have made a face when I looked at the strip because when I looked up Stacy and her husband were freaked.

"We're doing a C-section now," I told Stacy.

"No. I don't want that," she told me.

"You want a healthy baby? Then we're doing a C-section. I'm sorry, sweetie, but this is the only way to get your baby out, she can't get out this way and we all want a healthy baby girl."

"What does that machine say?! What's happening?" she screamed at me. Her face turned beet red and her eyes bulged. The nurse looked at the strip and called for the NICU team and seconds later they poured into the room, there were about five of them.

I tried to tell Stacy that we just needed to get her baby out, but Dad was yelling too and I couldn't talk over him. "What the hell is happening?" he kept saying. He was holding his head with both hands and one of them had the little camera, the red light was on, he was taping. Stacy was screaming. It was surreal. This kind, freckled woman was screaming at me. And I couldn't see her because her husband was in my way, his bulk flexing, rigid. Get him out, I told a nurse. NOW. I was at my wit's end. My skin was tingling and my head was pounding and the big ranting miner wasn't helping. I settled myself down and just told Stacy to sit tight.

Then one of the NICU guys looked over the strip as we were prepping for the C-section and he whispered, "Why'd you wait so long?" And I didn't answer him. The anesthesiologist was setting up the spinal and I was getting the tray ready, but what he said stuck with me, like when I leave the house without my lunch or forget my pager. I had the sense that what he'd said was important but I didn't fully comprehend it.

As soon as the spinal was good I did it. I was on autopilot. There must have been ten people in the room. Her uterus was a little odd; I had to cut across vertically, and she won't be able to labor that uterus again, she'll need another C-section if she gets pregnant. But I delivered her a live healthy baby, and that was a great relief. The APGAR wasn't great, it's a measure of how healthy the baby is, but the NICU team said she'd go to the nursery instead of the NICU because she was breathing well and looked okay.

We showed Stacy her baby. She said, "Hi, Miranda!" and then the team took Miranda to the nursery and Stacy fell asleep. While I was closing Stacy, a nurse brought back her husband. He stood in the doorway and apologized to me. "I shouldn't have gone off on you, you were right to kick me out." And I realized why I wanted him out of the room so badly. His face was unshaven and he looked menacing, like my father sometimes. I closed Stacy and told him I'd look in on them again the next day. I was exhausted and wanted to go home.

Before I left I put a needle in one of the arteries in the umbilical cord and aspirated some blood. It's routine. I sent it to Respiratory to get pH readings. They're more accurate than APGAR scores and tell us how acidotic or hypoxic a baby is. When a baby doesn't breathe it can't dispose of carbon monoxide and it builds up; the baby gets acidotic and the pH goes down. Normal pH is about 7.3. After I sent it to the lab I went and did my chart notes. When I was done I checked the labs I'd sent. Miranda's pH came back at 7.04. Low, but not terrifying. I went to the nursery to check on her. I thought it would be a pleasant thing to do before I left.

When I got in there the neonatal intensive care team was all around one of the bassinets. They'd closed the curtain so that people out in the hallway couldn't see into the nursery. There was an attending, two residents, and two NICU nurses huddled around the bassinet. I couldn't get close enough to see what was happening. There was commotion. And a terrible smell. Like sulfur. Then they whisked the baby off to the NICU. Five of them running next to her.

A pediatrician was there too. He's an older practitioner, he's been in the community for years and was one of my attendings when I was a resident. He told me Miranda had had a seizure while he was examining her. She'd been floppy; her limbs lacked the muscle tone you'd expect, and dropped when you moved them around. And then she'd seized, violently shaking. The NICU team had been called and appeared immediately. He asked about the labor and I told him.

When I was done he said, "Well, don't blame yourself. No way to know if it was oxygen deprivation." He put a hand on my arm as if we were at a funeral and he started to leave. I was stunned. I was still so tired. I didn't get it at first. I stopped him and asked what he meant about the oxygen deprivation. He said, "A seizure, the floppiness. We won't know for a while, but I've seen enough kids who started life like this. Don't hold me to it, kids' brains can do all sorts of great things, but my bet is she'll turn out to have problems."

"What do you mean?" I asked him. "Epilepsy?"

"Maybe. But seizures, the floppiness, I'd bet on cerebral palsy. Could be from the birth, but we'll probably never know what caused it." He shrugged and left.

The smell of sulfur was still everywhere. When I asked one of the nurses what the smell was she said, "What smell?" It was in my head.

Three weeks before I came to see you, Miranda's pediatrician called me. Miranda had been missing developmental milestones. There'd been feeding problems. She was late lifting her head up. Her limbs were stiff, spastic. An MRI had shown some scarring. The pediatrician wanted to wait but Stacy had pressed him for a referral and a pediatric neurologist had diagnosed Miranda with cerebral palsy.

"I thought you'd want to know," he told me.

I should have trusted my instinct to get Miranda out of Stacy sooner. I should have done the cesarean immediately, when I first felt that urgency. That moment is with me all the time now, I can't expel it from my head. I feel urgency. Like there's something I have to do right now only there's nothing. And nothing makes it go away. I've tried showers, sleeping, drinking, sedatives, screaming, eating, fucking, talking, nothing. Nothing. Nothing.

Amelia looked at me and winced.

Her face darkened. Her eyes unfocused as if she were back there in the nursery. I imagined her hunched over the bassinet. She doubled over onto her knees, coughing. She reached for a tissue and held it over her mouth and stayed like that for a long time.

My first urge was to get on my knees next to her and say that it could have happened to anyone. To put a hand on her shoulder. To say that there but for the grace of God go all of us. But she looked like she had more to say and I didn't want to interrupt. We sat for a long time.

She was quiet. And then she said, "Is it really healthy for me to express all of this?"

"I'm afraid so," I said.

"We used to think that drilling holes in people's skulls to release demons was good for us too."

"That's not good? We still do trephination in this department," I said.

She coughed a laugh. "There's going to be a malpractice case. When I canceled last week I told you I was meeting some people who made me an offer I couldn't refuse? They were lawyers."

I had my pager on last week. I wear it when I'm officially working for the university. For a little while every week I feel like a physician, but it hadn't gone off for four or five months. Then, last week, it did.

I answered the page and it was Michael O'Sullivan, the hospital attorney. At first I was disoriented; I expected to be talking to a colleague. O'Sullivan said, "We have to meet right now." I told him he'd have to wait. I wasn't in the hospital. He said, "We've already cleared it with your chairman. Please meet us in the administration conference room on the second floor, we'll be waiting." I asked him what it was about and he wouldn't tell me over the phone.

So I called you first and canceled our appointment. The meeting was in this nice conference room with leather chairs and oil paintings of the deans of the medical school lining the wall. I'd never been there before. My first response, sitting down, was the room. "How come our clinic waiting room looks like it's in the Third World and this room exists for the deans and the lawyers?" I actually said that out loud, and the two lawyers looked at each other. One of them wrinkled up his face, like he'd smelled something bad. The whole thing seemed comical to me. They acted like I was a serial killer they'd been asked to defend.

One of them, Michael, sat next to me, and the other one sat on the other side of the table. For a moment they both talked at once and I said, "Wow, lawyers in stereo." It was the littlest joke, but they didn't like that either. Michael said, "I represent the hospital, Wally here will be representing you. Most of the time we'll work together and we'll be on the same side. You do need to know that we may become opponents. There's hospital equipment involved, and our interests won't necessarily overlap. Do you understand?"

I said that I did.

"Fine. Could you start by explaining why you never called risk management after Miranda Paulsen's birth?" Risk management is the

lawyers. As you probably know, whenever we have a bad outcome we're supposed to call them so they can start to defend us from malpractice suits.

"What are we talking about?" I asked them.

"Ms. Paulsen's delivery of Miranda Paulsen on September third."

"Why didn't I call you? It didn't occur to me."

"You had an atrocious outcome and it didn't occur to you? Didn't you remember your orientation?"

"At the time, my patient's health was more on my mind than a lawsuit. A lawsuit didn't even occur to me."

"That's unfortunate," Michael said. "We can't defend you adequately if we're sideswiped with news we should have known about months ago. You realize that we're behind in our preparation."

Wally, the older one, interrupted. "Well, you're here now. That's fine. We're going to spend the next three hours together. We understand you have no clinical duties today. Is there anyone else you need to call?"

"No."

Wally said, "Good. Start at the beginning. Tell us everything about Ms. Paulsen." So I started to tell them about the day Stacy gave birth, and he interrupted me, saying, "No, from when you first laid eyes on her."

So then I started at the beginning and told them everything. I liked Wally more, he was in short sleeves, and he had a gentle way of asking questions. He had a Sun-Tran union pencil, that's the bus drivers' union in town, and I don't know why but I liked him because he had that pencil. It felt like he was just trying to do his job as well as he could. He had a yellow pad and drew diagrams on it while I talked. Then he opened his briefcase and pulled out a copy of Stacy's medical chart. It had multicolored tabs at different parts. He'd obviously been working on this case nonstop since they heard about it. The level of the questions was absurd. They looked for signs of mistakes at each of her visits. Thank heavens her pregnancy was healthy; I couldn't imagine what they would have been asking if she'd had a hard go of it.

He asked questions like, "You wrote here that the ultrasound showed development at fifteen weeks but your other calculation said she was fourteen weeks pregnant. Why is that? You note the fetus heart rate at one-twenty, is that high or low?" Questions like that. Every detail in the chart was examined. No matter what the question or answer, no matter what I said, Michael acted as if I'd just admitted to murdering someone. The older one just scrawled away. I kept reminding myself that they're lawyers, not obstetricians. They couldn't know if I'd made a mistake unless I told them.

Then we got to the birth. I told them everything I remembered, including the early deceleration, the lack of variability, and the C-section. Then Michael opened her chart and showed me the strip from the night before Stacy's delivery. I thought he was going to ask me another absurd question but there on the strip, plain as morning, were a series of late decelerations recorded at 3 A.M. I stopped breathing. I sat there staring at the strip, thinking it must be wrong. Someone else's. But there it was. September third, 3:17 A.M. Her medical record number and stamp on the strip. And further, long periods when Miranda's heart rate didn't change. Flat.

They showed me a few others. 2:12. 4:31. I felt like the room was spinning. If I'd seen them I would have done the cesarean immediately. Michael and Wally kept asking me questions but I couldn't even hear them. I felt that high-pitched ringing in my ears, like at night, and I thought I smelled ammonia. I started coughing. I felt like I couldn't get enough air. I knew it was psychosomatic. There was nothing really wrong with my lungs, but I couldn't breathe. Michael got up and brought me some water. I noticed the way he did it, like it was normal for me to be choking.

When I stopped coughing, I said I wanted to talk to Stacy. And her husband. I wanted to call them both. Michael responded to me like I was a passenger on an airplane asking for a bit of fresh air. He said, with the calmest voice you can imagine, that any interaction with them could jeopardize the case completely. That anything I said would be taken out of context and used against me in depositions and eventually in court. Anything approximating an apology would be dangerous, that even calling her, if I didn't normally call my patients this far after birth, would be damaging in itself. I told him this was a special situation. That I'd just discovered I was responsible. Michael looked at Wally and snapped, "You don't want to be in a deposition saying, 'I called as soon as I knew she was suing me' because the lawyer will say, 'To try to talk her out of it or because you felt guilty?'"

Wally interrupted, "Trust us on this. We've been doing this a long time. You could destroy your own defense if you called her."

They continued asking questions. After a while I started to feel relief. Like I'd been carrying a crime in my heart, something terrible I'd done years ago that had finally been discovered and exposed. I was Raskolnikov from Crime and Punishment. *The young ascetic who murdered his pawnbroker and her sister and was relieved when he was found out. At first I couldn't understand why I felt that way. But now, sitting here, I think I felt relief because I've known I'm a fraud all these years. My mistakes confirmed ideas I've had about myself throughout my medical training. It was only a matter of time before someone figured out that I wasn't capable of being a doctor.*

When I was in college I had enough money to travel to London but not enough to live there for more than a week without a job. I found work in a hotel. There were men and women from all over the world working there, from France, Ireland, Spain. One of my favorites was a dentist from Bolivia, but in London he could only wash dishes. He had unruly hair that set off in all directions after a day in the steam. As Amelia told me about the lawyers, her voice reminded me of the dentist's. She had the same resigned drop at the end of her sentences. The same humble shrug.

She paused. The stillness was broken by the central air-conditioner humming to life. Cold air descended on us. I felt a twinge in my back. I ignored it. She looked like she was going to say something, her chin quivered, but then she pressed her lips together until her face was calm. She squinted at the base of my chair and then looked at me. She was waiting for my response.

There is a moment like this in every good therapy, when the ice breaks, when the crystal surface cracks apart. It's usually uglier than the clean revelations in movies. Instead, there's usually dirt and bone, shards and confusion.

She wanted me to comfort her, to tell her it wasn't her fault. I was about to when something stopped me. What if Miranda were my child?

I'm hovering over a bassinet.

A younger Alexandra, my daughter, is in there, her feet and hands are floppy.

She can't move her head.

Oh my God.

What was she thinking that night? How had she missed the decelerations? What kind of doctor . . . And then I felt ashamed. She needed my comfort; anyone could make a mistake; why was I having such a strong response to this one? Who am I to judge?

Amelia was running a hand through her hair, her face slanted, but watching me. She caught my expression. Winced. Looked away. My mouth was parched. It was time for me to say something but I didn't. We sat.

How come she didn't tell me this before? She quit work because of this case. Why didn't she tell me about this during our first session?

I didn't speak soon enough. I sensed her panic rising, choking off our air. She had gray tentacles and her hopelessness reached across the room and suctioned my throat, my limbs.

She broke the silence. "I kept working after delivering Miranda. Consciously, I didn't blame myself. At that point, I didn't know about the late decelerations, but I felt in my heart that there was something wrong with what I'd done. Whenever I made a decision, even something small, I thought of the other alternative with more conviction. It didn't matter what it was. Picking out slacks for the morning, shampoo."

A week or two after I delivered Miranda I was assigned a new patient named Sophia. When we first met she held one of my hands in both of hers and said that she'd asked around and heard I was the best, she was thrilled that I was able to see her. I started like I always do, just sitting with her, asking questions about her life. She was a heavy hitter in optics, a vice president at Breault Research. She'd been on our faculty and on faculty at UNC at Chapel Hill. She'd only just moved back here. She radiated authority but said that she worried about her job; she'd been so career focused, this was a change for her, but she made it clear that she was excited to be a mother too.

She was about twenty-four weeks pregnant but still looked thin. She had blond hair and was about thirty-five. She was one of those strong women who talk fast and are used to getting what they want.

The intake was going along fine and then she mentioned that about a month before she'd had some bleeding. Spotting. She tried to get in to see her OB in Chapel Hill but the spotting stopped. Then in the flurry of the move she hadn't thought about it again. I put her on the ultrasound and saw a pocket of blood behind the placenta. And then I realized she was a previa. Her baby's placenta was growing over the cervix, the only road out of the uterus. Usually, placenta previas resolve on their own. As the uterus stretches to accommodate the baby's increased size, the placenta moves out of the way. But sometimes they don't resolve and that's potentially dangerous. We worry about rupturing the placenta and massive hemorrhage. It's rare but that's not what I thought when I saw it. I felt terror. This is how it's going to happen. This is how my career is going to end. It's happening right now. I'm going to lose her.

I tried to settle down. I looked more carefully. As I got better angles on the placenta it was obvious that it was resolving. False alarm. I must have showed it when I first saw the previa because my face was hot and she was saying, "What? What's a placenta previa?" She had a forceful voice.

Any resident could follow a case like this. At twenty-four weeks we just watch them. It was obvious that the previa was resolving. There was nothing to worry about. So I explained it to her very calmly. About previas and why I'd originally looked concerned and how it was going to be fine. If she had any spotting again she needed to get in immediately, but I didn't expect her to have any more and her baby looked fine.

The minute she was out of the office I started obsessing. I wondered if I'd really seen the previa resolving or if I'd just wanted to see it. I had a copy of the film; I hadn't printed the best angle, but I studied it over and over that day.

Over the next couple weeks I kept asking the staff to pull her chart so I could look at the film. I had this image of her awakening one morning, her sheets stained crimson. I looked her up on the Web. I wanted to know if she was the type of woman who would come in immediately if she started spotting. She'd ignored some spotting during the move; what kind of woman does that? From the Web I learned that she was at the top of her field. She had a doctorate from Rochester, one of the best optics programs in the country. She'd taught here, and then in North Carolina where she helped start a new company before she was recruited into Breault.

Two weeks after our appointment I called her at home in the evening to reschedule her follow-up visit. I wanted to move it to the end of the day when I'd have plenty of time after our appointment, just in case she was in crisis when she came in. It was awkward. She sounded flattered that I was calling her. She even said she wasn't used to physicians calling her directly, she usually heard from the receptionist. I wanted to ask if she was spotting. But I held it together.

A few days later I looked up her work number in her chart and called Breault. I didn't have a good reason to call. I wasn't sleeping much and I couldn't stop thinking about her. They told me she was out sick for a few days and I thought about going to her house—just in case she was bleeding. I didn't, but I called the next morning. I thought I was showing restraint. Her secretary must have recognized my voice, because before telling me if Sophia was there she asked, "Who's calling, please?" And I hung up.

When I saw her at our regularly scheduled follow-up a few weeks later I said, "You've been sick?"

And she said, "No."

And I said, "But you've missed work?" She looked at me like I was a freak.

"You've been calling me at work, haven't you? Why?" And I couldn't explain.

I didn't feel like a doctor anymore. I lied. I told her I hadn't called her. But I fumbled and coughed and sputtered.

She was very polite. She left and never came back. She started seeing Hugh, he's also on the faculty. I bet she thought I was a lesbian, attracted to her.

She must have told Hugh what I'd done because he was different from then on. It was subtle. He avoided me. If he saw me in the faculty office he thought of an excuse to leave quickly. I swear he once faked being paged to leave; we put our pagers on vibrate when we don't want the beeping to interrupt seminars and he suddenly looked down at his pager after I walked into the staff room and then he left.

I kept working for a few months after that but I consider Sophia my last patient. I saw her at the grocery store some months later, as big as a house. She was in the frozen foods. Just then I smelled something rancid, and I'm sure it was in my mind. Now whenever I'm really stressed, I smell things.

She looked up at me, a hint of embarrassment on her face.

I asked, "What's made you wait to tell me all of this?"

"I should be able to handle it. Cope. Seeing you these weeks I've kept hoping I would suddenly feel better. Maybe if I just had a nibble of therapy it would spread systemically and *voilà,* I wouldn't need to see you anymore and I wouldn't have to go into the details."

"But it doesn't feel that way?"

"It's like I'm getting sucked into the therapy vortex. The more I come here, the more I need to say, the worse I seem to feel."

"Maybe the things you need to say are like rocks that you're carrying around and letting them out will help you feel lighter." I knew I was relying on therapy truisms. The patient must talk about the deepest anguish to excise it. But it felt thin.

"I don't feel lighter. I feel nauseous."

"Maybe there are still too many rocks in there for you to notice any difference yet."

The session ended awkwardly. After a long silence she looked at her watch and said, "Time's up, next week, okay?" And was gone. I wondered if she'd be back.

I realized that I'd had shooting pains in my back for most of the session. They'd distracted me. In therapy, when it's going well, I often notice that my patient's gestures or postures mirror my own. I might rub a cheek and then see Amelia do the same. Or we cross our legs simultaneously or lean forward at the same time. But my pain had interrupted the natural flow of our movements. As Amelia had described her meeting with the lawyers I'd found myself rubbing my back, trying to soothe the pain.

Occasional shooting pain in my back is a steady part of my life. I was diagnosed with Hodgkin's disease, a lymphatic cancer, in 1987. I had six months of chemotherapy and a month of radiation. It didn't work. I relapsed. I had a bone marrow transplant, but it too was fruitless. The surgeries and radiation were unsuccessful.

My wife, Terry, and I went out to Stanford Medical Center, where my physician told me that he did not think he could cure me but that he was willing to try. I was put on an experimental protocol in which I had chemotherapy treatments twice a week. My body, already tired from massive treatment, weakened. I lost forty pounds. I had difficulty walking up stairs or opening doors. I aged.

When I was ten weeks into the protocol I awoke one morning to sizzling pain along my right shoulder blade. It was fierce and had no obvious cause. I took Tylenol but it didn't help. My skin was sensitive; even the slightest brush of fabric caused electric ripples across the skin of my back.

Two days later a rash, welts, and then blisters broke through and covered the right quadrant of my upper back. Terry recognized the symptoms of shingles. Also known as *Varicella zoster,* shingles is a painful, opportunistic virus that lives in the nerve roots in everyone who has had chicken pox. Our immune systems usually keep it in check. But in people who are severely immune compromised, the virus can "break out." If not contained quickly, permanent nerve damage, known as postherpetic neuralgia, is possible.

We quickly went to the oncology clinic. After waiting a few hours a resident was able to see me. He apologized for eating his lunch while we spoke. He had frizzy hair and a day's growth on his face. He took one look at my back, whistled, and wrote a prescription for acyclovir. I'd take one a day. The pain would be gone soon, he promised, and if I was lucky, I would only have mild nerve damage.

Two days later, the rash and blisters had widened their path. Shingles continued its march across my back like an old propaganda film showing the expansion of the Third Reich. I waited, giving the medication time to work. But soon I was unable to sleep or lift my arm without sharp protests from my skin. A week later my back was entirely covered. I looked and felt as if I'd been whipped. We went back.

This time I was seen by Dr. Hoppe, the director of the radiation oncology clinic. I was surprised. Why would an eminent member of the faculty take time now for a problem that warranted only the attention of a resident before? Hoppe, a tall man who looked about forty, sat in the corner of the cramped clinic room and calmly asked me detailed questions about how I was doing, the rest of my treatment. I wondered at first if he thought it was a psychological problem; he seemed so much more interested in my well-being than any previous physician I'd seen at Stanford. Had I had an unusual response to the acyclovir? Perhaps he wanted to write up the case? But then he clasped his hands together and said, "We owe you an apology. Our young doctor owes you an apology too. You were underdosed on the acyclovir. Here's the appropriate prescription," and he scrawled on his pad. When I saw the bottle in the pharmacy I realized I'd gotten only one-fifth the appropriate dosage.

Now, ten years later, a few times a month I have shooting pain, usually at night, along a nerve that runs across a shoulder blade. There's numbness back there, vast tracts of skin that will not have feeling again. Occasionally the nerve awakens, tries to fire, and sets my back ablaze. It's a little painful but not life changing. When I sit still, and consider it, I'm not angry. But maybe because I didn't lose that much. I was lucky to live, after all.

But why did my back flare during this session? I know the mind and body are more than just connected, they are part of the same system. Was my back expressing what I refused to acknowledge? That I am, beneath it all, still a vulnerable patient?

She'd expected me to comfort her and I hadn't. When she needed me to be a sympathetic doctor, aware of the burdens we all carry and the mistakes that can be made so easily, my back had reminded me of what happened to me at the hands of a careless physician. And unlike my mild nuisance, Stacy's and Miranda's lives were altered forever.

In most of my work with patients, having a history of cancer has been useful and positive. With medical patients I instinctively understand life from inside the experience. But when I started working with physicians I never anticipated the moments when my experience would be more like a wedge driven between us. My back was still hot and ablaze. I should have anticipated this, prepared for it. After all, I'd had a rehearsal once before, when I'd responded to someone else's medical mistake like the patient I am, with white-hot anger and not an ounce of empathy.

It had happened in 1994, the year after my internship at McLean, when I accepted an endowed fellowship at Harvard

Medical School. It was funded by a wealthy donor who asked only that we learn to counsel people facing medical crises. Through the deaths of two of her children, she'd learned that mental health professionals were ill equipped to counsel medical patients. There were four of us in the fellowship; together we functioned partly as a think tank and partly as a training group, refining counseling techniques designed for children and adults facing medical crises.

I was placed in the Brigham and Women's outpatient psychiatry clinic and the Dana Farber Cancer Institute's Jimmy Fund Clinic. In the Jimmy Fund Clinic I worked with children with cancer. Both placements were excellent. There were skilled supervisors and plenty of work.

In March of 1995, when I was nine months into the fellowship, the atmosphere at Dana Farber suddenly changed. I felt it before I knew what had caused it. There was an electric anxiety in the air. Staff marching off to this meeting and that. Angry whispers emanated from the "suits" clustered, waiting to go up in the elevator. I knew that as a trainee, I'd be sheltered from all things political, but I was still curious. Then, a few weeks after the change I was standing outside Andrea Patenaude's door, a psychologist and researcher who was supervising my work, when she stepped out of her office, a notebook in her hand. She apologized and said in a hushed tone that she had to cancel our weekly supervision.

"There's a meeting I have to attend. Emergency," she said.

When I was at McLean there'd been layoffs. Hospitals across the country were merging or reducing staffs. I asked if there was a budget crisis. She shook her head. "Come on in for a second." She opened the door to her office and we stepped inside. She closed the door behind us. She told me that one of the college students working as a data clerk on a research protocol had discovered a mistake.

Three months before, Betsy Lehman, a health reporter for the *Boston Globe,* was a participant in a research protocol for women with breast cancer. She was thirty-nine years old, a gifted reporter. The protocol required that she receive Cytoxan, a drug I'd had during my bone marrow transplant. I remembered that even at normal doses, Cytoxan could cause heart failure, nausea, vomiting, and reduced platelet and white blood cells.

An oncology fellow, James Foran, had misread the research protocol describing the dosing of Cytoxan. Or, Andrea said, there were rumors that he'd read the protocol accurately but that it had been written poorly. In any event, Betsy received four times the dose she should have been given for four consecutive days. She had horrible side effects and eventually died of heart failure. Maureen Batemen, another patient, had also received an overdose. She was a fifty-two-year-old schoolteacher who was now hospitalized with permanent heart damage.

Unlike other hospitals, Dana Farber didn't have a computer system to catch prescription errors. The fellows were supposed to know the correct dosage for all prescriptions. It was Dana Farber, after all. Harvard.

"I'm sorry, the heads of every department have to be at the meeting, we'll talk about your patients next week," Andrea said, and we parted.

After speaking with Andrea an unexpected fury had filled my chest. For five years, during that long battle with Hodgkin's disease, I felt perennially vulnerable to physicians. Dependent. I'd resented the above-the-fray smugness, the quiet knowledge that my death would have little impact on them, that as I flailed in the rapids they seemed so calm on the banks. I knew that if they really appreciated the level of vulnerability I felt, the bone-jarring fear that comes with a life-threatening illness, they would have been different, somber, connected. Betsy Lehman's death became a talisman for me, a symbol of everything wrong with the system.

But now in the quiet of my Tucson office, I couldn't help but think about the physician who wrote Betsy Lehman's order, Dr. James Foran. I hadn't thought of him in years. What had happened to him? What was in his heart? Had anyone told him it could have happened to anyone? What would I have said if he'd been my patient?

And then I thought of Amelia. Is it ethical for me to treat her when I can't stop thinking about how I'd feel if I were her patient? If she'd injured my child? I treat a lot of physicians, I don't usually imagine myself as their patient, but few of them acknowledged their mistakes. This hadn't happened when I treated other doctors who had cheated on their husbands or wives, or gone on alcoholic benders, or lied to their children. I'd thought about their spouses, considered their perspectives from an analytical, removed position, like a man surveying a chess set. I'd never fully imagined myself being their victim, filled with indignant rage and worry. Or become one, as I had at the end of this session, experiencing what I'd feel like if my daughter Alexandra had been born like Miranda. Perhaps I should excuse myself. There are some very competent mental health professionals in the area. It was comforting. Escape. That's it. I enjoyed a moment of respite with the thought. But what would happen to Amelia if I turned her over to someone else? It would be a rejection. I'd be telling her, indirectly but strongly, that her mistake was inexcusable. She'd be devastated. This is my job.

Session Eight

"Why do you think I want to know so much about cerebral palsy? Why can't I just let it go?" Amelia was asking. We were halfway through our session. It had started slowly. It's common that after an intense session the next one is slower, as if after swimming in the cold depths we all want to wade for a while. But now her intensity was returning.

There was a part of me that was surprised that she'd returned. I felt guilty, I'd rejected her by not offering her a soothing word when she needed me most. I knew she must have felt my withdrawal and expected that she might not return to see me again. But she was in the waiting room at the appointed time, hands patiently folded in her lap.

She leaned back on the couch and twisted her hair with one hand.

One of the strange things about medicine is that people think that if you're a doctor you know all of medicine. We don't. We only know our areas. I remember a few basic facts about cerebral palsy. That it's an umbrella term for chronic motor disorders. I know that it isn't contagious and that the motor problems generally don't get worse. It's usually caused by a problem in pregnancy or a birth injury. I vaguely remember that pregnant moms exposed to German measles can have a child with cerebral palsy.

Often the motor problems are severe and children don't reach developmental milestones on time, or, in some cases, ever. A four-year-old might be more like a two-year-old. They might not crawl, hold up their heads, or walk on time. Some of them have seizures and mental retardation.

But even though I know these facts, I still want to meet children with CP. I want to see Miranda for myself. I want to understand the full repercussions. Is that pathological? I told Jay and he asked why. Why would I want to do that to myself? What's the point? I couldn't answer him. Since the attorneys forbid me from seeing Miranda and her mother, I've been thinking of ways of meeting other children with CP. I've fantasized about spying on Stacy and Miranda.

On the Internet I read a few people's stories but they still didn't feel real. That's when I thought of Lee, a friend in pediatrics. He's Chinese American, one of those unmarried loner docs, an awkward guy. I think he's attracted to me—he laughs a little too loudly at my jokes, and whenever we see each other in Labor and Delivery our conversations go on a little longer than the content justifies. Anyway, he was the only person I could think to ask about CP without being interrogated. He's our local expert, I think he had a brother with CP. I didn't tell him why I was calling, only that I wanted to know more about the condition. He asked where I'd been lately.

"You pregnant? Is that why you're out?" Most of my colleagues only know that I disappeared, they have no idea why. My closest friends, Lynn and Elsie, have been good about protecting my privacy, but there have been rumors, most that I've been wooed away by a local private practice or another university and I'm just using up my sick time before putting in my notice.

I told him I wasn't pregnant and asked him about CP. Lee told me that he volunteered with a group called TROT, Therapeutic Riders of Tucson. It's a group that uses horses therapeutically for children with a number of disabilities; the largest group are kids with CP. They were having their annual riding show and barbecue—did I want to come? It sounded a little too festive for me, but I told him I'd go and he sounded thrilled. Then I worked into the conversation that I'd bring Jay and that I was disappointed that the two of them hadn't met, that they'd like each other. He said, "That would be great." But I could tell he didn't think so.

Jay didn't want to go. He's been working on a huge canvas that he hasn't let me see and he wanted the morning to work on it. He also said I was being morbid. I could have gotten him to go if I described Lee to him, but I didn't bother. I drove out alone on Saturday morning.

It was a hot, dry, beautiful morning. I rolled down the windows and enjoyed the air. TROT is located off Tanque Verde Road near the Catalina Highway that goes up Mount Lemmon. The land out there is at a slightly higher elevation; there are paloverde trees and white Arizona sycamores, and on the ground the desert chicory was blooming.

The show had already started when I drove in. It smelled like a festival, barbecue mingling with horse smells, hay, oiled leather, and fresh popcorn. There was music playing, bluegrass fiddling, and I could hear the muffled sounds of an announcer on a bullhorn. It was more crowded than I expected. Lots of parents and children, some in braces, some in wheelchairs, and horse people.

When I got closer I could see the setup. There were bleachers on one side of a large pen. Inside the pen there were children slowly walking their horses. Each horse was surrounded by four or five adults, one on each side to make sure the child didn't fall off, others holding targets and balls. The kids were punching and throwing and holding their hands up. Some of the children looked entirely normal; others had unusual postures. A man with a microphone announced each child.

I stood near the pen and some people behind me told me to sit down. Lee must have been looking for me because he suddenly appeared. He said he'd saved me and Jay seats midway up in the bleachers. I told him Jay hadn't come and he tried not to smile.

Lee explained that the kids in the riding show were all enrolled in equine therapy; he called it hippotherapy. I told him that was a silly name, a good example of someone taking an ancient language too seriously. He laughed. He explained that the goal is to improve children's walking. The horse's gait simulates human walking better than balancing on a therapy ball or using braces. It helps the children with muscle control and to learn the natural rhythm and sway of walking. Many of the people involved feel the therapy also helps children spiritually through bonding with a powerful animal. He apologized as he said it, as if being a physician and talking about anything spiritual was taboo. He ended by sharing that there was some solid science behind the therapy.

The guy with the microphone thanked all the volunteers and the Angel Charity, a group that donates money for the therapy. Then he described the children on horseback as they approached the front of the pen. The first one was named June and she had CP. June was five years old. She'd come to the program when she was three. At that time she still wasn't walking and had trouble controlling one of her arms. June was now able to walk almost independently. She was riding Thunder; the announcer said the horse was a blue roan Appaloosa.

June had a serious forehead and blond hair peeking out from under her riding helmet. She looked tiny on the big horse, her legs barely reached beyond the blanket under the saddle. But normal, too: I wouldn't have known there was anything unusual about her. When she got in front of the stands, the therapist in front of the horse put his hands over his head and then June raised her hands as if she were announcing a touchdown, one of her arms hovering lower than the other, and the crowd applauded. Lee said that before the therapy she couldn't raise that arm at all.

Then an eight-year-old girl named Stephanie came through. She had long black hair in a ponytail that curved out from under her helmet with exactly the same arc as the horse's tail. It seemed to defy gravity but that was the only part of her that did. She was hunched over the horse and her head was off to one side, her eyes up and away, as if the only way she could see forward was to twist herself around. Her right hand held the bridle and it was curled up near her throat. Her left hand held a ball. The adults were much closer to her and the horse than they were with June, as if they'd seen her fall off or panic in the past.

When Stephanie and her entourage got to the front of the ring the crowd hushed. The therapist on one side of the horse asked Stephanie to throw the ball. I could hear Lee drawing in his breath next to me. Stephanie lifted her left hand slightly and the ball dropped right into the therapist's hand. The crowd went wild. Everyone stood up and cheered and Stephanie had this twisted smile. I stood up too, and clapped, even though I didn't know why. Lee yelled over the applause that Stephanie didn't have consistent trunk or head control and this was the first time she'd thrown, or even dropped, the ball on command. "She asphyxiated on amniotic fluid during birth. She's doing great!"

Then, in that second, with everyone standing and applauding, I wanted to disappear. What if I were the mother? What if I were standing and applauding for my eight-year-old because she managed to drop a ball? Instead of sleepovers and soccer practice, college graduation and a big wedding, all the things I expect if I have a daughter, I'd be praying for a day when my daughter could drop a ball. I felt like I'd been kicked.

Lee looked at me and asked me if I was okay. I must have looked pale or something. "Are you dehydrated?" I told him I was fine. I must have sounded aggravated because he looked away, embarrassed for me. Doctors like Lee don't lose control.

Listening to Amelia left me confused. On one hand, I respected her. I could think of many physicians, many people in her situation who would avoid thinking about the full consequences of what they'd done. Me, for example. But as a former patient, I wanted her to get the magnitude of the consequences.

On the other hand, I felt nervous. When I had been an assistant professor for only a few months I met the psychologist for the Los Angeles Dodgers. He did a "Grand Rounds," a lecture, for the staff. He suggested that the difference between elite athletes and other professionals wasn't physical prowess. He thought, instead, that it was their ability to leave their mistakes behind. To learn from them and forget them. It was the men who tortured themselves after every strikeout, missed ground ball, or errant pitch who didn't last in the big leagues.

"I'm impressed that you're willing to face what happened to Stacy and Miranda, but I'm also curious—"

She interrupted me. "It's not what happened to them, Dan, it's what I did to them."

She'd never interrupted me before. She reminded me of a resident I'd given critical feedback to; she was studying every word for its flaw.

"Right. What you did to them. Okay. What were you hoping to get from going?"

She rubbed her knuckles against her lips and spoke into her hand as if it were a microphone, absently gazing at the floor.

"I don't know what I wanted. I know I felt horrible when I left. I still feel horrible. I don't like being stuck. I'm trying anything to find my way out of this. I'm not going to be one of those people who just freezes." She spoke with authority, she sounded like a marine. But there was a veneer of bravado, too. A hollowness. She was more like a boy pretending to be a marine.

Then she changed the topic. She brought up exercise, how she'd given it up completely. I encouraged her to start working out again and the session began to wind down.

When she was gone I left my office, taking the stairs two at a time to the reproductive endocrinology clinic. All the talk about exercise filled me with energy. The clinic was just a fancy etched-glass sign next to a series of offices on the eighth floor. I opened the door and saw my wife's hair, a long cascade of auburn and brown around her shoulders. Dr. Linden was running late as usual. When Terry saw me she nodded slightly. I smiled at her. I always feel a warmth when I'm near her. When I was the sickest, after the second relapse, she was my lighthouse. I followed her through cancer's darkest gales, and that response to her has never dimmed.

Lately, Terry'd been struggling. She'd been taking Metrodin to stimulate her ovaries to produce multiple eggs. Along with the drug came intense mood swings, as if each of those eggs was packaged with a month of intense emotion.

When I was twenty and first diagnosed with Hodgkin's, long before I was married, I'd banked sperm on the advice of another patient's mother. She'd warned my mother that the chemotherapy would render me sterile and that banked sperm was my only chance for biological children. She was right.

Eight years later, when Terry and I were in Boston, we'd used some of those sperm. At the time, I was finishing the fellowship at Harvard. After asking the physicians we worked with, we found the name of a reproductive endocrinologist who'd helped some of our colleagues with infertility.

Our Boston experience had been different from our fertility attempts with Dr. Linden. In Boston, we saw Dr. Alpert, who worked in an upscale outpatient clinic in Brookline. The first time we went, the waiting room was filled with couples. A sign on the door asked people with children not to bring them into the waiting room. Alpert was a big man in his fifties, balding slightly, with fleshy cheeks and tailored shirts. He wore a sports jacket and tie and took our history using an expensive fountain pen. He spoke without moving his mouth very much; the sound was something akin to a radio station just out of range. After studying the data on our sperm and asking me a few questions he sat quietly. Then he mumbled about a procedure called intra-cytoplasmic sperm injection, ICSI for short.

The procedure involved giving Terry shots of Metrodin to stimulate her ovaries to grow multiple eggs. Then the eggs would be "harvested" and a small amount of my sperm would be thawed and one lucky winner injected in each egg. Embryos would be grown in petri dishes. Then the best-looking collections of cells would be transferred back into Terry's uterus. Of the few embryos making the entire journey, hopefully one would survive. He said it was an aggressive approach but, given the limited sample of sperm, and that it had been more than eight years since they'd been frozen, he thought it offered us the best chance of pregnancy.

Then he looked at both of us, suddenly serious. He cautioned that even though he had a strong success rate, we should prepare ourselves for the long haul. There was no way to know how Terry would respond to the procedure. The psychological challenges of infertility had been compared to cancer treatment. We needed to be ready.

Six weeks later, Terry was pregnant. Alpert gave us the news by phone but cautioned that it was early. We'd see if her pregnancy held. He was right to caution us. A few weeks later, a follow-up test revealed that she'd miscarried. He told us that if we were not trying to get pregnant, we probably never would have known and that this happened naturally far more often than people realized. We'd try again.

On his second attempt with us, Alpert was successful again. He warned us again. We'll see. But the pregnancy held. Alexandra was born in Tucson in March of 1996, at term.

A year and a half after she was born, we met with Dr. Linden. She worked alone and there were no other couples in the waiting room. There were no signs warning us not to bring in children. When we met her, Dr. Linden was wearing a perfectly pressed white laboratory coat. She was tall and broad shouldered and spoke with the easy confidence of an athlete used to winning. She shared her impressive success rates and then took my hand and Terry's and looked squarely at both of us. She was certain Terry would be pregnant in no time. We soared.

It had been seven months since our first meeting with Dr. Linden. We'd had five attempts at ICSI with no success. Our most recent attempt was stopped before the harvesting of Terry's eggs because Linden had prescribed too much Metrodin and Terry'd been overstimulated, producing too many immature eggs, a potentially dangerous complication.

Terry was born an optimist. If we were ever lost, Terry would say quietly, "We'll find it." We met when I was twenty-one, and that quality drew me to her. I'd recently finished my first round of cancer treatment and the ongoing scans kept the illness in my consciousness. Growing up the grandchild of Holocaust victims and survivors, I am less naturally optimistic. When I was the sickest, septic and terrified, Terry's optimism held me up.

But now, we'd gone through the procedures five times. I was growing tired of the daily injections to boost the number of eggs Terry produced. We'd huddle in our little bathroom and Terry would break the lips of the glass vials, draw up the magic liquid, and hand me the syringe. I'd banter about something distracting until flicking my wrist, like throwing a dart, into the smooth skin that hides beneath her back jean pockets. Along with the spectacular number of eggs came moods. Terry's passions soared and crashed. She was sleepless and anxious and then weepy and tired. Then viciously angry, capable of hunting and killing with her bare hands.

I wanted, but didn't need, to have another child. Alex was eighteen months old when we started working with Linden. Alex filled the space in my heart that needed filling. The house never felt empty. She was also a considerable amount of work, energetic, social, and attractive, with dark skin and Bette Davis eyes. We doted on her with the fury of parents who'd worked hard to have a child.

Terry was paying a terrible price. For the first time in her life, her optimism was torturing her. Four weeks previously I'd found her in the bathroom, looking into the mirror, saying, "My breasts are swelling! I'm pregnant! I can feel it!" The next morning she'd sagged into bed, unable to go to work, another negative blood test still lingering in the dry air.

The previous week we'd hiked up to the Seven Falls and were temporarily lost when we couldn't find the new Bear Canyon trailhead. She dropped her head and said, "Figures," instead of laughing at our predicament and taking charge.

I sat next to Terry and we waited for Doctor Linden. She had her head in her hand, a weary girl. "How's your day?" I asked.

"Fine," she whispered. Terrible. As usual.

Lately I'd been acutely aware that we wouldn't be in those chairs were it not for my medical history. Though Terry would never say it, this was my fault. We sat quietly. A small pile of magazines sat on a corner table. I found a *Time* magazine and gave it to her. She thanked me but it sat on her lap.

Dr. Linden appeared and greeted us. She reminded me of a camp counselor; the stethoscope around her neck could have been a whistle. She smiled and then nodded, beckoning with her large hand. "Come on back. Let's play Capture the Flag," I misheard her say. Terry stood and we walked back together. I thought we might hold hands for a moment, or at least touch, but we didn't. She walked ahead of me and dropped into the chair in Linden's small conference room.

Terry's chart was on the table. After some small talk Linden fanned open the chart and read a column on the sheet from last month. "Okay. Well, we'd all agree that we took you up on the Metrodin too fast last time. I think this time we ought to take two vials on day one, and then one vial the next, and then two and then one."

Terry cleared her throat and spoke slowly. She'd rehearsed this part of the conversation with me already. "In Boston, Alpert monitored my estradiol every day instead of every few days like you do it. Then he'd tell me how many to take the next day. I felt managed more tightly; could we try that?" There was an edge to her voice, subtle, but knowing her it was impossible to miss. She was right, of course; Alpert had more systematically monitored her dosages of Metrodin every day. I expected Linden to reject the suggestion: in my experience there are few physicians, chefs, or pilots who like to hear how other people do it. I remembered a quote of Montaigne's: "You'll never see a physician approve of another's prescription without subtracting something from it, or adding something to it." There was a pause and then Linden nodded. Smiled again.

"No problem. We can do that. You'll start the first few days taking the vials like I've just suggested and then get your estradiol checked daily and I'll tell you how many to take the next day." Then she said, "Hey," looking into Terry's eyes and then into mine. "We're going to get you pregnant. I have no doubts." She nodded at us. There was a warmth to the smile, a comforting feeling. As if we were sitting with a favorite aunt.

Terry looked at me, her face thawing. When she smiles her brown eyes open wide and a person has been known to get lost in those pools. It was the first time she'd smiled at me in a few weeks, I realized. When we walked out she opened her mouth a tiny bit in a fake smile, it's a secret signal of affection we do when no one's looking. I returned the signal and she kissed me on the lips. "I'm getting Alex early, see you at home," she chirped, and was gone. I felt a warmth in my chest. I headed back down to the psychiatry clinic.

Session Nine

Amelia had jeans on, her hair pulled back. A loose T-shirt and sandals. I noticed that she was wearing a leather anklet I'd never seen before. She sat on the love seat and crossed one leg under her. I asked, as I usually do, where we should start.

You'll be happy to know that I'm finally back to swimming. Did I tell you that I set the record for the 400 freestyle in high school? Before all this happened I used to swim every morning before work at the Jewish Community Center. The pool there is outside, the lanes run north-south, and when you rest on the southern side there's an incredible view of the Catalina Mountains.

I'd get to the JCC at about 6:30, wearing my suit. After putting work clothes in my locker, I'd rinse and get out there. After a few laps Anton usually appeared. I don't know his real name. He has a tattoo on his shoulder with an eagle sitting on a globe and an anchor. I think he was in the marines. He's young and the ink is still fresh, the colors are bright, so it couldn't have been that long ago. He must be about twenty-four or twenty-five. He always took the lane next to mine. He's got a swimmer's body. Chiseled pectorals and a narrow waist. He's perennially tan, he's got incredibly short hair, and his face is angular. He looks hungry.

He swims fast, a little faster than I do naturally, but if I push it, I can keep up, and even swim faster than he does if I haul. I like swimming near him because my workout is always better. But there's another reason. I've got great goggles.

He wears swimmer's bathing suits. In high school we called them marble bags. It cuts above the natural contour of his rear, so when he's swimming in front of me it feels like I'm seeing a forbidden part of his body. He has these little curly hairs on the back of his thighs up on his rear.

Anyway, it was always a great way to start the day. Get in the lane next to Anton and catch as many glimpses as I could while stroking away all of my stress before the day started.

You've been pestering me to exercise and I knew it was a good idea so I tried to swim this morning. It was the first time in months. I got there like always, but at first I couldn't find my locker. The room was colder than usual and there was a flock of teenage girls, I think the swim team at the Jewish Community Center has decided to practice in the morning. Anyway, I came in and got turned around and couldn't find my locker. It was bizarre, I've been in there a thousand times. Meanwhile there was a chorus of teenage laughter and teasing surrounding me. The locker I thought was mine didn't have my lock on it and it stuck when I tried to open it. As it turned out, I was a row past my locker's row. After I found it I couldn't remember the combination to the lock.

I finally got out to the pool and Anton was already in the water. I don't actually know what his real name is. I made Anton up, because we've never actually spoken. I got into the water, stretched, and started. It felt like I was pulling through sludge and my breathing was out of sync. I usually crawl and breathe after three arm strokes, so I breathe on my right, and then on my left. It's a perfect rhythm for me, but I felt air hungry. I had to change the stroke and only breathe on my right and I quickly wore out. It was frustrating.

Then I had my first unobstructed view of Anton's rear as he swam by. I was going so slowly, he lapped me after only six laps. This was the worst part. His long body moving past mine, then the perfect view of his ass, and I felt nothing. Not even a mild quiver. His perfect body. Wasted on me.

Jay and I haven't had sex for six weeks. That's the longest we've ever gone since we've cohabitated. I had a urinary tract infection for a few days and we haven't had sex again since then. The worst part is that I don't miss it. I don't think about it at all.

You know, it's not being away from medicine that's so hard. It's the little things, like not getting coffee in the Java café in the morning before work, and missing the tired hellos with my friends. It's knowing that my life has no schedule. It's not being able to rely on my sleep, not knowing when I get into bed if I'm going to be awake for the next four hours. It's not knowing if I'll ever want to touch Jay again. I used to love his fore-arms, he's got painter's arms. I used to love when they were stained with oil paints, blue and green films on the little red hairs on his forearms. Is this going to change?

I didn't know.

As she talked I felt the same internal conflict. On one hand, she was just like any of my patients, she was struggling, and that engaged me, made me want to help her. On the other hand, I couldn't avoid imagining that Amelia had harmed my baby.

The session trickled on. She listed a series of events, an argu-ment with the phone company, feeling premenstrual, a flat tire, and how it had all come together to unravel her sleep. I gave her some advice about sleep hygiene, techniques she could use to sleep better: limiting caffeine late in the day, avoiding late meals, developing a soothing ritual before bed, and sticking to a consistent bedtime. I also told her to darken her house about an hour before bed to simulate dusk. She seemed eager to live in the shallow end of our experience and I allowed it, because part of me was nervous that she was going to bring up something that would cast me back into feeling like a patient, instead of her doc-tor. Then she said, "Oh, I forgot to tell you, something happened with my eating."

We went to the Renaissance Festival outside of Phoenix. It's a big carnival they have every year. It's a good place for Jay, he always sells a few pieces there. You know the line in Billy Joel's "Piano Man"? "They sit at the bar and put bread in my jar and say, Man, what are you doing here?" That's Jay. The tourists who know about art and see his stuff are always shocked to see someone that talented. So we went out there and manned the art booth in the morning when it was busy. People dress the parts, damsels in gowns with pulled-up cleavage and men in elaborate robes. In the afternoon it slowed down and grew overcast. I went for a walk. Past the jousters, a sword swallower, and a man dressed as a tree. I ended up at the carousel. It was huge, the largest carousel I'd ever seen. It had two levels, white horses three abreast going up and down, with feathered plumes, and tails with real hair. They appeared to be pulling carriages. There were thousands of lightbulbs. I just froze.

Mothers were standing next to toddlers who went up and down. Some of the children were somber, arms wrapped around the posts, others were waving and gleeful. It stopped and one group discharged and another filled in. When it started I had that feeling of moving. Everything was slow. The smell of cotton candy and fried food in my head, and tears filled me up. I realized I wanted to be one of the moms up there. Holding a child. Telling her to wave and hold on. That should be me. But how can I ever have a child now? I don't deserve a healthy child. I can't. And I felt suddenly hungry. Ravenous.

I was halfway to the fried shrimp booth when I stopped. I wasn't hungry. I was empty. And I thought, I don't need fried shrimp inside me, I need something else.

She looked at me. "It was the first time I've recognized and stopped the urge to binge, that's great, isn't it?" She was right about the binge. It was great. But not unexpected. I've found that when people identify the cause of their unhappiness, their bingeing diminishes. But I was more interested in something else right then.

"So until you forgive yourself, you're not going to be able to have children?"

"I've wanted to be a mother my entire life. I chose obstetrics.

That's part of life that I have to give up. I'm not going to be a mother."

"Did you tell Jay about wanting a baby?"

"No. I barely acknowledged it to myself. I did spend the afternoon pointing out adorable children. He says he doesn't want to have children right now. I think he's afraid that I'm not solid enough. I'm not mother material. He's right.

"Oh, I almost forgot, he wants to see you. Would that be okay? Not as a patient, he just wants to provide you with information you might need to be helpful to me. It's fine with me. He'll call, okay?" I nodded and she left.

When she was gone I sat quietly. I thought of Lauren, my adolescent friend, standing in the hallway with her books pulled tightly to her chest. I realized that Amelia reminded me of Lauren but I didn't know why. The stance was self-protective. Was Amelia protecting herself from me? Lauren usually comes to my thoughts when I'm overwhelmed by a patient's problems. Amelia hadn't said anything overwhelming. Why was I thinking of her? Amelia was as intelligent as Lauren. Possibly as sensitive. Their facial features were similar, both had warm eyes and the same slope to their cheeks.

On the following Saturday morning, Terry took Alexandra out to the park and I went to Supercuts, home of the eight-dollar haircut. Vy, a Vietnamese woman, about thirty or so, usually cuts my hair. The cuts are terrible, but I guess that's not why I go.

Vy was born in Vietnam and came to the United States in the mid '90s. She's short, buxom, and likes to complain about American men. "Men here think all Asian women servants. We're not all servants. I hate to cook, I never clean. They bore me." This attitude has not stifled her love life.

Vy has two boyfriends who haven't met. One, the older one, loves Vy with all his heart, worships her. He comes over to her house and does her household chores. He's always trimming her hedges, cleaning out her dryer vent, or adjusting the timing belt on her Honda.

The other boyfriend is in his late twenties. Smooth. A player. He likes Vy but doesn't want to commit, except to parties and dinners. In my mind, as she cuts my bangs, I imagine him in a white leisure suit with thick lapels, the reincarnation of a John Travolta '70s dance movie. "He's fun," she says.

I always ask her about having two boyfriends. Won't they eventually find out about each other? "I'm not worried," chirps Vy.

That Saturday morning, Vy told me about the ice cream debacle. For a while Vy had been fixated on ice cream. She'd been talking about ice cream with anyone who'd listen, singing out all the flavors on display in the ice cream place a few stores down: Rocky Road and Marshmallow Delight, Fruit Explosion and Peach Swirl. Well, one afternoon at around noon, the younger one showed up. He told her he was going to buy her the biggest ice cream they had. She giggled and, arm in arm, they left the salon to get their ice cream. She ordered the Ultimate Sundae. Three scoops, melted fudge, banana, and jimmies.

Outside the parlor they kissed and the younger lover ran off to his Mitsubishi convertible to get back to work. She returned to the salon alone, ice cream sundae in a plastic container in a bag in her hand, to find the older one waiting for her. "Hey, baby. I'm going to take you for ice cream," he said.

Vy handed the bag to her store manager, pretending to be delivering something, asked for another fifteen minutes off, and left with him, arm in arm. She was delighted to see him. At the ice cream shop she got a one-scoop cone. Peach Swirl.

"That's it?!" exclaimed the older boyfriend.

"That's it," said Vy. When she got back to the salon her manager was sharing her sundae with three of the other girls.

As Vy trimmed around my ears the girl at the chair next to Vy's said, "It was good, too. But next time, we want chocolate."

I love Vy's stories, and whenever I come she's got another one. About her parents, or her sister in California, or life in Saigon. She's had a lot of struggles for such a young person. Life hasn't gone her way. There were problems at college and with the immigration service. But she has a lightness about her, as if nothing that happens can harm her. As I sat in the chair I thought about Amelia. Why does Vy's life run over her like silk, easy and smooth, while Amelia's life chafes and catches? Then I realized that I liked being with Vy because her lightness is contagious. Nothing can hurt me when I'm with her. I love how breezy she is, and how her adventures entertain her.

But what about her boyfriends? The older one who dotes on her will be devastated when he realizes there's another man buying her ice cream. And that's the difference. Vy is free of fear. She's free of empathy, too. Maybe the two go together. Amelia feels the pain of those around her acutely, as if it's her pain. It's a gift, to be that attuned, that willing to imagine and respond to other people's anguish. Isn't that exactly what I wanted from my physicians and never felt I had?

But maybe it isn't a gift physicians should have. Could they make complex decisions if they were that keenly attuned to the gravity of each thought? Perhaps physicians are better at their jobs when they're more like Vy. Better when their patients' problems are like puzzles, no different from the Mensa quizzes in airplane magazines. Is that why surgeons have a reputation for being uncaring and arrogant, because it's necessary? But Amelia was loved because she always inhaled her patients, imbibed every fragrance, scent, and odor.

Vy snipped along my ears. She'd started another story. She was describing the time her father shot and missed an angry dog in their village. Vy barked and then grumbled, imitating the dog's yelped taunts after every missed shot and her father's groans while he tried to reload his rifle. I smiled, trying not to move my head (I wanted her to miss my ears), but I was near laughter.

Vy was born in Saigon during the Vietnam War. On the drive back up Swan Road, up and up into the foothills of the mountains toward our home, I wondered how someone born into that environment could have the lightness she exudes. I've met quite a few veterans from our war with her country and none of them have achieved that same lightness.

In 1990, I did an assessment of a veteran who had just returned from a visit back to Vietnam. He was forty-three years old, a big man with a long beard; black hairs commanded the upper part of his cheek, but gray hairs had taken over his chin and jawline. He looked like a biker, the kind of man who'd ride a Harley, but he had a higher-pitched voice than I'd expected and perfectly manicured hands. He was a dentist.

The patient had been referred by his physician, who said the dentist had been having concentration and memory problems. He had a history of post-traumatic stress disorder and his doctor wanted to know if the man's concentration problems were a product of PTSD or if he had an underlying early dementia.

I gave him the Wechsler Adult Intelligence Scales and the Memory Scales. If the initial testing was suspect, he'd have the full neuropsychology battery, which would take most of the day. The testing I did took two hours. When we were done we had a few minutes while we waited for my supervisor to join us. I told the patient that I wasn't supposed to say anything but I expected his results to be within normal limits. He nodded and told me he'd scheduled the testing months ago, when he was having problems, but that he was fine now. He'd just returned from a trip to Vietnam, organized by a group who set up tours for vets. He thought his memory was back to normal. There was silence for a few moments and I asked him about his trip.

Just the mention of Vietnam made him breathe a little deeper, speak a little louder. "It was the best goddamned thing I've ever done. I've had shakes since 1973. Not great for a man who works in people's mouths. I've had memory problems and trouble finding words for about three years. I spook easily. Loud noises. Darkness. I'm forty-three years old and dammit, I'm afraid of the dark. I've had nightmares and sometimes I wake up and swear I've just heard the click of a grenade pin being triggered.

"In 1986 I read a *Life* magazine article about a helicopter pilot who went back to Vietnam. It had never occurred to me that a person could go back. But ever since I read that article I've wanted to go. We've been in debt, I'm not great with money. But finally, last year, I scraped the money together and my wife's family even pitched in. I went for three weeks with a group of vets."

He'd been looking around the room and down at the table, but now his eyes focused on me and his voice lowered, gathering strength.

"I did search and recovery in Vietnam. After a battle I get choppered in. I take the dogs and I work my way through the whole scene until I find you." He pointed at me, his fingers jabbing the air in my direction. "I'm the best. I'd find all of you, no matter how far they'd blown the pieces. And I'd put you in a bag because your family wants all of you. I'd find your tags, too. Gotta find the tags. Then I'd carry you back to the chopper and bring you back to Graves Registration at the Twenty-fifth Infantry."

My jaw hung open. I didn't know such a job existed. He sat back and looked down at the table again, his voice softening.

"You get to Nam faster these days. I went to Da Nang, and China Beach, and I stayed in a hotel run by two former VC in Hanoi. I'd only been there a few days when I went to the bar, also run by a former Vietcong, and got drunk on his rice whiskey. The bartender was in the war and we told stories. I've got some shrapnel in my knee; I got it when I recovered a booby-trapped body. My wife jokes that I show my knee to everyone, even people I've just met. The bartender beat me to it, he showed me his missing finger. Then, before I could roll up my pants leg, he bent over the bar and parted his hair. There was a thick scar above his forehead. Shrapnel. He was blind in one eye.

"I started crying and apologizing. I'm so sorry. We should have never been here. He patted me on the shoulder over and over as if he was patting a baby. I wept and drank and wept and drank. It was a good time."

He leaned over and rolled up his pants leg to reveal a jagged white scar across his knee that spread onto his hairy thigh. I nodded. I wasn't sure of the appropriate response. He continued.

"I came back a different person. I think it was the rice whiskey and that guy patting me on the shoulder. He cured me. I still don't like noise but I haven't awakened to the sound of a grenade since I went. I learned that you have to go back to where it all happened; you're afraid of snakes, gotta pick up a snake."

Back from the haircut, I got out of the car. Could I apply what the veteran had learned to Amelia? She had to go back to work. But when? It wouldn't be like the dentist's trip back to Vietnam. When he went back he didn't have to hunt through the bush for body parts or dog tags. He could be a tourist, take his time in Da Nang and get drunk on rice whiskey. Amelia wouldn't have those luxuries. She was going to have to make peace with her past while simultaneously coping with her all-too-real-and-present fears of harming another baby. It felt too early to me. She wasn't ready. Could the vet have gone back to Vietnam in 1974, even if the politics had let him? Or did he need the slow tumble of years to pass first? I knew she wasn't ready. She still seemed bewildered. But her field of medicine moved quickly: she wouldn't have fifteen years.

Session Ten

On her next visit Amelia came into my office, sat down, and started talking before I could say a word. She had deep swaths of purple skin beneath her eyes; did she have black eyes? Her face looked swollen and the rims of her eyes were streaked with red. At first I didn't attend to her words, her appearance was so jarring; she was a few sentences in before I caught hold of what she was saying.

Your help with sleep was great, I've been falling asleep with no problem. But last night I woke up at four and I'd been sweating. I tried to get back to sleep but instead I lay there watching the ceiling fan make its slow, creaking circles. Jay was still asleep, his mouth agape. I take a glass of water to bed every night. The only other things on my bedside table are a photograph of me with my sisters and the clock alarm. When I woke up I glanced at the photograph through the water, and there, where Cora was supposed to be, was Rebecca.

About three years ago Jay met a gallery owner on Fourth Avenue. Rebecca. She's very cosmopolitan. She wears black clothing with silver jewelry, dangling earrings, and so many bracelets that every time she gestures she chimes. She's got to be forty or forty-five, she colors her hair black and she has tanned, smooth brown skin. She drops the names of artists whenever we see her. "Oh, Jay Jay, did you see Kozik's take on propaganda?" or "Craig Clements is showing some fierce new stuff." She calls him Jay Jay. It's more than the nickname, though, there's also a subtle insinuation that Jay needs to be more connected with the art community, that he lacks mentorship and that if he spent more time with her all of his artistic dreams would come true.

Our favorite places to eat are downtown, like the Barrio Grill. She's there a lot. About a year ago we ran into her there and she said she had a booth at the Gem Show in one of the exclusive dealer-only tents. She said she was willing to put a few of Jay's paintings up for sale. She priced them, sold two of the four he gave her, and one went for $4,500. It was far more money than we'd ever seen for any of his paintings. He was over the moon. She said it was a fair price and that if she'd had more time she could have asked even more.

Jay likes her. I don't. After we've seen her I find myself making fun of her. Once I told Jay that I thought she looked like a marionette. He says he likes her intensity—she reminds him of the art people he knew in Philadelphia. When I accused him of being attracted to her he said I was crazy. I know she wants him.

Anyway, I fell back asleep and had a dream that I went to Rebecca's gallery, only it was an aquarium. I thought I was alone. I went from tank to tank. The swordfish tank and the eels and the Portuguese man-o-war. The signs were on the tanks but they were empty. And then I found them. Becky and Jay having sex in the dolphin tank. Her body was incredible, she was about eight feet tall, and perfectly proportioned, her skin looked even better in the water, and Jay was wrapped around her. They looked perfect, spinning slowly, woven together, she had long hair and it drifted around their waists in slow motion. Little beads, air bubbles, gathered on the surface of their skin like a drape of silver.

Then Jay was standing next to me in a robe, toweling his hair, and she was still in the tank, spinning, only now we were in her gallery. He said, "Isn't she grand?"

"You fucked her, didn't you?"

"That's a disgusting way to say it, we made love," he said. "You're so uptight. What's your problem?"

When I woke up my jaw was sore. I must have been grinding my teeth. When he finally got out of bed I told him I wasn't talking to him and I waved a finger at him.

"What'd I do?" he yawned out.
I told him it wasn't any of his business.

"What do you think it means?" I asked Amelia.

"Isn't that your job?" A tired smile.

I waited. She picked up her backpack and rifled through it. She found a Chap Stick, pressed her lips into a kiss, and applied it. Then she threw it back into her bag and sighed.

"She's everything I'm not. I'm not artistic. I'm not an entrepreneur. I know I'm attractive, but not in the same way. I'm a girl next door. She's a goddess." I must have looked skeptical. My eyebrows rise involuntarily sometimes when I'm surprised.

"Honestly, she is. She's gorgeous. She's got those long legs and long arms and I don't think she's aging at the same rate as a regular woman. She's naturally dark. And sleek. When they get together they use words like *mood, composition,* and *texture.* They once spent forty minutes discussing how emotionally evocative a piece of metal could be. I interrupted them to joke that if it were a gun it would be more evocative. They smiled at me the way I smile at my niece when she offers an opinion of great movies."

The gun comment stuck with me. It was the kind of comment we often drop in conversation that appears to mean nothing on the surface. She'd warned Rebecca with that comment.

"The dream reminds you of what you aren't?"

"It's not just what I'm not. It's that I don't have parts that Jay needs. I'm not naive. I know that I'm not supposed to fulfill every one of his needs, but these aren't minor. These are big. I used to bring in the money that made it possible for him to be artistic. I gave him the freedom to do something society doesn't value but that he and I do. Now he's looking for work. He's always done a day or two of landscaping every week but now he's lining up job after job." She dropped her head. "The idea of him trimming hedges and arranging plants is abhorrent. But I'm also relieved, because we're running down our savings and soon we'll be in debt. I'm not bringing in anything."

I shifted in my seat, I hoped I wasn't showing too much curiosity. Despite centuries of speculation about the origin of dreams and even some science, we still have little consensus about what they are. Some scientists say they are nothing more than mind garbage, the place where memories and urges are disposed. Freud thought we fulfill our unconscious wishes through our dreams. Even today, there are those who believe dreams can be prophetic.

I don't know what dreams mean, but I was fascinated that Amelia's dreams were able to achieve what I was not. This was the first time she'd spoken to me about Jay's needs, Jay's perspective. I'd been surprised at how angry she was when Jay left her the note cards around the house. He'd been sweet to do it, she said, but she'd rejected him. My attempts to help her understand his perspective had been fruitless.

Even if she were right, and Jay had underestimated the impact of her mistake, he deserved more appreciation than she'd shown. Usually my patients complain that their spouses aren't attending to their needs at all. It's rare to have a spouse trying as hard as Jay. And I knew that if I were Jay I'd have let her sit with the guilt; my own anger would have prevented me from reaching out to her at all. He impressed me, and yet she kept him at arm's length.

The dream blew all of that away. It grabbed her, eclipsed her anger and disappointment, and forced her to understand how important Jay was to her. It was as if her mind had created a vivid, literal wake-up call that she shouldn't take him for granted.

"Has Jay called you yet?" she asked. I said no. "He will." I nodded. Then she looked into my face as if she were a desperate farmer and I the bank. "I'm losing him. Help me keep him. You have to help me keep him. What can I do? I need money. With money he could go back to painting." She rattled off ideas, her words abrupt and staccato. Then she slowed. Ran her fingers beneath her eyes as if she could rub off the blackness.

"Has he been doing any painting?" I asked. She said that he'd started on a new painting a few weeks ago before the hippother-apy. It was the first painting he'd done in a while. She added that he didn't seem as concerned about their lack of sexual contact as she was.

"Maybe he doesn't miss it?" she despaired.

She slouched. She was wearing a baggy dress and now it hid her form, as if she were sitting behind a curtain.

"This isn't the only dream I've had. I have to tell you about another one. This one is different. It's recurring. Stacy and Miranda happened in September. After Stacy and Miranda my caseload continued on like always, and I thought I was fine. A few weeks after Miranda was born, but before Sophia, the one with the previa, came to see me, I had a nightmare."

It's 4 A.M. and the lights in Labor and Delivery are flickering. There are moans all around me, I spin and see them for the first time, the room is filled with laboring mothers. My heart is in my temples, a nurse grabs my hand and pulls me toward a set of curtains, there's a mother behind them laboring and she's yelling for help, but when the nurse throws open the curtain there's no one there. She turns and says, "No, this way!" and she hands me an intubation kit for newborns. "We don't do those, the pediatricians do the intubations," I argue, but she doesn't hear me. She's pulling me across a long room filled with beds. The wood floors creak beneath our weight. As I'm dragged behind her, a hundred patients' hands pass over me, grabbing. Please, Doctor, only a minute, Doctor, help us, she's in pain, Doctor.

We get to a red curtain and she stops, and then slowly pulls it back to reveal a woman in labor. She's white-knuckling the rails of the bed. She has a cloth over her face, in the center there's crimson, her nose must be bleeding. A man stands behind the bed, I don't look at him but he says, "For Christ's sake, do something."

The intubation kit has turned into forceps. I ask if they've had other children. "No. This is our first." The nurse looks terrified, she backs away slowly. I yell to her to get warm water and sheets. "Yes, ma'am," she says, and she curtsies, still terrified. We're in a different era, maybe the Civil War.

I wring out a washcloth and I wipe the woman's brow, and there's something familiar about her forehead. I pull back the cloth on her face and it's my mother. She grabs my arm and pulls it to her chest, she's speaking with tenderness now, but her arms are so strong. She whispers, "Are you ready to come into the world?"

"I'm sorry?" I ask.

"It's time to push," she says. "You're coming."

"Momma?"

I don't know what to do. "I can't do this!" I say. I can't. I'm backing out of the room but I bump into someone. It's the nurse, and she's holding my mother's newborn, swaddled in a red blanket.

"I'm so sorry," she says, and she shakes her head slowly. She's telling me the baby is dead. But she's bouncing a little, as if to keep the baby settled.

"Let me see," I urge.

"No," she says. "It's forbidden."

"Let me see!" I start screaming and screaming.

"I'm having it a few times a week," she said. "Sometimes twice in one night. I'm scared to fall asleep."

"Amelia, that sounds horrible. I'd be afraid to sleep too. What do you think it means?" I asked. She leaned over and put her head in her hands.

"Do we have to do this? Isn't it obvious?"

I stared at her, blank.

"I couldn't deliver myself, even if my life depended on it. That's what it means."

"Wait, is that what the dream means, or what you really believe?"

"I've delivered fifteen hundred babies and if I had to I couldn't deliver one right now. I doubt everything I do. I can't buy cabbage without wondering if I'm making a mistake. You need clarity, confidence, when you're delivering. There's an art to knowing when to let nature do its thing or when to intervene. The ability to know the difference is what's missing. And the more I think about it, the more I know I've been a poser."

I suggested that before our next session, I wanted her to think about her earliest memories of being a fraud. A woman who had delivered fifteen hundred babies was not a poser. But better that she tear down that belief on her own. Together, we'd gather supporting details and, one by one, turn each over to find its true color and density.

Then, before I let her go, I taught her a technique for helping with recurring traumatic dreams, called dream rehearsal. I asked her to walk herself through the dream, step by step, remembering as much as she could, and then to alter one detail in her mind. After a few questions she said, "I'd like to change the color of the cloth on my mother's face to something other than crimson."

I asked her to choose another color and to rehearse the new dream three times a day, with the new color substituted, but to keep everything else the same. She'd probably continue to have the dream for a little while but its intensity would quickly diminish.

A few days later Jay left a message on my voice mail. It was clipped, to the point. "I'm Amelia Sorvino's husband, Jason. I'd like to see you soon, if at all possible." I phoned him back and we scheduled a half hour meeting for a week later.

Session Eleven

While looking at my calendar early in the day, I saw Amelia's name at 3:30. I didn't want to see her. During the last session, when she'd told me about the dreams, I'd felt stuck and frustrated.

I realized I felt misled. How long had she had recurring dreams before she told me about them? She also knew about Stacy and Miranda for the first two months of our treatment and didn't tell me. I'm used to therapy unfolding, my patients slowly sharing layers, but Amelia's secrecy is more intense, purposeful. What else has she hidden?

In explaining therapy to her, I'd used the metaphor of going together on a long winter drive. I didn't expect Amelia to make a turn familiar to her, while pretending to be lost. This work is confusing enough; it's hard to get where we need to go even when we share a look at the map.

Could she convincingly assure me that she was fine and then slide home and do herself in?

Is it the responsibility I feel for her that's gathering around my throat? The fear that someone will pull me from the wreck of our therapeutic vehicle only to point an accusing finger—didn't you see her driving toward the guard rail? It was icy, what were you doing up here?

I'm afraid of being a fraud. I recognized the feeling as a parallel process. It's a technical term; it means the patient has successfully helped me to feel what she feels. Was it genuine on my part? Feeling like a fraud assumes that someone else in this situation would be doing a better job. I've only been at this for ten years or so. There are many seasoned clinicians who would likely do better.

Maybe the truth of this situation is something more frightening, maybe anyone who treated her would have blind spots. All of us make mistakes. We are all human. The roles we've venerated—physician, psychologist, professor—are all myths. In the end, we have the same frailties we had before training. The same tendency to make bad decisions when we're exhausted. The same fear of failure, the same desperate desire to be loved, the same fierce need for respect. Even with lab coats and framed diplomas, even with the admiring words of relatives over Thanksgiving dinner, in the trenches of our professions all of us can fail.

But then, maybe this anger I feel comes from somewhere else, a deeper, more personal place. She reminded me of my own doctors. The way Brodsky stood at the end of my bed, his arms crossed, when I was septic and my fever had climbed above 106 degrees. My bones were refrigerator pipes, dots whirred across my vision, and the nurses and Terry looked scared. I will always remember the feeling that I was close to a precipice where warm, soothing water flowed below; I needed only to step off and relax, forever. Through it all Brodsky was so matter-of-fact. And I thought, *you knew this might happen, and you didn't tell me.*

I didn't want him to be calm. I wanted him to share my terror. To be surprised and then race off to pore over textbooks, lose sleep, call other experts, and convene a massive panel of scholars to sweat over how to keep me alive. I imagined Amelia the night of Miranda's birth and saw her casually standing next to the monitor, ignoring its potent warning, and I wanted to throttle her with my bare hands.

A few hours later we were in the middle of the session. She was garrulous. She'd taken Ambien, the sleeping pill, again, and had slept dreamless the past few nights. She looked better. Lack of sleep is a magnifier. It makes everything worse. I wondered if she'd stay away from intense content today. I hoped so. I knew I should push her but I was afraid of my anger. Would I push her now for the wrong reasons? When I'm confused about my motivations I resort to technique. I summarize, naming any emotion I hear, trying to accurately reflect what I hear and experience. I focused on Amelia's struggle, naming the minor anguish she discussed but not pushing her. She wasn't eager to work and most of the session was in the shallow end. We hadn't spoken about her feelings of being a fraud and the session trickled on.

Then she said, "I gave away my office in Obstetrics and I want to talk about that. The office wasn't much more than a windowless closet, really. I didn't even use it that often. It's about half the size of this office, and it has no feng shui. It's dreadful, but what happened up there yesterday surprised me."

During the last few years the department has lost two of its more experienced obstetricians, but last month we had four new hires. Young blood. I heard from Lynn, one of my closest friends, that office space was tight. Since I've been doing the quality assurance work from home, I called and offered my office to my chairman. He was very kind. He thanked me and told me that he'd find me space the second I decided to come back. "You've always been a real team player," he said. "Don't think I don't appreciate you. The minute you can come back I'll find you a bigger office if I have to share space with you myself."

So I went in and cleaned it out yesterday. I thought it would be a simple thing to do: get my personal possessions together, get my manuscripts into storage, and throw out what I didn't need. I'd forgotten how much stuff I had in there. My secretary, Elsie, and I had to keep raiding the research wing to get more boxes. Anyway, I spent most of the day in there, getting books packed away, and all my files and research papers. I was leaving and Elsie asked, "Aren't you going to take down your photos?"

I'd forgotten completely. I've delivered two hundred, two hundred and fifty babies a year, for six years, and their photographs cover a wall. Round, pink faces, most of them. Tired, happy moms looking straight into the camera. And me. Me in scrubs with long hair. Me in scrubs with short hair. Me during internship and residency and on faculty.

I started pulling them off the wall but I ripped one and Elsie put a hand on my arm. I realized there was a horrible, rancid smell. I knew it didn't exist, but I stood there, stuck. She slid in and replaced me, taking them down one at a time, gently peeling them from the wall as if they were Rembrandts or Picassos.

I stood behind her, she handed me the photos, and I put them into the envelopes. Suddenly, she handed me Samantha's photo and I felt like I was falling backward.

Samantha's was the first photograph I'd put up in my faculty office. Right in the middle of the wall. I was a senior resident when I delivered her. The attending was down in Emergency seeing a woman with a possible ectopic pregnancy. She had the intern with her. So I was "manning the decks" in Labor and Delivery. I had backup if I needed it. A woman came in, unannounced, in labor. Daphne Arbetter. She was about thirty-seven weeks along. One of the junior residents had followed her as an outpatient, but the chart said her prenatal care had been sketchy because she'd missed prenatal appointments. I brought her back into the evaluation suite and I had a feeling, a sense in my chest that something was wrong. I went to check her dilation and felt a rhythm in the birth canal. The umbilical cord was in her vagina. It was like a crimped hose, stuck between the baby's head and the pelvic wall. Daphne's oxygen-rich blood wasn't getting to Samantha. I put them on the monitor and the fetal heart rate was only 60.

I grabbed a nurse and had her lift the baby's head off the pelvic wall to relieve the pressure on the umbilical cord but the fetal heart rate went up only a few points. I could see the whites all the way around the nurse's eyes. Mom was growing anxious too, and I could feel the panic ratcheting up a few notches, but I was immune. I said quietly to Ms. Arbetter, "Sweetie, in about thirty minutes, you're going to have a baby in your arms." And I smiled at her. Then I went out and called the anesthesiologist. "Need you up here." I hung up and then called the neonatologist so I could hand off the baby after I delivered. "Need you up here." Then I was a woman in motion. "You, get Ms. Arbetter into Labor and Delivery." "You, get her prepped for a cesarean." "Dad, you can wait right out here, everything is going to be fine, I'll bring you in when we've got her ready for the cesarean and your job is going to be to talk to your wife about fun times you've had together while I get you a baby, understand?" "Yes, ma'am." "Yes, Doctor."

I scrubbed and then went in there on a mission. I did the incision and was cleanly into the uterus and had Samantha out in record time. She was fine. I could tell that the neonatologist was smiling at me because of the wrinkles around his eyes above his mask. He whispered, "Five more minutes without oxygen and she's Measure For Box. Good catch."

Ms. Arbetter had a little Versed on board, it's a drug that knocks you out. She smiled and said, "Hi, Samantha," and then she was out. The dad was on cloud nine. He pulled out the camera and snapped a bunch of photos of Samantha, and then of me holding Samantha. When I walked out of the OR my attending was there with the intern and they clapped. They actually applauded.

The talk about me joining the faculty started soon after that. I've been carrying that photo of me and Sam with me. Isn't it crazy? I keep rubbing the little faces, but no matter how hard I rub I can't bring back the doc who delivered her.

"She's still there," I said. "She's sitting right in front of me."

"No," she whispered. "She isn't."

When I got home Alexandra was in the backyard, using colored chalk to draw something on the brick patio. I put down the mail and Terry peeked in at me from the living room. "Now's a good time," she said. She went to the refrigerator and pulled out two vials of a clear liquid.

I threw my keys on the counter and followed her back to the bathroom off our bedroom. It was hot. The air-conditioner was battling the Tucson sun and losing. It's always warmest in Tucson in the late afternoon and the master bathroom was the hottest room in the house. I took off my tie, put down the toilet cover, sat down, and waited. Terry hunched over the counter. With a nurse's efficiency she liberated a needle from its paper wrapping, broke the lip of the first vial, injected air into it, and then drew up some of the fluid. She squirted a few drops out of the needle and then repeated the process with the second vial before handing me the needle. She turned around, unbelted her cotton slacks, dropped them, and rolled down her underwear. There were times earlier in our lives when this would have stirred me, transported me from wherever I was into the now. I've always been transfixed by the curve of her ass. Not today. She glanced back at me.

"You used the left last time," she said.

"No. I went right last time. This is my turf, just turn around."

"Are you sure? I could swear . . ."

I held the needle like a dart and weighed the throw. "So," I started. "Debbie, my admin, has been wearing colored contact lenses. She's got green eyes now."

"Green? How does she look?"

I flicked my wrist and depressed the plunger slowly. I remembered getting my own subcutaneous shots; it was less the breaking of the skin with the needle that hurt and more the fluid pressing into the tissue. Easy does it.

"Like a girl with brown eyes and green contact lenses," I said. Terry breathed out slowly, the hiss of air the only sound in the room. It shouldn't be. Damned air-conditioner.

"Not bad, Shapiro. You might have a second career here," Terry said. She pulled up her underwear and slacks and then began gathering up the vials and paper, took the needle from me, and put it in the red hazards-disposable box that had become as much a part of our bathroom as the hamper and scale.

She kissed me quickly, stayed close to my face, a Cheshire cat smile. Then she bounced out of the room. She was high on optimism, floating around our house in her own cloud of ether. Try to enjoy it, I told myself. Don't rain on her. I carried my tie into the closet and hung it up. She deserves a little hope. The crash will come soon enough.

Awake in bed that night, listening to the rise and fall of Terry's breath, I thought about Dr. Linden. I wondered how much time she spent thinking about us. Was she, like Amelia, standing next to the monitor, ignoring it? That wasn't fair to either of them. I should be more patient.

I was glad Linden had adjusted her plan with the Metrodin so readily when Terry challenged her, but then again, I wasn't. I didn't like the idea that I could approach the captain of our ship, suggest a new course to her, and watch her shrug and turn the wheel without even a pause. Was it so trivial a difference that whole vials of the medication didn't matter? They seemed to matter quite a bit. The number of eggs Terry produced and their maturity seemed directly correlated with the number of vials she recommended. Was it because she hadn't thought it through? Had she spent the time necessary to generate a careful plan?

I'm used to thinking about my physicians late at night. In the days when I was hunched over on the linoleum, wrestling with the side effects of the chemotherapy, I'd often wonder if my physicians had any idea, any real notion, of the anguish that came packaged with their medicines. Was it better that they didn't know? No, I always decided. It was best that they intimately understood; that way they'd never use them on someone who stood little chance of benefiting.

But I didn't think they understood. If they had, they'd have talked about it more. Like a lieutenant sending his troops into a smoky battlefield, they'd have provided some somber words of encouragement before starting treatment. There'd be no leaning back on a counter, arms crossed, with a chipper "How are we today?"

Then I thought of Amelia. How invested was I in her well-being? I hadn't thought of her between sessions for a few weeks. Was she awake, too, wondering about my treatment of her?

Session Twelve:
Jason Sells

Jay had on jeans with a turquoise belt buckle and a T-shirt. He shook my hand in the waiting room and I could feel his strength. A silver bracelet covered his other thick wrist while he scratched a day's growth on his cheek. His nails were dirty and I wondered if he'd been gardening. A landscaping job, I guessed. As we walked toward my office, he said, "I want to thank you for agreeing to see me," and he nodded a little. There was a pink rash on the crease where his neck met his jaw, razor burn. He was taller than I and bobbed with a broad stride, as if everywhere was home.

When we got into my office he gestured to the love seat and said, "Here?" and I nodded. He dropped into it and his legs splayed out. He had to be six foot four, maybe taller. I couldn't remember Amelia telling me he was tall. In the office I had a better chance to look at his face. He had curly hair, blond locks that framed a chiseled, windburned face. From farther away I bet he looked ten years younger. Up closer there were crow's feet running out from the corners of his eyes and straight gray hairs that didn't want to curl like the others. His eyes were steel blue. A good-looking man.

I ran through the business items. Confidentiality. I wouldn't be sharing anything he said with anyone else unless he was likely to harm an identified person or himself; I also wouldn't keep secrets from Amelia. If he wanted to tell me something sensitive I could help him figure out how to tell Amelia directly, but I wouldn't keep anything from her. Because he wasn't my patient, and we were meeting for Amelia's benefit, I'd record what was said in Amelia's chart. He listened politely and then smiled nervously when I was done.

"I've seen one other shrink when I was blocked in college. He was a lot older than you. I couldn't paint. His office was, well, more formal. This is homier." He scanned the enlarged photographs on my office walls, the lighthouse surrounded by waves and the esplanade that reminds me of Boston. Then he turned around and looked at the reprint of the water-colored snow leopard on the wall behind him.

"That's hot," he said. "It's by Milt Glaser, yeah? It's got energy. That's a deeply personal piece, isn't it?" He was right. I'd had it on the wall during my bone marrow transplant for inspiration. I felt revealed.

"Yes."

He was still turned away from me, his neck craned up at the print. "Water-colored. That's incredibly hard to do. I like your taste." He spun back and smiled at me.

"Thanks." There was a pause and he settled into the love seat.

"You wanted to see me?" I asked.

"And I appreciate your making the time." He squinted up at the photograph of the esplanade. In it the world has burst into spring. Colors hang in the air in the city park. He stared at it and said quickly, "Ames is getting worse. I don't blame you or anyone else, it's just, I can feel her slipping away." Matter-of-fact. "It's like she's on a ledge beneath me but she won't reach up and let me pull her out. I could. I know I could." He continued to study the photograph.

"She's getting worse?"

"It's anything. Everything. It's all worse. She's stopped cooking. Her rhythms are off, she sleeps late, can't sleep at night, she pops ibuprofen instead of eating. Has she told you about her nighttime habits?"

I thought he was referring to her binges but I didn't want to divulge anything sensitive. He caught me thinking about what to say.

"Her Jekyll and Hyde act with food is what I mean. The nighttime psychopath and the daytime abstainer. It's worse. She's hitting the fridge a few times a week after one in the morning." He stopped and looked at me. I nodded slightly, an acknowledgment that I knew. He looked back up into the esplanade print and continued, "We don't have sex anymore. I don't want you to think I'm here because of the sex. As a matter of fact, this new celibacy has been a jolt to my creativity, I'm busting on a canvas I only stretched two weeks ago. It's almost done, that's a new record. So I'm not sweating the sex, but it was an important part of her life and now it's gone. Have you watched her? She can't sit still. She's swimming again but I guess that's about all there is on the other side of the scale. No offense, Doc, but I don't think whatever you two are doing is making the grade. I don't blame you. My bet is that she isn't telling you everything."

I wanted to deny that, but of course I couldn't. Jay switched his view and started looking at the lighthouse. Then he looked at me.

"You didn't tell her to carry that heart tone strip with her, did you, Doc?" he asked.

I didn't understand.

"I figured. She hasn't told you that she's carrying a heart tone strip with her wherever she goes?" I was still confused. "You know, the tape that comes out of those machines. EKG, EEG, one of those. It's got the squiggly lines on it that represent how well a heart is beating? She made her own copy of her patient's strip and she's carrying it with her everywhere she goes. She keeps it in a pocket Shakespeare. When we got married, I gave her the entire Shakespeare collection in thirteen volumes, tiny books published in the 1880s. She used to keep one in the pocket of her lab coat just to remind her of all the world has to offer. She still carries one around, but now she's keeping that monitor strip in there with it. I'm no shrink, but that can't be a good sign."

I could see why Amelia was attracted to him. He was sensitive, smart, and he didn't lead with his intelligence, didn't realize how smart he was, and his naïveté about medicine must have been refreshing to her. I could imagine him nurturing her with food and soft words after a long night on call.

The heart tone strip scared me. I didn't know exactly what it meant. Most people carry things with them that give them faith. Rosary beads. A photograph of a lover. But she was carrying a cold representation of her mistake.

"I've been concerned that she's getting worse, too," I told him, "and I'm grateful for everything you're telling me."

"I knew it. She's been sandbagging you." He shook his head.

"I've known she's getting worse, that she occasionally omits details . . ."

"God's in the details, right? It's sure true of my work—it's got to be true of yours."

"I do appreciate having the details," I admitted. "But therapy takes time. She might not trust me enough to tell me everything. Look, you can do something for me. I want us to have a crisis plan. I'm going to give you my phone numbers, including my cell phone. If you're ever worried about her, call me immediately. I'll tell her you have my contact information. Don't hesitate, okay? From what you've said and what I've noticed, Amelia is struggling. If things get to be too much, I want you to have a low threshold for contacting me, can you do that?"

"You gonna make a house call if I phone you?" he asked.

"No."

"I get it, you mean if she's close to offing herself? You'd send out the cops or something. Put her away?"

I nodded.

"Jesus. I didn't realize it was that serious."

As I warned him I watched myself. Was I that worried? I nodded my head at both of us.

Session Thirteen

I need to reschedule," Amelia's voice said on my voice mail. "First deposition today. One of their experts. It was supposed to be at eleven but his flight was delayed so they've pushed it back and I want to be there. Any chance I can see you later in the week? Leave me a message."

I checked my schedule and didn't have any open times the rest of the week. Even my lunch hours were taken with supervision meetings with residents and a faculty meeting. I was already scheduled until 5:30, later than I like. It means dinner with Alex and Terry starts late and we all get moody when we're hungry. I thought about scheduling her into the faculty meeting but there were budget cuts coming. If I wanted to participate in the discussions I'd better be there. I couldn't schedule her that week.

In my caseload, there are always a few patients I worry about more than the others and Amelia had become one of those patients. Because she was potentially dangerous? Because I worried that I wasn't giving her optimal care? Regardless, we'd have to wait until the following week. I phoned and left her a message.

The next message on my machine was from Jennifer, one of the interns I supervise. The interns come to the university for their last year of clinical training before getting their Ph.D. in clinical psychology. Jennifer has been working with Alison, a patient, for eight months. Alison is a twenty-four-year-old woman who's been in my caseload for three years. She doesn't have insurance for outpatient therapy and our community lacks treatment for someone like her. Since my trainees can learn more from treating her than they would in a hundred seminars, I've kept her in my caseload and three different talented interns have worked with her. Jennifer is as good as any.

Alison was an inpatient on the second floor, in our psychiatric unit. Jennifer listed the particulars on my machine. Her last attempt was on Friday. Friends found her. She'd slit her wrists and her blood alcohol level was .14. She'd also downed all the Ativan she had on hand, about ten pills. Jennifer cleared her throat a few times on the message, as if she couldn't get Alison out of her throat.

I paged Jennifer and told her I had a few minutes, could she come up and we'd talk? Jennifer is tall, attractive, and articulate.

She's southern, from Georgia, but only the faintest trace of an accent sneaks out every now and then. When she came into my office she was rubbing a shoulder. She had rings under her eyes. She said, "Thank God you have time now, that's all I have to say."

"It's been scary, huh?"

"Oh"—her eyes opened wide—"I'm fine now that she's inpatient, but I've been terrified that any minute I'm going to get a call and hear that she's dead. When I got paged on Friday night I thought she was a goner. I don't know what I'm doing."

Jennifer is enormously competent. She's managed to get Alison to tell her about her history, the simultaneous abuse and neglect she suffered in a very religious household. She's gained Alison's trust. Alison has always been suicidal, and now that she cares about Jennifer, she's frightened. Everyone else has betrayed her; Alison expects the same from Jennifer. Alison's brothers and sisters have been very supportive but they don't know most of her history. The truth about her parents and uncle hasn't been shared yet. This hospitalization might give us an opportunity.

"You are doing a fantastic job," I told Jennifer. "But if our strategies haven't been effective, we should feel free to try something new."

Jennifer thought for a minute and then said, "How about a large family meeting, all the siblings? I think she gets suicidal when she feels isolated. In a meeting the brothers and sisters could learn everything that Alison went through. I think she might be ready to tell them. They'd see that she isn't crazy, that she's coping as well as she can."

It sounded good to me. But as Jennifer stood up to leave, I thought of her voice on my phone message. I said, "Jennifer, you can't keep her alive if she doesn't want to be." Her shoulders dropped.

"I needed to hear that." She smiled, and her eyes filled.

After she left I thought about my confident words. I can't keep a patient alive if she doesn't want to be. If what I'm doing isn't working, I should try something different. It sounded better when I said it to Jennifer.

The following week Amelia came in.

So I've now had my first deposition. The plaintiff brought in a physician named Logan from Georgia who testifies frequently. He's about fifty or so. We met in a hotel conference room near the airport. Everyone was in a suit except for me and the stenographer. Logan looked tired, and then I remembered he'd just stepped off a plane. What a job. That morning he'd flown from Atlanta to Chicago and then got rerouted through Dallas before coming into Tucson. He'd already spent a full day traveling and he looked it.

There was a male stenographer—I recognized him from somewhere but still haven't figured out where—the plaintiff's two attorneys, me, and Wally, the older lawyer. Stacy wasn't there. Her attorneys looked sharp. Gelled gray hair and Italian suits. They're from Phoenix, apparently. Before we got started we were all milling around in the same room. The hotel put out some pastries and juice for us. While we were standing there Wally told me that Tucson juries don't much like lawyers, and that they particularly don't like lawyers from out of state. They'll tolerate lawyers from Phoenix but only if they don't act like hotshots. He said it would be a mistake to wear a fancy suit into a Tucson courtroom. And, he said, nodding toward Dr. Logan, better to bring in experts from eastern universities than from California. Tucson juries hate California. I think he was trying to make me feel relaxed. He was funnier than at our last meeting.

I wasn't nervous. I was intrigued by the strategy. I loved that my lawyer was thinking about the other lawyers' suits and where they were from. That was cool. It was as if the entire show was about someone else's competence. Or a game. Both sides were polite and friendly before we got started. It could have been a supervisors' meeting at the university. I sat out of the way.

Wally spent the first twenty minutes asking Logan about his back-ground, from high school to now. They went through all the volunteering Logan did, all of the work he'd done with medical students. I noticed he hadn't published any research or done any editorial work, he had none of the credentials that would make him impressive to an academic physi-cian. He'd be laughed out of any medical school for calling himself an expert, but I could see how he would sound impressive to a jury who wouldn't realize he didn't have academic credentials.

The lawyers took copious notes. There couldn't have been that much to write. Logan trained at a midwestern university and had a few lecturer jobs. I didn't actually understand how he made a living until Wally asked him how often he testified. He's a professional witness. He travels around the country testifying in B level cases. Wally told me afterward that it was a good sign that they could only recruit an expert of his level. My lawyer has already lined up the chairman of obstetrics at the medical school in New Mexico. The doc from New Mexico's in his sixties and has an impeccable reputation. Wally said, "He'll blow Logan out of the water." He also said he had a lead on getting a hotshot from Delaware who only treats kids with cerebral palsy.

Then they got to the part about me. Logan attacked every aspect of my care of Stacy. From the first minute I laid eyes on her I was making mistakes, according to him. I hadn't done the ultrasounds at appropriate times, hadn't ordered a level II ultrasound early enough or discussed the amnio with her as early as he recommended. My nutrition counseling had been substandard, he attacked my coffee suggestion, and he said I should have anticipated birth problems given her size and Miranda's likely weight. He went on to say that not doing a cesarean section after late decelerations was unconscionable.

I was honestly fine with everything he said because it was so absurd to attack all of my decisions. Wally's questions jumped around. He focused on what Logan had done during the past three months. He made him list every case he'd testified in and his fees. The guy was making a fortune jetting around testifying for plaintiffs. Then he asked him how many babies he'd delivered himself in the past year. None. Is it possible, given the HMO permeation in Tucson, that standard care decisions to limit unnecessary tests and procedures might be different in different parts of the country? Yes. Is it common that nutrition counseling is conducted by nurses in many clinics? It's possible. And on and on. It was enormously satisfying to have someone arguing my side.

When it was over everyone shook hands. Then Wally and I spoke for a few minutes. I told him I was impressed with how calmly he shot down all of Logan's attacks.

"Look, this is a long process, people are going to say some nasty things about you during all of this, try not to take it personally." I thought it was a strange thing to say.

It wasn't until later, on the drive home, that I began to dwell on the few things Logan said that Wally hadn't shot down. He said that I should have anticipated having problems with her birth because of Miranda's size relative to Stacy's pelvis. He said that not doing the C-section earlier was unconscionable. Logan was right, on both counts.

Amelia rubbed her arms, as if she was cold. "I was so bummed that I didn't have an appointment to come in here last week. I tried talking to Jay about it but he doesn't get it. And then he left town on Thursday. You've become my lifeline, there really isn't anyone else I can talk to. I spoke to Lynn and briefly with Elsie, but they both say the same thing. Don't take the case so seriously. It happens to everyone. Stay out of the depositions unless you want to torture yourself. It was good advice, but they don't understand."

"You didn't tell them you thought the expert was right about the important parts."

"Exactly."

"Hard for them to understand you without all the information."

"Maybe."

"I wonder, sometimes, if you don't do that in here too. Not share everything going on in your head."

She surveyed me. "You sound like Jay. I almost forgot, how was your meeting with him? He said he liked you. That I should trust you."

"He told me you've been having a harder time than you've been letting on in here."

Amelia snapped her fingers and pointed at me. "Oh, shit. That's where I know the stenographer from. He's an artist. He knows Jay. They aren't friends, but I think they had pieces in the same show. Damn. They must have to keep things confidential, right?"

"I assume. Can we get back to that telling me everything bit?"

She tilted her forehead toward me. The portrait of sincerity. She smiled. "I'm telling you everything." I could smell apricots. Her fragrance? I was hoping she'd say something about the heart tone strip but she didn't.

Okay, here's something honest. Over the weekend I painted part of our bedroom. It's always been too bright. It faces east and the morning sun fills the room. I bought this rich burgundy paint and threw down painter tarps, got the ladder and the rollers and paint trays. I put on some Shawn Colvin and was grooving. Jay was out of the house, he took a trip back east with three of his canvases, including the one he just finished, to visit one of his mentors. They get together every few years. The guy is one of the only people Jay trusts about his work. He always comes back fired up and eager to return to his art. We're worried about money, as you know, but I couldn't take the trip away from him. It would be too big a signal of how far we've descended.

Anyway, the house was all mine and it felt good to be painting. I was excited to have Jay come back and see it. Colors are important to him, I knew the color would make the room more sensual and that he'd get it. I think I've wanted him to know that I understand the toll our lack of intimacy has been taking on him. I knew he'd understand that the color was about intimacy, that I was trying.

As soon as he goes away I long for him. His touch, the way he holds his coffee cup—he calls it his "mug of life"—even his scent. I just felt human again. Productive, for the first time in such a long time.

I was also thinking about sex again. How fun it would be to get intimate with him when he came back. Maybe surprise him. When we were young we used to play roles. We'd pretend to be characters thrown together and then one of us would seduce the other. It was his idea at first but I loved it. I'd be the language teacher and he my student. Or he'd be the soldier and I a nurse. The scenarios sound funny when I say them, but they were intense and passionate. In those roles we had a chance to be desperate with each other.

I think they also helped us deconstruct traditional roles. In those games we learned that we could take turns being dominant, and that it was okay for either of us to be aggressive, or lazy, or more horny. The first time he suggested it I wasn't into it at all. I felt timid enough just being me, let alone trying to be someone else. But we had some wine and stayed up late and he had some aggressive rock on and he told me to take him if I could catch him. He was leaping around my little apartment in his overalls, this lean body. I finally tackled him on the couch and sat on his chest. "You're mine now," I told him. It was fantastic.

We've lost all of that. I thought that maybe when I finished the room I'd go down to the secondhand store, Buffalo Exchange, and find some outfits for a first-class seduction. I was thinking of doing the transforming librarian. The pent-up woman who suddenly breaks free. It felt appropriate.

So I'd just finished one coat on the longest wall. Not the detail work, but most of the wall, and already the room felt different. I'd just moved the ladder and was up on a fresh wall when the phone rang. It took me a few secs to get to it; I had to come down off the ladder. I lazily picked it up, I expected Jay. A strange voice, a woman, said, "Dr. Sorvino?"

I thought it was the paging operator. I said, "Yeah, I'm not on now." I've been off for months, don't those people realize I'm not on service? But the voice said, "This is Stacy Paulsen. I'm sorry to bother you at home. I've been wanting to call you for a long time. Is this Dr. Sorvino?"

I didn't recognize her name. But then I felt a sudden heat in my chest as if my body knew the name before I did. The line was silent for a minute.

I said, "Yes?"

"I was hoping to talk to you about what's going on. I feel . . . Well, I feel terrible about it, but I want you to know some things." I could hear a male voice in the distant background yelling something. I couldn't make it out. Stacy must have put her hand over the mouthpiece because I heard that sound of a hand scraping the phone and then silence.

Then she said, "Sorry about that, are you still there?"

I felt like I was on a roller coaster just crossing the top of the first peak. Then I was screaming downward. Vertigo. The whole room spun. Burgundy and white. In the haze I remembered what the lawyers said. Don't talk to her. As I held the phone up over the receiver, I could hear Stacy saying, "Are you there?" again and again. I dropped the receiver. I hung up on her.

I stood there in a quarter-painted room, unable to move, feeling so small. And suddenly tired. Just exhausted. I needed sleep. I took the phone off the hook and went and slept in the guest bedroom. It was only the afternoon but I slept right through the night.

When Jay came back a few days later I hadn't painted again. The ladder was still up. A half gallon of dried paint was still in the paint tray.

He was sweet. He was in a terrific mood, but that made it worse. He stood in the middle of the room holding the dried-up paint tray, saying, "Great idea," and "Nice work." As if I were a five-year-old holding up a lumpy art project.

She looked at me. "I hung up on my patient. She needed me. Wanted me. She was reaching out."

"Your lawyers told you not to talk to her, right?"

"That's just it. I've become a defendant. That's my new identity. I'm defensive. You just said before that I'm avoiding talking about myself, and I am. I don't want to think about everything that's going wrong. But isn't that healthy? To live fully even in the midst of struggle? See, I play these games with myself. I'm a professional defendant now. Maybe I could go around defending myself as a profession. On the other hand, that doesn't sound like much of a life either. Have you ever felt like you're running out of options?" She reminded me of a woman I worked with right after Hurricane Andrew, who stood in her roofless kitchen rattling off a list of chores she was going to do. I must have looked worried because Amelia said, "Hey, chill. Nothing to worry about. I'm fine. You don't need to call the white coats."

"Are you thinking about hurting yourself?"

"No. I promise," she said. "God, you piss me off sometimes. I finally start telling you the truth and you're so caught up in the possibility of me killing myself that you don't listen. Are you listening?"

"I'm listening." Her indignation effectively moved me off the topic of suicide, but I stored away that she wasn't surprised by the question. Maybe she's right. Maybe I was too worried to concentrate. "Okay, so you're a professional defendant. Whose choice is that?"

"The lawyers'."

"No. You're making the choice not to talk to her. You're choosing to be a defendant."

"What are you saying? They told me not to talk to her."

"Still your choice."

"Oh, you're saying I could just ignore them? They said she could take everything I have. That any monies in the suit beyond what the insurance covers will come out of my personal funds. The equity in our house. The cars. Mutual funds. Even Jay's paintings could be assets."

"Fine. You've still made the choice. By not talking to her you help your case and potentially save money. The cost of doing what they say is you give up feeling like her physician. You don't get a chance to have an honest conversation with her. I don't care which choice you make, I just want you to see that you're making one."

"But it's not just my choice. It would also affect Jay if they cleaned us out. I can't take that risk just because I grandiosely reject the identity of 'defendant.'"

"Fine," I said. "It's a choice for both you and Jay. Have you asked him what he wants you to do?"

She rubbed her arms. She reminded me of a referee signaling the end of a period.

"It's cold in here. You could hang meat in this room."

We're done for the day, she was saying.

"This case isn't going to help your feelings of being a fraud. Next session, let's start by talking about that. I want to know what kind of fraud you are. Are you technically incompetent? Are you emotionally incapable of caring for your patients? What is it?" She nodded in agreement. She'd say anything to get out of this room.

After she left I wrote a chart note and checked my calendar. I saw the note from myself, the reminder to look up research on physicians' responses to malpractice. Gayle, the psychiatry resident I was scheduled to supervise during the next hour, had just had her baby and was on maternity leave. I wondered why I hadn't sent her a congratulatory card. I usually do that. I turned on the computer.

Throughout my training I've heard medical professionals tell one another, "It's not a matter of *if* you'll get sued, it's when." It was such a casual phrase. It's the cost of doing business. Like dues to the American Medical Association or license renewal fees. But I realized that, although I knew a number of physicians who'd been sued, I knew almost nothing about what they felt during the experience. They simply didn't talk about it.

After turning on my old Macintosh I logged on to Ovid, the university library databases, where I could search a few thousand scientific journals simultaneously. I typed in a few search terms. Fifty-four abstracts appeared, summaries of articles. They were organized by date. I settled in and started to read.

The results were surprising. The majority of physician defendants described their malpractice cases as traumatic, and about one in five described the suits as the most traumatic experiences of their lives.

I e-mailed the articles to myself from the search center and waited a few moments before checking my e-mail, where I could print them out. I wasn't sure what to make of the findings. I bristled at the use of the word *traumatic*. In psychology and psychiatry, trauma refers to horrible experiences that are outside the natural range of human experience, like living through a fire or a war or a terrible car accident.

The physicians in these studies must have led charmed lives if a malpractice case was the most traumatic experience they'd had. How could being sued be the most traumatic part of a life unless one had never suffered real loss, a real threat to life? My bone marrow transplant was terrifying and challenging, but other than a few frightening bolts into wakefulness I wouldn't call it traumatic. And what about that veteran I'd treated who'd done "search and recovery" in Vietnam, the one who carried corpses of dead soldiers back to processing centers? Black helicopters had ruled his sleep and he woke to the smell of diesel fuel. That was trauma.

I continued reading. Researchers in most of the studies concluded that the malpractice cases had a profound impact on litigants' satisfaction with their careers and frequently resulted in serious family problems. Many had left medicine, and there were suggestions that the divorce rate might be higher among litigants than other physicians. Those who stayed in medicine usually practiced defensively after their cases were resolved, ordering too many expensive tests and avoiding doing procedures. One study concluded that malpractice defendants who didn't get counseling hadn't returned to baseline stress levels even two years after litigation.

Some of the articles were about problems in the malpractice system. When experts did massive reviews of medical charts and then tracked which negligence resulted in malpractice cases, the authors concluded that the wrong cases went to trial. Mistakes were more often missed than not, and the cases that were brought in front of juries frequently lacked merit.

If I were designing a malpractice system I would want it to remunerate Stacy, so that Miranda was guaranteed to have medical care costs completely covered in the future. The system should also assess Amelia's care of other patients to ensure that her mistake was an isolated incident and not the tip of an iceberg. And the most important part of the system should evaluate if systematic changes in medical delivery might prevent the problem in the future. Destroying a caring physician who makes a human error should never be the end result. Ideally, the system would offer services to both the physician and her patient, automatically referring Amelia for help, and Stacy too. This current system seemed to be consumed with remuneration but did little to address the other goals.

It was sad but validating to read that most patients who are harmed never know. It was something I'd always suspected when I was a patient and it was confirmed during my career. Patients are not sophisticated enough to recognize when dosing mistakes are made, when tests are omitted, or when procedures have gone awry because of physician error. Health professionals know that they could lose their jobs, their homes, and their lives if they tell the truth and are motivated to keep this information from their patients. As a result, many patients who are most egregiously harmed in medicine are never remunerated, and further, they never know.

The white cloak of secrecy had always enraged me. But what I hadn't considered before treating Amelia was the other side of that secretive story. That the physicians who make the mistakes could be devastated. The cost of secrecy for them is that they never get a chance to talk about what happened. There's a reason people go to confession, scrawl in journals, and whisper to friends on the phone in the middle of the night. A reason why they spend hard-earned cash to talk to psychologists. Secrets are burdens, some dense enough to destroy the people carrying them.

When I got home Terry was sprawled on the couch watching CNN. There was a mudslide in California. We watched as a house slid down a hill as if on a sled. They showed it a few times from different angles.

"Look at that," she said. "It's a sinkhole. Those poor people." Then they interviewed the owners, who shrugged and wiped their eyes. I turned and was walking back into the kitchen when Terry said, "It's negative."

I stopped. Turned back toward her. At first I didn't understand. She still faced the television.

"Oh," I said. As I walked back into the kitchen my legs felt heavy. I'm walking through the mud that has filled my home. Here's part of our dining room table, here's my grandfather's chess set, here are the refrigerator photographs, Alexandra with bits of white icing on the corners of her mouth and Terry's dad sitting on the lawn tractor, laughing in his white T-shirt.

I'd gladly take the mud over the pregnancy result.

Back in our bedroom, hours later, I turned off the fan and listened. I was waiting for Terry to return to our bed, after putting Alexandra down again. Alex is attuned to our moods, like an orbiting satellite that drifts and clings as our gravity varies. I've noticed that if Terry and I argue over something, even something quiet, Alex's sleep is more disrupted. She'll come into our bedroom at 11:00, and again at 1:00 or 2:00. "I'm hungry," she'll say, her code for "Someone help me get back to sleep."

Right now, the house is silent. Terry has been in there for twenty-five minutes. Alex sleeps on a bed we call Magic Car, in the shape of a VW Beetle. It's a little plastic monstrosity that she loves. The few nights that Terry's fallen asleep in Magic Car she's regretted it in the morning. Back pain.

I wanted Terry to return to bed, I wanted to talk with her about the pregnancy result and our plan, but all evening she'd evaded me with banter about CNN, her work, and Alex's latest exploits at day care. This was our fifth try. Or was it our sixth? Is it time to call it off? We could count ourselves lucky because we have Alexandra and I'm alive and not tempt the fates any further with more medical adventures?

At 4 A.M. I woke up. Something was jabbing me in the back. It was my book. I must have fallen asleep while I was reading. I slowly lowered my arm next to me and touched Terry's pillow. No Terry. She'd slept with Alex rather than talk with me.

The cafeteria in University Medical Center is on the second floor. There are the typical hospital cafeteria offerings: overcooked vegetables and meats, whipped potatoes or lasagna. But there's also a salad bar, sushi in plastic trays, subs made to order, and Java City. Java City offers specialty coffees and gourmet sandwiches. I'm not a coffee drinker but I like the wraps and homemade breads they use. I like the fragrances on this side of the cafeteria, ground coffee beans and fresh breads.

The lines are long at lunchtime. A few days after the mudslide I was standing in the Java City line behind two women, nurses. I didn't know one but recognized the other. Gloanna. She's a pediatric nurse practitioner who works with kids with cancer in the outpatient clinic. Terry works on the bone marrow transplant unit and they often share patients. Gloanna sends a lot of patients to me. I like her, she's energetic and maternal. The other nurse looked about twenty-five, her uniform was crisp and white. She was a little plump, in that ambiguous state where it's dangerous to ask if she's pregnant. She had the timid look of a girl new to hospitals. I didn't know her. Gloanna's smock had pins all over it: the sign of the experienced nurse.

Gloanna was saying, "I think the best females up there are Lynn Coppola and Kathy Reed. Amelia Sorvino delivered my best friend's babies, she's fantastic too. The bummer is they're all hard to get in with. When Janet called they told her she'd have to wait until November. The trick is getting around the receptionists. I say just call the doc's office you want in with and tell them you work in the system."

"I tried to get in with Sorvino but she's not taking new patients," the new nurse said.

"All the receptionists say that, you have to call the doc direct. Call Sorvino direct." Gloanna looked at me. I was obviously eavesdropping. "Hey, Dan, am I right on this or am I right?"

"Uh, absolutely, as always."

Gloanna smiled at the new nurse and pointed a thumb at me. "This is Dr. Dan Shapiro. He's a sweetie. It's hard to find good disciples." She looked back at me. "Who delivered Alexandra?"

"Uh, Lynn delivered Alexandra. Lynn's great," I said to the new nurse.

"They're all great. Sorvino delivered Katilin and Ro Bagatell's babies. Have you met Dr. Bagatell yet? No matter, call Sorvino again direct." She turned to me. "Oh, Dan, sweetie. I just thought of something, I know you're incredibly busy but I want to ask a favor. Pretty please. We've got an eleven-year-old girl who needs some of your magic."

Her tone dropped to just louder than a whisper. "She's a great kid with osteosarcoma, her cancer has wrapped itself around her knee. We've tried to save her leg with chemo but it's not working and the leg needs to come off. Soon. We're all worried about fractures. The procedure is scheduled for six weeks from now. Make my life and tell me you'll see her." When Gloanna asks I feel like it's my mom asking for something.

"Of course," I said.

Gloanna's voice was back, strong. "So, wouldn't you just call the physician you wanted directly?"

"Sure," I said. I smiled weakly. The line wasn't moving.

Gloanna looked back at the nurse next to her. "So, do we know yet? Boy or girl?"

I wasn't hungry anymore. It was bizarre to hear someone talking about my patient without being able to participate. I excused myself from the line. My hunger is usually reliable; why was it gone?

I looked back at Gloanna and the pregnant woman. The pregnant nurse ran her hands along her belly and it was obvious. It felt unfair that Terry was at home, catching up on sleep after a negative pregnancy test while all around us, the fertility gods were smiling on others. I know that there is no such thing as fair. Given my cancer history, we were lucky to have a child. But still, I wanted desperately to laugh and lunch with Terry, hash over obstetricians, and plot our perfect delivery.

Session Thirteen

I t's fraud day," Amelia started, "but I'm unprepared for class." I didn't know what she was talking about. My confusion must have registered on my face because she continued, "You remember? You asked me at the end of our last session to tell you why I think I'm a fraud."

Now that she'd said it, I remembered. What had I been after? My memory was slow. Sleep deprivation. I'd been consumed with thinking about pregnancy. I still hadn't spoken to Terry about my reservations about continuing fertility treatments, and life in our house felt dense and slow. Meals were quiet. The corner of my left eye was occasionally fluttering and a thin crease of skin on the inside of my cheek burned. We needed to talk.

I tuned my attention back to Amelia in time to hear her say,

My father had one talent in the kitchen. He could bake. He could bake circles around my mother. Focaccia was his bread of choice. I baked focaccia last night. I bake sometimes when I'm upset. I can think when I'm doing it and there's an honesty in baking bread. Nothing you say or think can make the bread better. The only way to get good focaccia is to take your time. It forces my mind to slow down; there's a natural rhythm to it.

I love working warm dough, the fragrances of yeast and olive oil, oregano and butter. Scents that take me back. I told you my bedroom was right off the kitchen when I was a kid. At one time my bedroom had been a large pantry but the people before us had put a door on it and installed a window. My grandfather lived in there until he died. When I was a girl I'd play in there until my father's loaves were ready. He used to top them with Parmesan and pecans or sometimes with browned onions and rosemary. I can be anywhere and smell Parmesan or rosemary and instantly picture my father in his apron. Mr. Serious. He was always stern when he baked; I think he did it to prevent us from touching his loaves before they were done.

So last night, Jay was in his studio and I was in the kitchen. I was working the dough. I had the radio on, that alternative station. I felt a tickle in my chest, I tried to ignore it but it grew. Slowly. Ignore it. Work the dough. Pounding. Jackhammer. Ignore it.

Then I couldn't breathe. Everything was in slow motion. What's happening? Tachycardia, pain in my arms and chest. I was having an MI, a heart attack. No breath. I got over to the phone and I dialed 911. When the person answered I realized that it wasn't a heart attack, it was a panic attack. I hung up without saying anything and they called back. Jay came in as the phone was ringing. I forgot that they know

where you're calling from. I had to tell them I was okay and that they
didn't need to send anyone. When I hung up Jay asked who was on the
phone. I told him it was 911 calling back.

"But we didn't call them."

"Yeah, we did. I'm in the middle of a panic attack." When I heard
my voice it sounded so much calmer than I felt on the inside.

"You look fine."

"I'm not."

"Should we take you somewhere? Should we call Shapiro?"

"No. I'm okay now, sweetie. Go back to painting." Then I started
trembling. I opened a bottle of Chablis. I was trembling so much Jay had to
help me open it. I was going to call you but I couldn't bear the humiliation.

She was wearing a leather necklace with a silver heart hanging
from it. She played with it, twisting the necklace. "I'm cracking
up, aren't I? So what should I be taking? Which medications
stop panic attacks? I could do benzos, and there are a few SSRIs
approved for anxiety, right?"

"Yes."

"Well? What are my options?"

"There are drugs you can take," I said. "But I don't think we
should be focusing on medications just now."

"Why not?"

"Because you're in the middle of uncovering some important
parts of your life and it's natural that you're having some intense
reactions. And frankly, I don't want you to medicate any of it
away."

"Did you miss the part about the full-blown panic attack? I
could go over it again. . . . You just want to torture me? Is this,
like, 'Psychologists go bad?'" She held her hands palms up and
waved them in the air.

"Behavioral approaches to panic work more than eighty-five
percent of the time. I bet you panicked for a good reason. Let's
trust it."

"But it was miserable. I was literally choking. I thought I was dying. You don't know what that's like to worry that you're dying." I felt my cheeks get hot. Oh, but I do, I almost said. Something passed between us. I'd never told her about my history of cancer. It wasn't a secret, hell, I'd written a book about it, but I don't typically talk to my patients about it unless they bring it up. If patients learn I've written a book about my experience I usually advise them not to read it until our work is over. Our work is about them. But sitting with Amelia, I felt a flare of anger. After an awkward moment I spoke, as much to relieve our awkwardness as to get to my point.

"Let's focus on what you were thinking about before the panic started. Can you remember?"

"I was baking. Just thinking about the bread. Carole King was on the alternative station. I had all the ingredients on the cutting board, I'd set the oven and oiled the baking pan. I felt fine. Then I was thinking about my father for a while, wondering if a child would ever feel about my baking the way I felt about his. Dad never baked unless everything was going well in the world. I bake when I'm anxious. But that wasn't a big deal."

"You bake when you're anxious. So you were anxious before you started. About what?"

"Nothing. I don't remember."

"Did thinking about your father make you think about having your own children?"

"Maybe." She said it like "no."

"Are you having thoughts about having babies? Could that be it?"

"Nah."

I wanted to linger here, explore her fertility issues more. Or did I? Was this my issue or hers?

"Can you remember worries from earlier in the day? Other things that concerned you?"

"Nothing stands out." She opened her bag and rifled through it, then suddenly stopped. "Wait a minute. I did think about something stressful. And then I spent most of yesterday trying not to think about it. That makes it important, huh?"

I awoke in the middle of the night a few nights ago. I came out of a dream feeling as if instead of sleeping in our bedroom, I was in that twin bed in my bedroom near the kitchen back in Philadelphia. It was a comforting memory. Vivid. I could almost hear the hum of the refrigerator, and the creaks of the floorboards upstairs where my sisters slept. I imagined there was a breeze outside my open window, like late September when the weather in Philly has just changed and autumn is readying. There's a fragrance to autumn that mingles everywhere.

When I was fourteen or so, I awoke after only sleeping for a few hours to the whispers of my parents in the kitchen. There was some quiet laughter. They hadn't gone to bed yet, it must have been about midnight. I slowly dropped out of bed and tiptoed to the door. I slid to the floor and looked through the crack between the bottom of the door and the floor.

I could see my mother's feet, they were always in woolen socks; it could be 80 degrees, she'd still have them on. I could see the bottom of her cotton nightie. She was doing something near the stove. And my father's bare feet were lit up by refrigerator light; he was taking something out, maybe something to drink.

Dad had just teased her, she was laughing. She said something like, "Come on. Answer me. I want you to come with me. She can do harder work. Won't you come?" There was a melody in Mom's voice; when she wanted something she sang it out to my father.

My father whispered something I couldn't hear. He closed the refrigerator and they must have walked over to the kitchen table, because I heard the drag of the metal chairs being pulled back over the linoleum, and a glass being put down on the table. Dad said something in a low voice and Mom said, "The principal will listen to you if you come with me. Paolo. Come on. Say you'll do it." Whatever she wanted, he wasn't having any of it and she was still flirting to get it.

"Paolo, she's smart. Smarter than both of us. She's got a chance. But not if she stays in those classes. Things are different for them, they've got classes for the smart kids and classes for the dumb kids and even though she does

well in the dumb classes it ain't going to show for nothing. We gotta get them to put her in the harder classes." Mom was practically pleading with him.

Dad grunted something and then Mom got pissed.

"Bullshit she is. She's smart. I swear she is. Paolo, don't be such a shit." I heard the scrape of the chair, and saw my father's feet standing away from the table.

"Everyone thinks their kid is something special," he barked. *"They got tests at that school and she did normal. There's nothing wrong with normal. That's why she's where she is. She ain't going to college, she ain't gonna be a nurse. Stop filling her head with your dreams."*

Then Mom said, "Susan thought Amelia was smart too. . . ." That was it. Just the mention of my aunt made Dad growl something else, and I could see his bare feet march by me and then I heard them pounding up the stairs. I heard a sharp inhale in the kitchen. My mother. And quiet sobs.

My face was pressed against the cold floor. I curled up in a ball. I wanted to tell her that I didn't care. That it didn't matter to me. I didn't mind the easy classes. That she was more ambitious than I was.

I remember looking at my notebooks the next day. I methodically went through my notes. There were doodles in the margins. Faces and stars, loopy ink drawings of flowers and eyes with long eyelashes. No more. I bought new notebooks and copied my notes into them. There'd be no more gazing at the pretty boys in class, or doodling. Over those next weeks I developed a cough. It was like there was a ball of doubt that hardened in my throat, and I couldn't get it out.

I'd had B's and a few A's before then. Even a C or two. Thinking about it made me cough. So I got serious. I did well that fall and winter.

It was Christmas break when I learned that I'd be switching to the harder classes. When my mom opened the letter with my new class schedule on it, she took it to my father, beaming at him, but he said, "So what? She hasn't done squat in them yet."

When he said that I knew I'd be first in the honors classes if it killed me. Best, from then on. I wouldn't just get A's. I'd get the highest A's. I'd be the best. The absolute best. And it wasn't just to earn his love, or respect, or prove him wrong, or anything. It wasn't only about him.

When he said that, I felt myself change from being a soft unfocused girl to something harder and fiercer. I wanted him to know that I'd become someone different, someone he didn't know, someone he'd never known.

I became disciplined. From then on I awoke an hour earlier. I got up before Dad got up and made sure I was showered and at the breakfast table working when he got his morning coffee. I think that's when the voice was born.

"Voice?"

"His voice in my head. When I studied at the kitchen table I heard his voice saying, 'Sure, anyone can do that for a few days, let's see you do it regularly.' And so I did. I made sure I was doing homework before school every day. Even if it was done, I came out there and worked on something for extra credit. Later, in college and medical school, I had a work ethic that set me apart."

"Tell me more about that voice."

She looked down at her shoes and said quietly, "I've never spoken about it out loud. It's a challenger, a critic. It's been good for me, it's made me work hard."

"And the doubt? The lump in your throat?"

"It's always right here." She touched her throat and swallowed. "The doubt. It's so familiar to me. It's been with me since that night. I can almost taste the dust on the floor. After that night I wanted Dad to notice how hard I was working. I wanted him to see that I could hack it, that I was smart.

"He came to my college graduation, clinging to my mother's arm. Even though I knew he was suffering—my dad's been demented awhile—I still wanted him to see my diploma. See, you bastard? I did it! Phi Beta Kappa! Valedictorian! After I walked across the stage I found him and Mom. She was so proud, but that didn't matter to me. I wanted him to say he was wrong. That he was proud too. My mother said, 'He's proud of you, dear.'"

I kept expecting tears to stream down Amelia's face but they didn't. The skin beneath her eyes was blotched pink and white as if her face had heated, expanded, to keep back the tide of emotion.

"That voice, that critic, is part of me. It was with me throughout high school and college. When I walked into my first class in medical school, it was with me. And in organic chemistry when we were getting weeded out and at the MCATs and when I filled out the med school applications. And every time I walk into a patient's room my father is there telling my mother that I'm only average. Stop making a big deal. I'm just a normal kid walking into some poor pregnant woman's room without the sense to realize that I've no business being there."

She sat back and looked at me. Her torso was rigid, frozen, as if the roots anchoring her to those days had just grown thicker.

"It's easier not to think about this, isn't it?"

"Yes."

"Maybe this is what your panic is about? Your body can't deny your anguish about this anymore?"

"I know this is all ancient history, but it's still unpleasant, and it's still with me. I'm not anguished. My problem is that I don't feel anything. I'm empty."

"You look like you're about to cry. I think you're full to over-flowing."

"I am?"

"You are."

She shook her head. "I'm just tired."

"This is important," I said. With too much energy. I sounded like I did when I rehearsed in my head how I was going to approach Terry about the fertility plan.

"I'm tired," she repeated softly. "Look, I'm sorry but I need to cancel our next session. I'm going back to Philadelphia for Memorial Day to see Mom. Can I see you in two weeks?" Her bringing up the schedule signaled the end of the session. We had a few minutes left.

"I think you'll find you'll have fewer panic attacks if you think and talk about this more," I said. She nodded quickly as if dismissing an intrusive salesman, and was gone.

Terry, Alexandra, and I also left town for Memorial Day. I get together with Eric, Joshua, and Chuck, friends since college, every year. This year Eric's wife, Nicole, invited everyone to Torch Lake outside of Traverse City in northern Michigan.

Alex slept through most of the first flight. She sat on my lap during the second leg, looking out at the farms and rivers below while I tried to prevent her from kicking the seat in front of us. Terry and I still hadn't spoken, but when I was carrying Alex toward the security line she reached over and ran her fingers through Alex's hair, and then through mine. She said, "I love my little family." And she nodded at me.

We stopped and bought two pounds of sweet purple cherries from a farmer manning a stand on the road between the Traverse City airport and the cottage on Torch Lake. He packed them into a green Styrofoam container and when I went to eat one he slapped my hand and laughed at my surprise. "That one wants to stay with the others," he said. We picked up some peppers and corn, too, and got back on the road.

When we got up to the lake there were hugs all around. I went onto the back porch with Chuck and Nic, Chuck's boy, who's Alex's age. Together we all looked down from the porch into clear lake water. I could see the minnows and feel Chuck's hand on my shoulder, I felt the warm breeze and knew I was already starting to relax.

The next afternoon, after a night of bottled beer and white wine in plastic cups, Terry's shoulders had already sun-darkened and my toes were sporting pink polish with glitter that Alex had applied. Terry took my hand and we walked down to the dock together. Alex was napping and Joshua and Eric were out on a wooden raft, about a hundred yards away, trying to knock each other in. I told Terry I had my money on Joshua.

"I'll be okay, you know," Terry said while we watched Joshua grab for Eric's long, outstretched arm. I looked at her. "If it doesn't work out. I'll be okay. If I don't get pregnant. I don't need to have another one. I'd just like it. Okay? So don't worry." She squeezed my hand.

I felt a warmth gather in my chest.

"Go on out there," she said. "Eric needs your help." And she pushed me into the cold water.

I treaded and watched Terry walk back up the dock, her strong upper arms swaying. She looked beautiful and weary, this wife of mine. I felt the last month's insecurities and angers, insults and hard swallows melting under the sun, glacial ice trickling into fresh cool water.

When I came back to Tucson I felt refreshed, energetic. There was a message on my machine from Charlotte's mother. Charlotte was the eleven-year-old with osteosarcoma. Her mother said that Charlotte seemed to be doing well. She'd met with the surgeons and with the prosthetics people and her mood seemed fine, but she worried that when Charlotte awoke after the amputation without a leg, it would be a massive shock. "Please call me back," she'd pleaded. I phoned and scheduled her for later in the week.

Session Fourteen

Amelia entered my office wearing black leggings and an oversized black blouse. She sat taller in the love seat, radiating a confidence I hadn't seen recently. Then I realized that she reminded me of the women I trained with in Boston. She was dressed more like an easterner than a person from the Southwest.

It's rare that women in Tucson dress completely in black. It's too hot here. But on the East Coast, in the cities, it's the one dress code that endures, season after season.

"How was Philadelphia?"

"Terrific," she said.

It was the first unbridled enthusiasm I'd heard from her.

I think I told you, my dad has Alzheimer's. I don't talk about it much. When I was in high school and he started having memory problems it embarrassed me. I stopped talking about him to other people, or bringing friends over to the house. I'm ashamed of that behavior. Jay accuses me of erasing him.

It happened slowly. There were little signs when I was a sophomore in high school. He lost his keys. He drove right by our house when he was driving us home. He couldn't tell my swim coach our phone number. We ignored it all. Dad was just a goof. But then in February of my sophomore year, he awoke in the middle of the night, went down to the kitchen, and opened the back door. It must have been 20 degrees outside, but he went out into the snow in his pajamas. Mom came down at 4 A.M. and found him sitting in a foot of snow on the back porch, the door wide open. She said the house was so cold, the cat's water dish had a thin layer of ice. But then a few days later he seemed totally himself.

The next few years were hard. We all knew he was deteriorating but he'd go for long periods of time when there were no signs that anything was different. He'd get enraged occasionally but most of the time he was just bewildered. My senior year he lost his job at the garage. I threw myself into schoolwork and tried not to think about it.

Mom should have put him in a home years ago but she still looks after him. He's occasionally incontinent, he can't feed himself most of the time, he'll go for days without speaking. But then there are these periods when he's almost lucid. He talks, eats a little, recognizes Mom. He hasn't recognized my sisters or me for years. I'm used to it now.

Some people with Alzheimer's are enraged all the time, but he's nicer now. He can be sweet. When he came to my college graduation, he met people he'd never met before. He said things like, "Where've you been? God, if you're not the spitting image of your father. . . ."

When he met my academic adviser, a very quiet chemist, Dad said, "You look good, you've trimmed down." My adviser looked down at his belly and didn't know what to say. Dad looked at Mom and said, "Don't you think he's trimmed down?" And Mom said, "Oh, absolutely." My adviser looked startled and made a quick exit.

I was there this past weekend. I helped out with Dad and the chores, anything to feel useful and needed. On Saturday morning I was folding the laundry in the basement and the house was quiet. My father was puttering upstairs in the kitchen and I heard my mother shoo him away from the stove and then I heard my father say to her, "Annie, have you seen her?"

And my mother said, "Whom, dear?"

And my daddy said, his voice low and urgent, "There's a sad girl in the house, Annie. A very sad girl."

And I realized he was talking about me.

Cora, my little sister, lives about a mile from Mom's. Cora has a two-year-old, Brittany. She's a pistol. Cora and I were going through some of the old games we had packed in Mom's attic. The attic isn't much more than a crawl space, so Cora was up on the ladder handing things down to me. Brittany was going through all of it. There was an Operation game, some old stuffed animals, and a big steel top that you spin to make sparks.

The first time I spun it, Brit was terrified. The sparks shoot off inside a tin-and-plastic container. She grabbed my legs and hid behind them. Then I showed her how to do it. I told her it wouldn't hurt her, and she tried it. She was enthralled. Her eyes opened up and she giggled every time she got it to spin. With one hand she held my leg, and with the other she pushed down the top to make it go. I was standing looking up at Cora, feeling Brit holding on to my leg, hearing her giggle, and I felt a twinge. How natural it felt to have that little hand holding me. Cora looked down at us and said, "You know it's a lot of work, too, it's not all spinning tops."

I said, "What?"

"Is Jay ready yet?"

Then I realized what she was saying.

"No. I don't think so."

"Tick tock. Tick tock," she said.

She was right. Those feelings flooded over me. I do want children, but I'm afraid I'd just screw them up too.

Then Cora pulled down some photo albums. This is the thing I really want to tell you about. Cora came down the ladder and we all sat in the hallway and went through the photos. There were a bunch of old black-and-whites, my grandfather holding my father when Dad was a baby. My father and mother posed next to their first car, a Chevy Impala. And my favorite, my father in shorts and an undershirt, smiling at me while he tosses me above his head. Our faces are radiant, our eyes locked together, me caught forever in midair.

My childhood memories of my father are intermingled with the smells of oil and aftershave. He had massive hands and they were always covered in spots of grease he couldn't quite get off. Across the street from the garage, there was a five-and-dime with a candy counter. Dad loved candy. He used to bring it home in brown paper bags. Shoestring licorice, hot spots, jelly beans, jaw breakers. As soon as I saw him get out of the car after work, he'd pull one of these bags out of his blue work pants.

I remember racing up to Dad once, but he said he didn't have any candy. I thought he was teasing and started begging and laughing. He sometimes pretended to forget where the candy was. He suddenly screamed at me to clean off my shoes, to not be so stupid. I was going to track mud into the house. I remember the veins in his neck were throbbing. I started crying and ran off to my room. Then I realized he was never worried about cleanliness when he was working, and not having candy, I added it up.

In the album, there was a photo of one of my birthdays, I must have been about eight. We are all on one side of the table except my mother, who must have taken the photo. My grandfather is laughing, my sisters are laughing, but my dad is only smirking. His hands are resting on *the table, they're spotless. His hands were never spotless when he was working.*

Dad lost his job twice when I was growing up. Three times if you include the final one. The first time was when the garage changed owners, and the new guy laid him off along with a few other guys. Dad eventually got his job back, but for a while things were tight. I don't know the financial details. I think my grandfather must have carried the family.

That first time he must have been unemployed for a year or so. He started fixing cars at the house. Neighbors left their cars in the driveway and Dad used a pile of planks off the back stoop to elevate them. For a while, there was a different car in the driveway every afternoon when I got home from school, but there were dry spots, too, when Dad couldn't even get side work.

What I remember most is the confidence I had that things would be okay. Even though my parents were fighting more I knew Dad would keep us going.

So I was sitting there looking at the album, thinking with such pride about my father, when I thought about myself. I wasn't fired. They want me at work. I'm not working because I'm a coward. No, seriously, that's what I am. I'm not being hard on myself, this is the reality. I need to get back on the horse.

I think this therapy is part of the problem. You make me feel like I'm normal to be transfixed by my mistake. This isn't normal. It's cowardly. So I don't think I'm coming back. No offense, I just think you're too understanding about all of this. What I need is a good swift kick in the pants. If my dad were lucid he'd say, "What the hell are you waiting for?" It's not your fault, I just don't think this is the right thing for me.

An awkwardness settled over the room. We're seventh-graders. She's breaking up with me. I said, "Are you sure you're not running from how intense things have become in here lately? I've felt you were getting close to some important revelations." Are you sure you want to leave me?

"Thanks for being here. Really. And if I ever need this again I'll be back," she said.

We can still be friends.

She stood up and offered me her hand. I stood and shook it.

"I'm not convinced that this is the best thing for you, but you know where to find me."

She smiled her wide-open smile. Then she spun on her heel and was gone.

It felt so sudden. Maybe this is the right decision. There are many paths to wellness, maybe therapy isn't the right one for her. Sometimes therapy is indulgent. For some people it's easy to sit and talk about problems when what they really need is to *do something*.

I usually get that feeling with people who are too comfortable living in their heads. Who have turned a situation over so many times like a diamond that they've seen every facet, every cut, and they've lost where they started. Sometimes they've generated solutions or actions they could take, only to balk at following through. Or they've tried only one thing and failed, and retreated into talking. At those times I will intervene: "We've rowed across the river, now it's time for you to get out."

I didn't have that feeling with Amelia. Was it too early for her to go back? It felt like a flight into health. It was rare that people could pull themselves up by their bootstraps to overcome intense anguish so quickly. Usually therapy was harder than that. But then again, I wasn't sure. I considered it as I headed to the reproductive endocrinology clinic.

Terry and I waited in the little room. One of the fluorescent lights above flickered. I tried to read the details in *Entertainment Today* about Rush Limbaugh's hearing problem under the flickering light. No wonder Rush Limbaugh said the moronic things he did. He couldn't hear anyone else's point of view. Terry leaned her head back against the wall.

Linden eventually walked another woman out. As she opened the door for her the woman turned and smiled. Linden smiled back. "See you next week." And they waved like old college friends leaving a reunion.

When the woman was gone Linden turned and smiled at Terry. "Come on back." We followed. Back in her little office she opened Terry's chart, scratched her ear, and said, "What are you doing to my success rate?" She smiled. Oh, a joke.

Terry was, as usual, faster than me.

"I got pregnant the first time in Boston, what are you doing to mine?"

"Ah-hah," she said. "That's good. That's good." She studied the chart for a few minutes, turning pages and contemplating. "Look," she finally announced. "There is no reason why you aren't pregnant right now. I honestly don't know what's wrong. You're healthy, you've responded well to the Metrodin, the ICSI is producing good cells, I'm sure this is going to work. Nature gets to play her role, she's stymied us a few times, but I've got a good feeling. Okay?" Her head bobbed on her shoulders but her curly hair didn't move.

Terry asked a few logistical questions and then Dr. Linden said, "I know you must be going through a lot. I know how hard this is. But remember that in the end, we're going to get you both another baby. So don't fret. No frettage." She smiled. "Let me walk you out." I stood up. And she walked just in front of us, as if she were with us. One of us. In our fertility battle completely.

When we were almost at the door I glanced into the waiting area. A couple was sitting there. The woman had her face in her hands.

The next day I met Charlotte, the eleven-year-old with osteosarcoma, for the first time. When I arrived she was standing in the waiting room, dancing a little in place. She was looking out the window, and then turned in a slow circle. Her mother sat watching her. Charlotte was bald from the chemotherapy; as she turned I saw her face, she was all freckles and floppy hat, tall for her eleven years, one of those girls who would tower over her peers soon. I watched the elegant, slow way her hands flowed in midair; I could almost hear the music. I didn't want to interrupt her. Her mother watched her too, and the few other people in the waiting room.

I said Charlotte's name and the spell was broken. Charlotte shook my hand. Grinned. Businesslike. And then she waved a quick good-bye to her mom and turned to me with the trusting ease of a girl used to random medical professionals taking her here and there. Her mom emitted a tired smile and she stood, lingering an extra second watching Charlotte, who sensed the extra attention, and said a gentle, "See ya back here in an hour, Ma."

"Right," her mother said, and pushed open the door out of the clinic.

Charlotte looked at me. "Are the babies on this floor?"

"Babies?"

"Yeah, you know, the new babies." She chewed the end of a finger.

"Labor and Delivery is down the hall; you want to see the nursery?"

"If that's where they keep 'em, that's where I want to go. Can't we talk down there as much as in your office?"

"I'll tell you what. Let's sit in my office for a few minutes and get to know each other and then in about fifteen minutes we'll go check out the newborns. Deal?"

"Deal." She shook my hand again.

In my office Charlotte's voice was singsong. Topics came and went, the serious and casual mixed together. I had to concentrate to ensure I didn't let something serious drift by. She told a knock-knock joke in the same breath as telling me she thought she'd heard her father crying in the bathroom after one of her treatments. She shared her fear of losing her leg while running her hands along the love seat. When she'd finished telling me about the man with the ponytail who was making her first prosthetic, the training leg, she sighed and said, "Now can we go see the newborns?"

We walked past my door, down the corridor, through the security door, and back out onto the main hospital corridor. We were lucky. The nursery was full and the shades were open. There were seven newborns, each in a plastic, rolling bassinet. Their names were written on note cards taped to the bassinet if they'd been named, or just their last names if they hadn't. Rodriguez and Connors, Muchio and Croteau were present. Pink, olive, and brown little faces. Right in front of the glass a newborn was slowly kicking his legs, as if riding a tiny bicycle under the warming lights. I told Charlotte he probably had a low body temperature, so they were warming him.

Charlotte was engrossed in all the activity, the nurses bending here and there to check a belly button clip or to bundle a baby. She pressed her face against the glass and pools of fog gathered around her cheeks on the glass.

Miguel, the boy under the lights, twitched in his sleep.

"Do you think he can dream?" Charlotte asked.

I was adrift, thinking about the fertility treatment. *Quit it. We've got an amputation to prepare for.*

"Uh, sure," I answered.

"What do you think he's dreaming about?" she asked.

"Milk?"

"I think he's dreaming about a dog," she said.

"A dog?"

"Yeah. A border collie. One of those smart dogs. I bet he'd love to have his own dog."

"Really?"

"Absolutely. He's dreaming about a dog."

We watched for a while and then it was time to meet her

mother in the waiting room. I was relieved. I needed to be away from the babies. I turned from the nursery glass and saw a child running toward us. He was laughing. He was Hispanic, about ten years old, and wearing an Arizona Wildcats cap. His mother, she might have been his grandmother, lumbered behind him. She carried a big purse and panted. He ran his hand along the wall and then I realized it wasn't his hand, it was a prosthetic. His feet were gone too; where the lower parts of his legs should be there was a mass of steel and sneaker. He had four prosthetics and could have been bionic, given his speed.

I look at Charlotte as he passed. She was transfixed.

"*Mira*! Look!" the boy behind us said to his mother, tapping urgently on the nursery glass. We turned, he was pointing his prosthetic into the nursery. "Miguel! Miguel! *I've got a little brother!*"

On the walk back to the waiting room Charlotte was silent. Then, as I pulled open the door to the psychiatry waiting room, Charlotte spoke, her voice not more than a whisper. "If that kid can do four, I can do one. No problem."

We met every day over the next week. Charlotte and her family were as prepared as any of the families I'd worked with. My first research supervisor in graduate school pioneered the study of children undergoing medical procedures, so this situation was familiar.

Charlotte's parents had done a splendid job. Charlotte had met the surgeon herself, as well as the people making her prosthetic. She understood as much as most adults about the procedure and life after. She was honest about her fear and expressed it. From our conversations I learned that she was already thinking about how she'd get around her house and school and what she'd tell her friends. We rehearsed how to respond to gawking kids and considered how she might strengthen her other leg through swimming.

I hadn't done much for Charlotte and it occurred to me that this was one of those times when she and her family needed to hear that they'd done everything they could, more than they needed me to do anything specific.

After our last session I sat down with Charlotte's mom and told her I was confident that they'd done everything they could. Her mother seemed grateful to hear it. And then she said, "I'm just worried that she's going to awaken a different kid. It's one thing to talk about losing a leg, another to wake up and it's gone, you know?"

I told her we could only do our best and that I thought Charlotte was going to be fine. Her surgery was scheduled for the following Thursday, a week from our last meeting. The family was going to Sea World in San Diego and would be back on Wednesday. I promised to meet them in the postanesthesia recovery unit after her surgery.

Thursday Night

The bow dips, icy water pours over. There's snow in my face. Wind screams through the sails and the waves are huge, white monsters that crash just off the deck. I cling to the wheel but I don't know which way to turn it. The world is white, each flake is a shard that stings my wrists, throat, and ankles. I look up, there's blue ice in the rigging; the sails and ropes are heavy with crystals. I fight to breathe. Everything is cold.

The waves are growing, something high above creaks a warning. Straining metal. The sails are going to come down, there's too much weight. *What am I doing? I don't know how to sail.* I look up into an angry wave.

What's that sound? I see the familiar outline of my pager and the little light flashing on the screen. My heart pounds. I'm alive. The clock reads 2:17 A.M. *I'm in bed. It's still night. That's it. No more reading about storms before bed.*

Terry sat up, blinked a few times, and whispered, "Is that mine?" I held the pager and stopped it from bleating.

"No, sweetie. Go back to sleep." She dropped soundlessly and was out.

I got up and shuffled down the hallway, listening to my knees make popping sounds. If they're doing that during my early thirties, what will they sound like ten years from now? I ran my hand along the wall so I wouldn't have to turn on the hall light and risk waking Alex. The floor seemed to lurch like the deck of the frozen ship. *That dream felt so real.*

The page is probably from Jennifer, the intern. I bet her patient has tried to kill herself again. With Amelia gone, Jennifer's patient was the only patient in my caseload I worried about. I stumbled over a stack of books at the base of my desk, swore a few times, and turned on the desk lamp. Bright light. I fumbled for the phone.

I keep a cell phone and a house phone in my office. That way, if I need to, I can stay on the phone with a patient and simultaneously call the Mobile Acute Team, a group of mental health paramedics who travel with the police to dangerous situations. I dialed the digits on my pager and it rang and rang. Eventually it clicked and a grandmotherly voice said, "Paging operator."

"Dan Shapiro returning a page."

"Good evening, Dr. Shapiro. Hold please." Her voice was melodic. No one should be that chipper at this hour in the morning. I played with my desk lamp. I turned it off. Turned it on. Turned it off. There was a full moon and when my eyes adjusted I could see deep into the desert. I anticipated Jennifer's voice, like the melody of the next song from a familiar album starting in my head before the music. I could help her cope with anything that might have come up.

There was a click and I heard a voice.

"Sorry to wake you up." Not Jennifer. Monotone. Who? Whoa.

"Amelia? Where are you?"

"Not so fast," she said. "Lez talk first." *She's drunk. Or worse.* I turned on the cell phone.

"What have you taken?"

"Nothing too serious. Some vodka. But it gave me a headache, so I took a few Tylenol number threes, jus' four of 'em, I promise."

"Tell me where you are."

"You're so excited. Calm down. . . . Hey, I sound like a therapist." She giggled.

"Where are you?"

"You're no fun. Let's see. Yup. No doubt about it. I'm in Tucson." She was laughing again.

"Dr. Sorvino. Where are you?"

"I just told you, silly."

"I'm getting off the phone."

"Okay. Okay. No need to throw a snit. I'm at the Blackett's Ridge trailhead."

"Are you serious?"

"Let's see. Hmmm. Dirt. Prickly pear cactus. Bats. Great city view. No doubt about it. Blackett's Ridge trailhead."

She was a mile into the hiking trails of the Santa Catalina Mountains but within range of emergency vehicles. She must have walked into Bear Canyon from the Sabino parking lot, and then taken the Phone Line Trail. The MAC team has gone to stranger places. I looked out the window again. It was bright enough to hike outside. They could see the trail well enough to get up there if one of them had been there before. Had she told me that she hiked?

"What are you doing up there?"

"Haven't decided."

Silence.

"Amelia?" I could hear her breathing. I glanced up at the window but in the reflection I saw my school friend, Lauren, standing behind me with her books pulled to her chest. I spun around but there was nothing there; the edge of the door frame had looked like her shoulder and hair. I started to dial 911. Stopped. *Empathy,* I told myself. *Rouse some empathy. Find out what she's feeling.*

"It must be lonely out there." *Oooh. That sounded pathetic.*

"It is lonely. But it's also calm. I can see the twinkling lights of the city. I forgot my contacts so all the lights are a little fuzzy. It's colder up here than I anticipated. I forgot a sweater. Silly, huh? I figured I wouldn't need a sweater where I was going."

"I don't think you really want to die."

"I don't think you have any idea. Thinking about it has been the most comfort I've had in months. I've been planning all afternoon. I've actually felt productive again, getting all the details down."

Her voice sounded like a drunk soldier readying for a drop into enemy territory, phoning only to announce her deployment.

I didn't know what to say. *I am an overeducated man with a cell phone.*

She broke the silence with a groan.

"Are you okay?" I asked.

"My stomach. I've got some pain. Just enough vodka to be painful on an empty stomach, not enough to do any real good. And this rock is uncomfortable. This is the first time I've wished my ass had more padding. Hold on." And then, "Okay. I'm back. I'm on a new uncomfortable rock."

"Why don't you come down here and we can talk about this? I could meet you in the—"

"Oh. The good Dr. Shapiro. You're sweet. You've kept me alive much longer than I expected, but the magic's gone. I'm really done. There's nothing more to say. There's nothing left. You're not even my official therapist anymore. I'm sorry. I shouldn't have called you."

"What happened? Did you go back to work?"

"In a manner of speaking." She coughed. "Look, that doesn't matter now. None of this matters anymore." I heard quick breaths into the mouthpiece, as if she'd been running.

I pressed the first number: 9 . . . Once the call went through, the MAC team and police would race out there. The Blackett's Ridge trailhead is 2,500 feet higher than the city's ocean of lights. From her elevation she'd see the flashing lights coming unless I told the team not to use them. Would she kill herself if she saw them coming?

"Dr. Dan, I'm a fallen star. A black hole. We've never said this in session, but here's the simple unflinching reality. I destroyed a child's life with my carelessness. You want to hear something funny? You can buy a pacifier in a gas station. I've found them in supermarkets, drugstores, hardware stores, even the goddamned Laundromat. I see them everywhere. They're even in the hospital gift shop. Each one says, 'You hurt a baby. You hurt a baby. You hurt a baby.' Oh my God." There was a sharp inhale and she coughed, an ugly hacking sound.

"Look, why do it now? We haven't seen each other in a while. Give us some time to deal with whatever happened when you went back to work. You could always kill yourself tomorrow if you still want to." I heard a quick snort and a tired laugh, and then I was laughing too.

"That's ridiculous," she said, still laughing. Then, "You're stalling. You've been stalling." She caught me still laughing. I had to switch gears quickly. Suddenly all was tenuous, crumbling.

"You're right, I've been stalling," I started. "I don't know what happened since you stopped working with me. I don't know if you went back to work or what happened there if you did. I can't help you see that you're still a competent physician if you won't let me. Or that what you did could have happened to anyone." I paused, unsure of what to say next. She didn't say anything. A good sign? "Bad things happen despite our best efforts. Part of being human is making mistakes that we can't take back or make better." *God, I'm a talking Hallmark card.* I felt a rush of adrenaline, and in my mind I saw Rachel hanging from the fire escape, Epstein sitting in the chart room sweating in his coat, my cousin Andrea alone at Thanksgiving. My leg tapped away under my desk. My mouth was dry. I'm going to remember this moment for the rest of my life. *Suppress the panic. Speak softly. Be clear.*

"Amelia, I'll miss you so much if you kill yourself. I'll be devastated. Jay will never recover. I'll never recover. Please. Don't do it. Come on down. Can you give us some more time? Can you do that for me?"

I heard her rapid breathing again.

"I had this all planned," she said softly, as if I'd just called to say I couldn't make dinner.

"You'll come down, then?"

"I'll come down, but it doesn't mean anything, okay? No long-term promises."

Is she just getting off the phone? Is she going to kill herself anyway?

"I'll be in my office at seven. I'll expect you to see me then. Promise you'll wait until you're sober before you come down."

"Yeah. Yeah. Good night," she whispered. The phone went dead.

I switched my pager to vibrate so it wouldn't awaken Terry again, carried it back to the bedroom, and climbed into bed. The room felt hot. I couldn't get comfortable. Then I was back up and out of bed. I walked to the dining room and out the sliding glass door onto the brick patio. I closed it slowly and sat down. The moon was bright; moon shadows from the patio furniture made speckled patterns on the brick.

Was this my fault? I'd had difficulty throughout my treatment of Amelia; the natural empathy I usually feel for my patients was often evasive. I had let the image of her harming Alexandra invade my treatment. But now, as I tried to conjure up the picture of Alexandra, floppy in the bassinet, it felt foreign and forced. I felt scared for Amelia, I do care about her. What have I done? I've botched this treatment.

What would a real therapist have done on the phone with her? Arthur Klein or Gerry Koocher, my supervisors at Harvard? What would Nana, my grandmother, have said? Would they have sent out the MAC team for a dramatic confrontation on Blackett's Ridge? This wouldn't have happened to them, they wouldn't have been in this situation. They wouldn't have over-identified with the parents of the child who was hurt. They would have told Amelia from the start that her mistake was understandable, forgivable. And then Amelia would have been fine?

Is that realistic? I've overromanticized my mentors, painted and fluffed them into what I want them to be—omnipotent. I need to believe that there are endless rows of scholars and gurus to solve every therapy problem, because I don't want to face that my professional path could end in thorn and scrub. I don't want to know that there aren't answers in some situations, that some anguish is terminal.

Why was Amelia suicidal? It didn't make sense. But then, with the exception of terminal physical illness, it rarely made sense to me. Lives change, it is the one constant. Even if we are miserable now, chances are that our lives will be different in the future. Suicide is saying to all the future versions of ourselves that we are certain they will be miserable, too. Twenty, forty, even sixty years from now. Who has that level of certainty? Amelia couldn't have it. She was young. Too young to say that without being a doctor she had no hope.

After my aunt Gwen killed herself, my mother tells me, attacks flew around the family. Gwen's sisters thought Gwen's husband, my uncle, was to blame. My grandmother suggested that Gwen's father had been abusive. Over the years, as we moved into adulthood, accusations were still whispered at family gatherings and they filtered through the family. The turmoil was palpable.

But I had always felt that it was Gwen's fault. She was the one who had murdered herself. And the reasons were impossible to know. People kill themselves for a variety of reasons; just like every other action people take, some make sense, many don't. I should feel better. Maybe there's nothing I could have done to keep her off that ridge. But if there's nothing I could have done, this field stinks.

I looked out across Tucson's city lights. The air was crisp. Amelia was only a few miles away in the high desert. Deciding to live or die.

Session Fifteen

A t 6:20 A.M., the office suite was still quiet. I turned on the lights in the waiting room, the hallways, and in my office. I turned on my slate fountain. It was low on water and sputtered a high-pitched spitting sound. I carried a plastic cup down the hall to the sink in the bathroom and filled it. In the bathroom I looked at myself. Dark half-moons sagged beneath my eyes. I needed a haircut. My hair grows too fast. I had a mound in the middle of my head. I came back and poured the water into my fountain. It gurgled happily. It was comforting. She's still alive. Isn't she? Maybe the smells of the high desert—the sage, mesquite, and creosote—were soothing. I sat in my office chair and felt the heaviness in my limbs. I hadn't slept since I spoke to Amelia four hours before.

I tried to remember what I'd said to her and wrote it down. Had I really not hospitalized her? What if she'd told me she would come down just to get me off the phone? I wrote a chart note. *Phone contact. Patient paged at 2:20, acutely suicidal with intent, reported ingesting 4 Tylenol #3, ETOH x 4.* Had I asked her about taking anything else? I couldn't remember.

I left my office to check the waiting room and realized I was grinding my teeth. Maybe I should get one of those nighttime mouth guards. I could carry it around with me all day. Part of me wanted Amelia to be in the waiting room, but part of me didn't. I desperately wanted her to be alive but I didn't want to have a session with her. I was still raw.

She wasn't there. Was she dead? I walked around and sat at the receptionist's desk, playing with a stapler, waiting. How would I react if I got a call that she was dead? Would I quit? Would the call come in to my direct line or the receptionist's? Probably the receptionist's. The receptionist's message light was blinking.

Why didn't I call the MAC team? What the hell was I thinking?

I didn't have the receptionist's security code to check her voice mail. If I call the administrator of the system and tell them it's an emergency will they give me the messages? Then the electronic doors swung open and a hunched-over figure trudged up to the receptionist's desk, hair chaotically leaping this way and that. She was fumbling in her wallet for her insurance card. She looked up to find me sitting there and did a double-take.

"Budget cutbacks? You're the early-morning receptionist now, too?" Her voice was baritone.

My heart pounded. *Thank God.* I felt myself welling up. Her face was drawn. There was dirt on one of her cheeks. She brushed hair out of her face and I could see auburn powder beneath her nails, the color of the dirt up on the trailhead.

"I guess I'll do the insurance later, okay? Can we go back?" she asked. She zipped her backpack and walked the short hallway to my office. I followed. She went in and paused before sitting down, as if seeing the office for the first time.

"Good morning," she said.

"Morning."

"You look awful, too. My fault. Sorry."

"I'm glad you came down."

"Thanks, I guess."

The fountain trickled.

"What happened, why did you go up there? Did something happen when you went back to work?" She looked at me. She rubbed her eyes and yawned. I wanted to yawn, too.

"We can talk about that later. You don't know the best part. After we got off the phone my night got really interesting."

"It wasn't interesting enough already?"

"I didn't kill myself, but I did destroy two mailboxes, end the life of one cholla cactus, and also assassinated a Waste Management trash barrel and its little friend, a blue recycling bin.

"I had a little accident driving home. One minute I was driving and the next I was stopped on the side of the road. I was sober, too. Honest. I just didn't have my contacts in. Eventually, a cop drove by and spotted me. He was a regular Sherlock Holmes. He parked, came out of his car with a flashlight, shined it on me and said, 'Ma'am, is that a mailbox sticking out of the front of your car?' I told him it was a new hood ornament, and then I couldn't stop laughing.

"He made me get out and he did a full field sobriety test. I thought it would only be putting a finger on my nose and walking a straight line, but he broke out the full gamut of tricks. One minute I was thinking about dying and the next I was a circus animal: standing on one leg, guessing how long thirty seconds was, and turning in a circle with my eyes closed.

"He did a Breathalyzer. It read at .08. Just at the legal limit. I said, 'Congratulations Officer Friendly, you just bagged a physician.' He told me it gave him no great pleasure and that Driving Under the Influence was serious. 'Doctor or not, I have to report all of this. You could have killed someone. This mailbox could have been a kid.' At first I thought what he was saying was ludicrous. After all, what kid would be out at 3:30 in the morning on a desert road? But then I told him he was right, I could have killed a kid."

She looked at me. This was the first time she'd said that. She scratched her cheek.

"Bottom line. I'm going to have a court date, isn't that exciting?"

"Congratulations, you certainly had an interesting night."

"Hell, I think I could make the cover of *Interesting Night*

Magazine. It won't be my first foray into the legal world. I've enjoyed the civil proceedings so much, why not explore the criminal justice system?"

"Hmmm."

"I wonder if they give frequent flyer miles? Maybe I could win a free civil suit." The jokes came one after another, and she laughed for a second but then the jocularity evaporated, like desert rain in a time-lapse film.

"Amelia, I don't understand how you ended up on the trailhead. What happened?"

"I don't feel like talking about it now. I just wanted you to see that I was still alive. I owed you that. I know what it's like to be tortured by a patient. I'm here because of you, okay? Let's just leave it at that. I want to go home and sleep." She looked down. Sheepish. "I want you to be my therapist again. Can I come back in and we can pretend this didn't happen? I'll be fine. Promise." She brushed the hair from her eyes and looked at me. She was exhausted. I picked up my appointment book.

We settled on a time for our first session and I told her we'd be seeing each other twice a week for a little while and then asked if she could do that. She nodded. "Good. Before you leave, take ten minutes and tell me what happened, why you went up there. You have to understand that it's too hard to sit in the passenger seat without knowing where we're going and where you've just been."

She looked like she might stand up and leave anyway. One of her legs jittered, as if she were a schoolboy waiting for the bell to ring.

I gave up. "Okay. If you aren't going to talk to me now, I want you to call and leave messages on my machine. I want to hear from you twice a day tomorrow and over the weekend, so I'll know you aren't planning to imminently harm yourself. Or no deal."

"I have to check in?"

"Last night was a suicide dress rehearsal. If you won't promise to call me, then I'll hospitalize you right now."

"You wouldn't do that against my will. I'd never talk to you again." She said it plainly, no drama. Matter-of-fact.

"Promise you'll phone. I expect my first call around seven tonight."

"It's infantilizing."

"Promise me you'll make the calls, or we start the hospital thing right now."

"What do you want me to say into your machine, that I'm not going to kill myself in the foreseeable future?"

"Right."

"So you're my suicide parole officer now?"

"That's right. Officer Shapiro. Do we have a deal?"

"When I did a psych rotation they had padded rooms. Do you still have padded rooms?"

"Deal?"

"Deal. Now can I go?"

I held my hand out toward the door like a cruise director offering the presidential suite.

The messages over the weekend were timed just as I'd asked.

"It's me. This is a waste of time."

"This is Sorvino's pizzeria. We are still very much alive. You have a pepperoni pie to pick up."

"This is parolee Sorvino calling in. Next time, maybe you could get me one of those zappers that unruly dogs wear. If I stray too far, I get shocked. Talk to ya tomorrow."

And on.

Session Sixteen

I received Amelia's voice mail messages a few times a day, even over the weekend. They were funny, they softened me. By Monday I was looking forward to seeing her. She came in first thing, she was wearing trendy slacks and an emerald blouse. She looked like a lawyer. She came into the office, sat down, and started in, sounding rehearsed, as if she'd practiced what to tell me all weekend.

Okay, after our termination session, the last time we saw each other before Friday, I called my chairman and told him I wanted to come back. He was thrilled. I was still riding the determination from my trip to Philadelphia and I remember I had confidence. He was great. He got right into the practical details. Said he'd find me an office and that I should call Kathy Reed to talk to her about picking up some outpatients and supervising residents.

I spoke to Kathy and she was terrific too. No drama. No questions. It was as if I was just returning from vacation. We talked about clinic days and she told me about a resident she was worried about, a slacker who'd been cutting some corners. It didn't have anything to do with me, but it was her way of letting me back in the club. She was treating me like a faculty member, getting me up to speed.

Her tone was changing, losing its rehearsed effect, she was pausing and thinking, the normal pace of her narration returning.

Then I called Sanchez. He's a unit clerk in Labor and Delivery. He's one of those people who knows everything that's going on with everyone. He's a little guy with boundless energy. He's the one who sets up the office pool when the basketball tournament comes around, and remembers the patients' names and the staff's birthdays. He's a human bulletin board. I knew that once I'd told him word would shoot through the department. He said, "Dude, you know what this means." (He even calls the women "dude.")

I said, "No, Sanchez, what's it mean?"

"Party. PAAAARTY. No worries, Doc. I'm on it. I've put together parties in four hours. Can you make it tomorrow night?"

So on Thursday there was a party at Bob Dobbs, the burger joint on Sixth Street.

Jay has never liked these places but he went for me and I was glad he did. It was so good to see everyone. Bob Dobbs was busy but we had one corner to ourselves, a bunch of the docs and nurses packed around a few rickety tables. I love Bob Dobbs because it's unpretentious. There's no fake western theme or sports memorabilia on the wall. It's always filled with regulars and college kids having a good time. The walls are covered with messages and markered drawings. Things like "Milo X lost his beer virginity here October 5, 1993," and "What if the Hokey Pokey really is what it's all about?"

A bunch of the residents were there, and Lynn and Hugh and Kathy. Elsie. I remember that Bonnie Raitt was playing when Sanchez got up there with a marker, shook his butt a few times, and scrawled, "Doctor Amelia Always Delivers." And then Lynn took the marker and wrote, "Because she can't do anything else" in small letters. The entire group howled.

I had a few Harps and enjoyed the sea of friendly faces and the smell of the grill. Everyone took a turn getting ribbed. Lynn is really skinny and Hugh called her "stick girl" and we toasted her new nickname. We laughed a lot, and I felt accepted again. It was like I'd never left. Elsie was the only one who wouldn't play along. She didn't drink anything. She just had a diet Coke and sat quietly. At one point I leaned across the table and asked her what was wrong and she said, "Nothing, sweetie." And she smiled one of her "talking-to-the-boss" smiles. "Come on, Elsie," I said, and she said, "I'm just hungry is all. When is that veggie burger getting out here?"

I noticed that the place was mobbed. When had it gotten so crowded?

I found my way back to the bathroom line and waited—and waited. You know what that place is like back there in that little hall. I finally got in and was peeing when I overheard people in the hallway. A couple guys were talking about breast implants versus the natural look and then I heard familiar female voices. Two of the residents were talking. One of them said, "Can you believe they said she always delivers? Kind of inappropriate, wasn't it?"

"She looked okay with it."

"Why rub it in her face?"

"Do you think she'll be ready?"

"Put it this way, I wouldn't want her delivering my baby on Friday."

"You gotta get back on the horse, baby."

"Yeah, but not my horse . . ." They were laughing. I thought about hiding. I even checked the size of the window up near the ceiling, with plans of escape. Instead, I opened the door. We all hesitated, looking at one another, and I brushed by them.

"Oh shit," one of them whispered.

I got another Harp from the bar and went back out and sat next to Elsie, who was still mopey. To cheer her up I started singing "Jeremiah was a bullfrog" as loud as I could. It's a little thing with me and Elsie. I call it musical virii. The object is to implant an obnoxious song in Elsie's head and she tries the same with me. I once got her to hum Barry Manilow's "Mandy" to herself for three weeks. She's a little more clever. About a year ago I came into the office one morning to find a child's tape of Barney's "I love you, you love me" playing in my dictation recorder. She'd gotten her son to dub it six times on a minicassette and she'd left it playing in my office when she knew I'd walk in on it.

So I was singing "Never understood a single word he said" at the top of my lungs when Elsie finally smiled at me. I took it as a sign that everything was going to be okay.

My first day was Friday. I had two C-sections scheduled in the morning and then I was the attending in the residents' outpatient clinic in the afternoon.

The on-call suite is right next to Labor and Delivery. It's four little rooms with beds and lockers. They're off a larger, common room that has a television, refrigerator, coffeepots, and two computers where we can see the fetal and maternal heart rate strips and search the library's medical databases. Williams Obstetrics *is on the coffee table in there—it's the bible of obstetrics. When I'm in the mood, I can catch up on obscure birth injuries. I like that space. It's like a doctors-only pod. I've spent so many hours in those rooms, sleeping while on call, talking to Jay on the phone, or watching television. It's a second home.*

When I got to work I changed in one of the little rooms. The bed was made. Someone's socks were hanging off the top of the locker, as if the locker had ears. There was also a coffee cup with lipstick smears on the bedside table. I liked seeing those things. I was home.

In the common room I met two second-year residents, Karen and Eleanor, who were going to assist me. Karen had been a midwife for a year before going to medical school. She was my age, very sweet. Eleanor was younger, eager. Karen had seen the mom for her prenatal visits. The mom was at thirty-seven weeks along and had been having mild vaginal bleeding and some pelvic and abdominal pain. We were concerned about abruptio placentae, when a normally located placenta separates too early. In severe cases it can harm the fetus but her baby was doing well. Her bleeding had intensified during the past couple of days and the C-section was scheduled.

While the anesthesia folks met with the patient the three of us sat in the doctors' pod and talked. I'd forgotten how great it was to talk with residents. First we talked through the classification scheme for abruptio placentae; my guess was that our patient was only Class One, it characterizes about 50 percent of cases and the risks aren't that high. Then I asked them about their experiences in the residency.

Eleanor was excited and still caught up in the magic of deliveries. Karen had done hundreds on her own before medical school and we compared notes. I told them about my first delivery, and working with Sally. I shared my mantra about this work, that it never gets old.

I almost always like female obstetricians. They aren't like the female oncologists or surgeons, who seem to get cold over time. These two were kindred spirits. They were there to bring children into the world.

And I liked how they treated me. That easy respect, it's subtle, the way after speaking they looked at me for a nod or agreement. Or the quick way they laughed when I described the wonder I felt after my first birth. I didn't have any of those thoughts of not deserving or not belonging. I did belong. Then we went to meet the patient.

The patient's face was a sea of freckles. She was obviously uncomfortable, and nervous, but excited to be a mother. Karen introduced me to the patient as the most popular faculty member in the hospital. I felt a twinge then. I couldn't think of what to say next for a moment.

We went over the procedure, what was going to happen. We'd bring her back alone first, and the anesthesia folks she'd already met would start a spinal. She'd be awake and we'd put up a screen, just a blue drape hung between two steel poles, between her and us, so that she could see me at all times but not the surgical field. The patient's mother was her surgical partner. She was going to be there with us; she'd come in after the drape was up, and the spinal was running. There'd be a few other people in the room from the pediatric team who would show her child to her after the delivery. When I told her about the pediatrician I felt something. A glimpse of Miranda, floppy. I dismissed it and continued. I told her the whole thing would take about forty minutes, tops, probably closer to twenty.

"She's incredibly quick," Karen told the mom. She'd heard about me. Karen offered a few more bits of information about the C-section, about how we would proceed, and I realized that she must have observed other C-sections. We went back to the OR and masked up with hair masks, face masks, and plastic screens in case of splatter. Then we scrubbed in. I like that ritual. The hot water. The soap. The big silver sinks. While we scrubbed we talked through C-section options. The benefit of a low transverse cut over a classical C-section is that it gives women the option of having a vaginal birth later; we call them VBACs. Anyway, the risk of rupturing a good transverse scar is very low. We talked through the different possible cuts, inverted T's, low verticals, and classicals, and I told them how to know you're in the right place for a transverse. Take two

fingers above the pelvic bone, stretch your fingers as wide as they'll go and that's the distance for the incision. I felt fine. Put me in, coach. I've never been more ready.

When I went into the OR the screens were set up, mom's epidural was running, and we were ready. The room was very bright, I'd forgotten how bright everything is. A nurse screwed two green holders into the two lights that hang like orbs over the surgical field. Then she moved them around and asked if I liked where they were. I thought, *Oh yeah, this is my show.* "Fine," I said. I asked the patient how she was feeling and she said she was comfortable. Both of her arms were splayed out away from her, like Jesus. *Helpless. Hardly comfortable.*

The anesthesia resident and attending stood next to the patient's head and gave us the thumbs-up. The pediatric folks stood at the other end of the bed, at her feet. Next to them was the Labor and Delivery nurse, who manned the tray of clamps and scalpels. Another nurse stood next to the suction machine behind us, the long tubes running from the suction cylinders where her blood and waters would go, to the straw in the surgical field.

Then I realized that the anesthesia attending was Ann Jones. *I couldn't believe it took me that long, because even behind a mask she's easy to recognize. She's great. I think she knows what happened with me, but she didn't show it.* She smiled at me from behind the clear plastic mask.

We stood up to the surgical field. Karen and Eleanor stood next to me. The patient had one hand in her mother's, and the other was open toward the ceiling. That hand trembled; it was almost imperceptible, but I could tell. *This is barbaric. I'm about to cut open a perfectly capable mother. What are we doing? She could probably deliver this baby naturally. And then I thought, stop it. She needs this.*

A last check to ensure we have everything. *Suction. Clamps. Scalpel. Anesthesia. Pediatric folk. Lamps. Bucket for the placenta. Tools for a breech delivery wrapped in towels.*

Ready. Let's do this. First, the Allis test. I took an Allis clamp and pinched mom's skin all around her belly, hard. It's to test her for anesthesia. If she could feel it she'd leap off the table. She didn't move. I told Eleanor to take the straw and get ready to suction for me.

Scalpel. I made the first incision. The bikini cut. A thin ribbon of blood descended down her belly. I went below the layer of fat to the fascia, the connective tissue that holds everything together. I dissected through the fascia and arrived at crimson muscles. The six-pack. Using my thumbs I spread her muscles apart. It took work. They're thick like cables. Then I slid her bladder aside and a large pink uterus revealed itself. There is a live child in there, in a perfectly tuned environment.

I found her pelvic bone and used two fingers to measure above it. I showed Karen and Eleanor what I was doing. Then I stretched out my fingers. This tells me where to make the incision. Low transverse. Then I asked for a scalpel and made the incision.

Warm water gushed over my hands. I could see purple legs intertwined. Breech. Shit. I need to get those out. I didn't want to touch the legs. The baby wasn't moving. I could tell he was floppy. There's something wrong.

Everything slowed down. Blood and waters from the incision trickled and pooled on the lower drape. It didn't seem like blood. It looked like a black Pennsylvania lake. I felt my pulse in my forearms, and then my temples. The walls of the room were peach and they started to fold inward on themselves. I looked back at all the blood. Eleanor was suctioning as fast as she could. The first cylinder was almost full. So much blood. I couldn't remember if that was normal.

What am I doing?

Karen said, "Dr. Sorvino?" The smell of the antiseptic filled my head. The overhead lamps swayed and I saw all the faces. Ann Jones and the anesthesia resident. Karen. The patient. The moment extended into hours. Eleanor asked if she should go page Lynn? Karen said no.

Karen stepped up, reached in, and held her hands like a quarterback receiving the football, grabbing the baby by his pelvis. She pulled hard. It took some muscle. She got him partially out and Ann Jones told her to wrap him in a towel to get a better grip. Eleanor handed Karen a towel the size of a large washcloth and she wrapped it around the baby. She moved with authority. She grabbed him around the pelvis again and pulled him out the rest of the way. I knew he'd be silent. Floppy. But he was good and pissed, writhing his arms and legs. He squealed and shook his head as Karen suctioned him. He was angry. Strong. Dark-skinned. His cries shattered my coma. I woke up. She scissored the cord and handed him to the pediatric resident. Then she stepped back into the field.

She didn't know what to do. I told her to reach back into the uterus and scoop out the placenta, the bright purple mass of tissue, and give it to the nurse, who whisked it away to get stem cells from the cord. I told Karen to pull the uterus out of its home, rest it up on the patient's belly, and sew it up. It's just a blown-up balloon now. I told her to look it over for bleeders. Nice. Now push it back in there. Don't worry if it won't go in at first, it'll go soon. When it settled back under everything she slid the bladder in place, and massaged the muscles back into place, too. Now stitch the bikini. My voice quivered with each word but Karen was fantastic. I noticed that I'd wrapped my arms around myself as if I weren't scrubbed anymore. Then we were done. We said good-bye to the patient and we walked out. I pulled off my masks and gloves and we walked back toward the doctors' pod. My arms were still wrapped around myself, the smell of antiseptic still in my face.

The moment we got in the room Karen inhaled deeply and covered her face. She was trying not to cry. I stuttered that she'd been brilliant. Eleanor looked pale.

"What happened?" Karen asked me, just a whisper. Then I noticed there were two other faculty in the room, Lynn and Jim. Then Ann Jones came in. She must have been right behind us. She complimented Karen and then put her arms around my shoulder and turned me toward the wall, away from everyone. She whispered that before every procedure she feels nauseous. Her eyes looked so maternal. I told her I would never put her in that situation again. Then I turned back and thanked Karen. And Ann and Eleanor. I told Eleanor to call Elsie and have her cancel the rest of my day.

I ran down to the room with my locker, grabbed my clothing, and scurried out. Down the stairs, all seven floors, and out of the hospital, still in my scrubs, full to my throat with a frantic energy. I didn't realize until I was halfway to the parking garage that there were blood splatters on the shoulder of my scrub top. I must have looked a sight.

On the drive home I knew what I had to do. I went to the golfing store

*on Campbell and bought a sweat suit. The salesgirl was afraid of me, I
don't blame her, I looked deranged.*

*I changed in the car. Then I went to Beyond Bread and got a table
outside in the heat and waited. I tried to read the papers and nibble but I
wasn't hungry. When it was late I went home. I didn't tell Jay what
had happened. I pretended I'd worked the whole day. It felt good not to
have to explain what happened to anyone. Ever again. I just erased it.*

That's when I started planning the hike up to my favorite ridge.

*I thought about coming to see you. I did. I missed talking with you. I
felt badly about stopping our treatment so suddenly, but I couldn't face
you. I couldn't take the humiliation of having to explain it to you after
stopping therapy. And I didn't want you to get blamed after I was dead.
I knew if I went back into treatment and then killed myself, you'd suffer.
Better that it not happen on your watch.*

"But something changed your mind," I said. "You called me
when you were up there."

"I don't know." She looked at the wall. "I wanted to hear your
voice. . . . I wanted to hear your perspective. You have such a
calm way of talking about horrible things." She looked at me.
"You know, you don't talk about it, but I read your book. When
you had cancer you fought to live. That spoke to me. It made me
realize that I shouldn't be so willing to throw it all away. But at
the same time, I didn't want to talk to you. A part of me really
wanted to die."

I felt exposed. But complete. A patient. Her doctor. Both at
once.

"What about now?"

"Now I just want to forget."

"You might need an inpatient stay. What do you think?"

"What would that do?" she asked, skeptical.

"You'd be in a safe place, you'd get some sleep. Maybe some
antianxiety medication." As I spoke I realized I wanted her to go
in for me. So I'd be in a safe place and get some sleep.

"I'm safe now. I called you, didn't I? And if I went in I'd just sing and dance until they let me out. I know what to say." She was right. She could get out easily by assuring the staff that she was fine. Even a sophisticated staff can only do so much in this age of three-day inpatient stays.

"I'm glad you called. And if you assure me that you'll do it next time too, then I won't push the hospitalization. We're on for Wednesday, but I want you to keep up the check-in calls."

"Dan?" Amelia looked straight into me.

"Hmm?"

"Will I ever be a doctor again?"

The hair on my arms stood up.

"Yes, you will."

"I don't think you really believe that."

"Dr. Sorvino. You will be a doctor again."

"You're afraid I'll kill myself if you tell me the truth."

She tossed her head and her hair fell around her face. She brushed it away slowly with her hand.

"You care desperately about your patients. You have the technical competence. You've delivered fifteen hundred babies and allowed one bad delivery to color your entire sense of yourself. If you'll just give yourself some room, I know you'll be a doctor again."

She smirked at me. She didn't believe a word.

"I mean it," I added, and the words hung, alone, in the room. I let her leave.

I'd promised myself to take real lunch hours, but there is always something to squeeze in. On Monday we had a faculty meeting at noon so I was trying to muster the appetite to eat before the meeting. My session with Amelia was still with me; it had eclipsed my desire for food. I was walking into the faculty meeting when my pager beeped to life. I went back to my office to answer it.

Gloanna's voice greeted me. "Hey, sweet thing."

"Hey, Glow."

"So tell me, how's our princess doing? She ready for business? The excitement is in two days." Charlotte's amputation was scheduled for Wednesday. I'd almost forgotten.

"I think she's as ready as she can be," I told her. "There's no way to tell how she'll respond after it really happens, but I think her parents have done everything they could have. You've done everything you could have. I think I have too." Switching gears was hard, first Amelia, then the faculty meeting, and now Charlotte were all swirling together.

"She's a princess," Gloanna said.

"She's great."

"Thanks for doing this, I know you won't get paid. Anyway, she loves seeing you."

I awoke Wednesday morning knowing it was Charlotte's day. It's one thing to think about an amputation, to meet the kind faces who'll be doing the procedure, the surgeon, the anesthesiologists, the operating room nurses and prosthetic people, and another thing to experience it. I had nine surgeries during my five years with cancer. I woke up once with broken ribs, another time with a tube running into my lungs, a third time with plastic tubes running into my femoral vein. It's bizarre to wake up and find your body different in any way, let alone without a leg you had before you went to sleep. Some things can't be anticipated.

It was going to be a busy day. I had to give a lunchtime talk to a group of physicians concerned with burnout. I had five patients to see, and a few residents to supervise. And a session with Amelia was at the end of the day.

On the morning drive to Alex's school, she sang at the top of her lungs in the backseat while I ran my hand along my thigh, imagining it gone.

I got down to the post anesthesia care unit, the PACU, at around 11:00. Charlotte's surgery had been the first case, at 7:00

A.M. The unit is on the lowest floor, away from the main tower of the hospital. It always takes me longer than I expect to get there. The unit is a long row of beds, where patients who have just had surgery recover from anesthesia. I figured she'd be waking up around then.

I walked the rows, looking from bed to bed, and finally found Charlotte's mother sitting on a stool next to a bed where wires and IV bags disappeared beneath a blanket.

The PACU feels high-tech. Cold. There are computers on every wall, monitors showing the patients' heart rates and oxygenation. IV bags hover everywhere. The professionals are all in scrubs, there are nurses with clipboards and anesthesiologists and surgeons with stethoscopes and charts. Charlotte's mother looked glad to see a familiar face.

The tip of Charlotte's bald head peeked out from the blankets. If I hadn't seen her mother I wouldn't have known there was anyone in the bed. She's so tiny, I thought.

"She's still asleep," she said. "I know she'd love to see you. She hasn't woken up for very long yet. She's awake and then asleep again and she hasn't spoken yet. It's been more than two hours since the surgery but no one seems worried. Her dad just went to get some coffee." She looked at the bald head and said, "Charlotte? Charlotte? Look who's here."

I walked closer. Charlotte stirred. Eyelids fluttered; she sat up and looked around.

"How you doin', champ?" I asked.

She rubbed her eyes, squinted as her eyes adjusted and said a soft "Hey." She swallowed. "My throat is so dry. Water?"

Her mother handed her a paper cup with a straw. Charlotte sipped a little and then put the cup down on a bedside table. Then her eyes opened a little wider, she reached under the covers and felt around, looking down. She must have found the stub at the end of her thigh because her hands lingered in one spot for a long time. Eventually her hands came up and folded together over the blanket.

"I have a question," she said with a low, quivering voice. Her mother and I stared. Uh-oh.

"What is it, honey?" her mother asked.

There was a long pause. Charlotte swallowed, took another drink of water, and looked into each of our faces, urgency in her eyes. "Can I have a dog?"

"What?"

She said it again, her voice a little louder. "A dog. A border collie. I'll take care of it, I promise."

Her mother looked at me and grinned. "Her timing, it's impressive, isn't it?"

"Impeccable."

"You're working it, Charlotte, aren't you?" her mom said.

"I really want a dog. Say yes, Mom. Please."

Her father appeared, two coffee cups in his hands. Charlotte's mother gestured with her head toward Charlotte and said, "Listen to this. Go ahead, tell Dad your biggest concern now that your leg is gone." His eyes opened wide.

"Dad, can I have a dog?"

Walking through the long maze to get back to the main elevators I remembered I'd be seeing Amelia at the end of the day. I didn't want to. I was tired of worrying. Charlotte's resilience was a thick oak tree. Amelia was a sapling. Was it the lifetime of self-doubt that made Amelia struggle so much more? Had her medical training rendered her an unforgiving perfectionist? Was it some genetic fluke, some tiny double helix spiraling in her DNA, that made her want to give up?

Or maybe the difference between them was that Charlotte and her parents were willing to admit their fears, to talk about them openly, while Amelia paved hers over. It has always been odd to me that in our culture, and in medicine, strength is associated with silence. In reality, it takes true courage to acknowledge our fears, to talk about them. It's true that none of us wants to spend time with someone who talks only about his fears, but Amelia lived so far on the other end of the spectrum that this was not a concern. When we talk openly, we can begin to understand that we are all in the same cosmic soup, that pain and crisis are a universal part of life. This is health. The ability to laugh and cry easily, to acknowledge our emotions, whatever they are.

Charlotte was coping with a lifetime change without even a trickle of self-pity, perhaps because she had squarely faced the fullness of her loss. Amelia hadn't lost a leg. Her challenges weren't permanent, but she struggled partially because her anguish was still buried. I knew it was an oversimplistic summary but as I found the elevator I didn't care.

Session Seventeen

Amelia arrived at 4:35 for our 5:00 session. The receptionist called and told me she was there. She'd never been early before. I was in the middle of supervision with a resident. "She'll have to wait," I barked into the phone and then caught myself. What's this anger about? What's my problem? Coming early is her way of saying that she's trying.

When I walked into the waiting room at 5:00 she smiled at me and I was surprised that I felt glad to see her. And ashamed of my outburst on the phone. I'd have to remember to apologize to the receptionist. Amelia looked good. There were no circles beneath her eyes. The warmth was back in her smile. For a moment I forgot the 2 A.M. phone call, the check-ins, she looked so competent, vibrant.

"Hi," she said, when we sat down.

"Where should we start?"

"I'm feeling better."

"That's great."

"The case is heating up. Can I talk about that? It's on my mind. I had a deposition yesterday and there are more scheduled over the next couple weeks. My lawyer said that after the next few depositions we'll know how strong a case they have."

Yesterday they deposed a nurse who was working the morning Miranda was born. She's a traveler, she works in obstetrics units all over the country. She's about fifty. I didn't recognize her at first—her hair had been longer before. Then I remembered her. She was a great nurse. She'd come in to assist when we were all exhausted. She was the nurse who had said that we were all wrecks.

Since the DUI Wally has been a lot less chatty with me. He did say that he wanted her to testify because she had a lot of experience and could attest to my excellent reputation and skills.

She was my height, slender, with bushy gray hair that was probably red when she was younger. She was in scrubs for the interview. It was such a contrast to the experts in suits who had been deposed before her. She had a scar on her throat. I wondered about that. She'd had thyroid cancer, I guessed. She didn't look glad to be there, or as comfortable as the lawyers. She kept scratching her cheek and clasping and unclasping her hands.

They went through her background; she'd been a nurse at Johns Hopkins for twenty years before her divorce. She raised three children in a Baltimore suburb, she'd been married to a surgeon. Then she divorced him when her kids were all in college and she hit the road. Six weeks here, six weeks there. She'd worked in over twenty hospitals in a dozen states, mostly in the West. Colorado, New Mexico, and Arizona.

She was on from 7 A.M. on the morning Miranda was born. They asked her about her work habits, references, and why she worked as a traveler. Then the plaintiff's attorney asked her to describe the morning of Miranda's birth. She looked at me and said, "First thing I want to say is that Dr. Sorvino is a good doctor." The attorney smiled at her and nodded.

"*Thank you,*" he said. "*So you'd worked with Dr. Sorvino prior to the birth of Miranda Paulsen?*"

"*Yes.*"

"*How would you describe her behavior?*"

"*Excellent. She's a good doctor, like I said.*"

"*Forgive me if I don't say it right, but how many births have you assisted Dr. Sorvino in? Prior to this one?*"

"*Maybe five. Seven. I don't know exactly.*"

"*That's fine. Fine.*" He looked at his pad. "*How did those births turn out?*"

"*Okay. One of them had to go C-section.*"

"*Fine. Did you ever have reason to expect that she might have a substance abuse problem?*" He was slick, he just slipped that in.

The nurse looked surprised. "*No. Absolutely not.*"

Wally said, "*Object, Leo, you know that's not going to fly.*"

The plaintiff's attorney said, "*Let's move on. You don't have to answer that. Turning now to the day in question. Miranda Paulsen's birth. Have you discussed this day with anyone?*"

"*You mean talked with anyone about it?*"

"*That's right.*"

"*Yeah. I guess.*"

"*Whom would that be?*"

She fidgeted. You would have thought she was on trial. "*My boyfriend, my daughter. A few of the nurses at work, Marla Maritzer, and one other person, one of the nurses who works in the NICU where Stacy was for a while, her name is Ellie Cunin. Then I've spoken with Dr. Sorvino's attorney.*"

"*Mr. Whittiker.*"

"*Right. Mr. Whittiker. That's it.*"

"*You haven't spoken to Dr. Sorvino about this case?*"

"*No.*"

He scratched away in his legal pad. He looked as meticulous as a bookkeeper.

"*So could you tell us what happened when you came on shift on September third?*"

"Right. So I came on and got the change of shift report from Melissa, she was the nurse on before me."

"Melissa Amador?"

"Right."

"Was she a student nurse?"

"No, she was a new nurse, fresh out of training."

"And what did she tell you?"

"She told me they'd all had a rough night. That Sorvino looked like she'd been through a war. You know, exhausted."

"What else did she say?"

"That her baby needed to come out now."

"What did she mean?"

"I thought she meant that for everyone's sake, Miranda needed to be born."

"So it was a medical necessity?"

"Object to form," Wally said. I didn't know why.

"It was more like they were all exhausted and it was just time." The nurse looked scared of saying the wrong thing.

"What did she tell you about the fetal heart rate monitoring?"

"She didn't say anything."

"There was nothing about late decelerations?"

"No."

"Is it the nurse's job to check the heart rates?"

"Yes, but usually we just look for rates that are too low or too high or flat."

"So whose job is it to look for late decelerations?"

"It's everyone's. If she had been a more experienced nurse, she would have looked for them, but she was fresh out of training."

"So I'm sorry, I'm a little confused. Was it Dr. Sorvino's job to know there were late decelerations happening given that she knew there was a student nurse on the night before?"

"She wasn't a student."

"Excuse me. A relatively young nurse?"

"Yes. It was also Dr. Sorvino's job."

"*Thank you. Turning back to when you first came into the room. You told the patient and Sorvino that they looked like 'wrecks.' Why did you say that?*"

"*They were exhausted. They'd been up all night.*"

"*Were you present when Sorvino first suggested she wanted to do a C-section?*"

"*Yes.*"

"*What did you think?*"

"*It sounded like a good idea to me.*"

"*Why is that?*"

"*They were all on edge.*"

"*So at that point you didn't know that during the night, there had been a series of radical late decelerations?*"

"*No.*"

"*Melissa Amador hadn't shown you the strip from around 3 A.M. or drawn your attention to it in any way?*"

"*No.*"

"*No?*"

"*She didn't show me the strip.*"

"*When did you see the strip showing the radical late decelerations for the first time?*"

"*When the anesthesiologist showed it to me right after Miranda was born.*"

"*And what did you think when you saw it?*"

"*I didn't think anything.*"

The lawyer changed pads again. Flipped through some pages. Then he said, "*Didn't you say, and I quote, 'Oh, that poor baby'?*"

"*I might have said that.*"

"*And what would you have meant if you'd said that?*"

"*That it was too bad.*"

"*Fine. Were you surprised to learn that Miranda Paulsen has cerebral palsy?*"

"*No.*"

"*No? Why not?*"

"Because of the strip."

"So if Dr. Sorvino had been on top of the monitoring, and had seen that strip from 3 A.M., the same one you saw, what do you think she would have done?"

"You'd have to ask her."

"I'm asking you."

"I'm not a doctor."

"Okay. Have you ever seen a strip that looked like that in the past from other births?"

"Yes."

"And what happened, did the physician deliver the babies immediately?"

"Sometimes."

"Sometimes?"

"Usually."

"So you've been in this situation before? When late decelerations have happened and the doctor has delivered the baby right away?"

"We all have."

"But at 7 or 7:30 the morning after the decelerations, she was still only talking about a C-section? Four hours later?"

"Is that a question?"

"Yes. I'm asking you. You heard her talk about, but not do, a C-section, at 7 or 7:30?"

"She did it later."

"When she did finally see the decelerations she did the C-section immediately?"

"Yes."

"So is it safe to say that if she'd seen the same thing on the strip four hours earlier, you don't know of any reason why she'd have done something different?"

"I don't understand."

"She saw late decelerations just before she delivered Miranda. If she'd seen those same decelerations on the strip at 3 in the morning she would have done the same thing, right?"

"Probably. Yes."

"Fine. Fine. Thank you."

When the nurse got up, she didn't look at me. She shot out of there.

Wally told me he'd call me. Then he gave me the name of a good DUI lawyer and shuffled out with an armful of books and legal pads.

I waited. She looked at me. "So what did you learn from this deposition? How did it impact you?"

"It was just sad. That poor nurse had to come in and rat me out. She didn't want to be there, she was just doing what she thought was right. I could tell that the case really pained her. She'd been thinking about it. She sagged in the chair through the entire thing. I did that to her. I forced her into that situation. The nurses often get screwed in these cases when they do what the doctor wanted them to and it was the wrong thing. In the back of her mind she was also defending the night nurse. The whole thing was just sad, you know?"

"Any other responses?"

"Oh. Yeah. I think I'm gonna lose the case." She shrugged and then changed the subject. I brought us back twice. Saying, "I wonder if we might get back to talking about the case?" And then, when that didn't work, "I'm still curious about the deposition. . . ." She dodged me, focusing on a friend who hadn't called her for a few months, and the hour drifted on.

Before she left I asked her if she was feeling suicidal now; she shook her head quickly. No. Absolutely not. For a second I felt silly for asking. Her denial was so vehement and she seemed so strong. Somewhere in the recesses of my clinical brain a voice was saying, "She protests too much. Ask her again." But I didn't.

"Why don't you come down here?" Terry asked. She was four floors below me in the bone marrow transplant unit, where she worked as a nurse practitioner. It was Thursday morning. Her pregnancy test was in the computer. She wanted me to come down to the unit and look it up with her. A shared experience. She was certain she was pregnant, but trying to stave off her hope. Her breasts had swelled again, this time impressively; it was obvious to me and everyone else. Her face was rosy. I tried to quell my own hope, but it was rising like a phoenix.

I took the stairs to the third floor and then walked down the long hallways of Disney characters to the bone marrow transplant unit. I turned onto the corridor with transplant rooms off to one side. Between each room are counters with health professionals hunched over charts or computers, like air traffic controllers for individual lives. The concentration level felt high. A few patients, bald and masked, plodded the halls holding on to steel IV poles. The routine was familiar. I was a bone marrow transplant patient once.

I spotted familiar long brown hair at the end of the hall near the coral fish tank. Terry was standing with Adrienne, an oncologist from Alabama. "Here's your cute husband now," Adrienne drawled when I was in earshot. Adrienne had been trying to get pregnant too.

Terry spun around, an electric smile filling her face.

"Ready?"

"Sure," I said.

She logged in to the lab and typed in her name and password. I glanced back at the fish tank. Fish lazily cruised through purple coral. It might be fun to be a fish. Goldfish don't have good spatial memory; every place is new to them. I looked back, Terry was entering her name in the patient field and selecting the most recent blood test. There were a series of other screens that appeared and disappeared too quickly for me to understand. Then she arrived at one screen and stopped; there was a long series of numbers.

"What?" I asked.

Adrienne said, "Next time, honey. Next time." She put a hand on Terry's shoulder, patted a few times, and then walked away.

"What?" I said.

Terry covered her nose and mouth with steepled hands. "I was so sure. I was so sure. Danny, what are we doing wrong?" A lone silver tear descended down her cheek. I wrapped my arms around her from behind and she sagged, tired.

That night at dinner the phone rang. Terry answered. I'd just told Alex that her mouth might not like the broccoli but her body wanted it. She didn't believe me. She wasn't eating; she moved her small fork around the broccoli as if it were an unstable toxin that might erupt if grazed by metal. Terry picked up the phone in the kitchen and I heard her say, "Yeah, I know." When she came back to the table she said it was Linden's office calling to share the negative pregnancy result.

"Adrienne told me that Linden's lab guy quit, the one who was doing the technical part of the procedures. She also heard a rumor that Linden's been thrown out of Southern Arizona Physicians for accounting irregularities."

"Really? Fraud?"

"She didn't say, but obviously it was bad enough for her to get booted. There's something wrong with that woman," she said. "I know five women who go to her, none of them have gotten pregnant."

"It could be that we're a tough bunch, you know, that she takes hard patients." Careful. This is dangerous ground.

"I got pregnant the first time in Boston. I know I'm fertile."

"You were younger then," I said.

She gripped her fork as if it were a knife. I could see a vein on her knuckle. Not a smart thing to say. I wanted to tell her that I couldn't do it anymore. That it was ripping us apart. Alex was enough. I let the urge pass.

"Did you know that she's lost track of our samples? Every time she tells me about your sperm samples she has a different number;

she hasn't kept track of them. Dan, she's sloppy with everything except her billing. She's a con. Adrienne told me about a Web page where you can look up everyone's success rates. Remember how she told us her rates were competitive with any in the country? Before you got home I looked her up. On the Web page she says she has an eleven percent success rate. She's among the weakest in the country. It's not me. I know it's not me. When I left work today she passed me in her new Lexus. The more procedures she does, the more she gets paid."

It was natural for Terry to be angry. She was disappointed. I wanted to lash out, too, but my feelings were more confused. I blamed her as much as Linden. I wanted out. But what if she was right? What if Linden was incompetent? Could I forgive myself if we didn't try again with someone else? I did want another child. But at what cost?

"You said that Web page lists success rates. Do you remember what we did when I was sick?"

She looked at me blankly.

"Let's go to the best."

"You have to pay out of pocket. Linden's the only reproductive endocrinologist on our provider list. We'd have to pay cash. We only have the fifteen thousand or so we've been saving for the house; just one try will cost that, maybe more. That money is for an emergency."

We sat in silence. Neither of us said the obvious. This was an emergency.

Saturday morning. Alexandra was working on a project; scissors, cotton, and glitter surrounded her on the dining room table. Newspaper was spread on the floor beneath her and she was in toddler heaven. Terry was sprawled on the couch, a paperback in her hand. I was reading *The New York Times*.

A space had opened up since the pregnancy result crashed home. After a horrible sleepless night, Terry got on the Internet.

The most successful physician in the country was in Denver. She'd phoned and managed to schedule a consultation with him in a few weeks. Her hope filled the house like a melody. We'd already had breakfast and the smell of scrambled eggs lingered in the air. *Weekend Edition,* the NPR program, was on the radio somewhere; soft voices came in and out of earshot.

I'd already checked on the fate of my beleaguered Red Sox. The Sox were clinging desperately to their respect, with no hope, even this early, of winning a pennant. The damned Yankees were in first place, as usual. Arizona was making noise in the National League. Maybe they had a chance.

I flipped back to the front page and worked my way through the headlines. There was an article about South Africa. The Truth and Reconciliation Commission was still meeting regularly. The story explained how busy they were and what they were doing. It didn't say how they were structured, but from the article it appeared that the perpetrators of various human rights atrocities were voluntarily coming forward and disclosing what they'd done.

The idea of such a commission fascinated me. It's such a novel method for resolving conflicts, so different from American proceedings. I went into my office and logged on to the Internet. I searched for Truth and Reconciliation and found South Africa's official Web site.

Unlike conventional Anglo-American proceedings in which prosecutors gather evidence and indict perpetrators, it is the perpetrators who apply for amnesty. If they tell the entire truth of their participation in a politically motivated act, omission, or offense that harmed someone, then amnesty could be granted.

If perpetrators don't come forward, they risk being uncovered by a separate board who investigate abuses and do not grant amnesty. South Africa created the boards because they recognized the dangers of a continued cycle of vengeance and secrecy.

It occurred to me that this might be an appropriate model for malpractice. Imagine a system in which instead of paying malpractice insurers, health professionals paid into a truth and reconciliation reparations and rehabilitation fund. Those who made mistakes would come in front of the board and argue why his or her patient deserved compensation. If the physician participated in truth and reconciliation fully by telling the entire truth about their mistake, amnesty would be offered and the physician wouldn't have to compensate the patient out of personal funds. If the truth and reconciliation commission agreed with the physician that harm occurred, the patient would be compensated by the board. Unlike jury awards that are inconsistent, there could be uniform, national guidelines for compensating patients. This board might also refer the health practitioner for counseling or retraining.

Empowered to conduct random chart audits and investigate medical errors or substandard practice of health professionals who don't come forward, the commission would also find more mistakes than state boards (who rely on the malpractice system to identify mistakes). Physicians like Linden might be more quickly weeded out. Because more mistakes would be identified the commission could also look for patterns and transmit the findings to the medical community to prevent as many future mistakes as possible.

How could I apply this to Amelia? If Amelia were participating in a truth and reconciliation system it would be better for her and her patient. Amelia could unburden herself and feel that she was continuing to act in her patient's best interest. Stacy could get some reimbursement for Miranda's injury and Amelia's personal livelihood would not be threatened. Simply by existing, the commission would communicate to physicians like Amelia, the genuinely committed doctors, that mistakes are going to happen and that there is an ethical way to handle them without risking all of her assets. Perhaps she wouldn't be wrestling with the sense that she's a fraud.

What if Amelia followed the spirit of these principles rather than participating in the civil system as she'd been ordered by her lawyers? What if she told Stacy everything she knew about her mistake? What if she gave up trying to win the case, and instead tried to win back her sense of being her patient's advocate? What if she acted like a physician instead of a defendant?

Session Eighteen

D uring our next session I explained the truth and reconciliation idea to Amelia, how it might help her feel like a physician instead of a defendant.

"My lawyers still aren't going to like it," Amelia said. "They're convinced we'll win. They have some hotshot expert coming into town for a deposition who's supposed to save the day."

"Would you feel better if the day was saved?"

"I made a mistake. That's what I think." She sat for a moment. "You're right that this system is screwing with my head. The moment I hung up on Stacy, that time when I was painting, that was the end of my career. I think about it all the time. The paint and the room spinning and everything I had worked so hard for all those years, just evaporating.

"I didn't talk with her because they told me not to. They've been adamant. I could screw up my entire case if I talk to her; they keep reminding me that it's potentially a multimillion-dollar suit. After the insurance money is gone it's up to me to make up the rest. We have twenty-five thousand dollars saved and a house worth three hundred thousand, with most of it mortgaged. They keep insinuating we'll be homeless if I'm not careful."

"What is feeling like a doctor worth to you?"

She rubbed her eyes.

"Not much. I have a lot more experience these days as a defendant. Did I tell you I was in court again yesterday? I got my day in court for the DUI."

They aren't kidding when they say the civil and criminal courts are different. For the preliminary hearing I was in a massive room with forty other people accused of felonies. I kept thinking of the Arlo Guthrie song "Alice's Restaurant." Where he sings about sitting in prison after getting arrested for littering. Some of my fellow accusees were undesirable. There were a bunch of methamphetamine addicts who had stolen everything from mail to cars. Then there were a few deadbeat parents, both men and women, I'm happy to report. A few underage drinkers, one guy whose dog had mauled his neighbor. A delightful group. And me. They brought us in one at a time and we had our brief trials.

Officer Friendly wasn't there. I was charged with driving under the influence of alcohol and destruction of property. Everyone looked bored. The prosecutor stood up and said they were dropping the driving under the influence charge because the results of the field sobriety tests weren't available. The judge asked him what he was talking about and the prosecutor said he'd spoken to the officer that morning and he'd had a death in his family and was out of state. He'd be unable to provide information about the nature of the sobriety test.

The judge didn't seem to care. Then my lawyer tried to get the damage of property part dropped too and the judge told him not to push it. The judge read a list of all the property I'd destroyed and asked me what I was doing on the road at 3 A.M., nowhere near the hospital. I told him I'd gone for a moonlight hike. And he said, "I'm sure you were drinking or under the influence of something. I don't know what your problems are, Doctor, but this community needs its physicians to have their act together. Do you understand that? Stay out of my courtroom." He sentenced me to community service and ordered me to pay $1,420 for the property I destroyed, as well as the court fees. My lawyer told me that it was only a misdemeanor and that BOMEX, the medical board, wouldn't have to be notified. He was very proud of himself.

So next month I start working at the animal shelter. I owe them a hundred hours. I owe the lawyer $3,600. I joked that it was a $5,000 mailbox, but in reality, I know I was lucky. If the DUI had stuck I'd have gone to jail and lost my driver's license for a year—and my medical license, too.

My eyebrows rose.

"Not that I care . . . about the medical license." She smiled at me.

I'm not a great traveler. Some people travel easily. Their internal compass comes with them. But when I leave home I always feel a little lost. Particularly if I'm traveling without Alex, who structures my life with her needs. A few days after my session with Amelia I went to San Antonio to give a keynote lecture to a thousand nurses. I'd become interested in health professionals' self-care and had been lucky enough to get invited to share my ideas at a number of conferences. This would be easy; I'd fly into San Antonio one day and come back the next.

At the airport I discovered that my plane was delayed so I decided to get my scarred brown loafers polished. I found the shoeshine chairs in the terminal and climbed up. The shoeshine woman was working the rags on another man's shoes and I sat next to him, perched above the airport crowd, and watched her. She was about fifty; she wore a pair of sweatpants and a flowered smock. She had on white hospital worker sneakers. Her hair was gray, shaped like a mushroom, and it fell around her face. There were bifocals resting on the base of the oak shoeshine stand. The man sitting next to me was in a suit. His face was fleshy and pale. He had the day's *Wall Street Journal* on his lap and expensive shoes on the stirrups.

She greeted me with "And how's your journey today?" and then went back to talking to the man she was finishing.

"Well, the way I see it, you should be glad they delayed your flight."

"I really need to get to Chicago," he said. He was flustered. His face was reddening.

"You'll get there, boss. You'll get there. You ought to calm yourself down, getting all excited about this is like yelling at the wind. There ain't no sense yelling at the wind, now is there?" Then she put down a rag and said, "You hear me?" She wagged a finger at him. He nodded. Then she said, "All right, Mr. Impatient, you're all done." He stood up and sheepishly handed her a five. Then he grabbed his small bag and briskly headed back toward the gates. "You'll get there. I ain't seen a single skeleton in one of those seats."

She turned back to me. "Well, hello there." She put my feet more securely into the stirrups and rested one hand on a shoe while the other hand went to work. It reminded me of the way people lean comfortably against their own cars; for now, my feet and my shoes belonged to her.

We talked. She said she'd started "rubbing feet" ten years ago. "Then I was sexier," she said. "Now I'm just built for comfort." She looked up at me and smirked. She asked where I was going and how I felt about my plane being delayed. I told her I wasn't all that concerned about it. "That's smart," she said.

She told me about the guy from Chicago she'd just finished. "He complained from the moment he sat in my chair. Said he was 'really irritated,' said the airline bastards ought to get their act together. I told him there were tornadoes between here and Chicago. If they decide to fly into the tornadoes, then you should get irritated."

I was surprised. Usually people working for tips are fatiguingly polite. At least I was when I was in college, working room service in a hotel and tending bar. I was polite to everyone, even the most annoying people. I showed my surprise in my face. She looked up at me and continued, running a cloth around my shoe. "I figure his mama ain't with him, if she was she would tell him, but since she ain't I'll do. There's near a thousand folks down there waiting to fly out, he ain't the only one." When she was done I got up. She surveyed me. "You got a piece of food on your collar. Saving that for later, are you?" I brushed it away and she smiled. "All done now. Look good. Don't forget your bags now, ya hear? Have a safe flight." And then she added, "Don't worry about it, you'll get there too."

I found my money and was handing it over to her when she waved at a man pushing a large trash barrel. "Hey, Lee." He wore a striped short-sleeved shirt and had a heavy red patch on his shoulder. He called out to her, "Hey, Trish, keepin' it real?" and she called back, "Keepin' it real, Lee. Keepin' it real."

I thought about Trish all the way to San Antonio. In those few moments with me she did something rare and important. She was human first, and a shoe shiner second. She was willing to sacrifice her tip in favor of calling it like she saw it. She wasn't willing to let her job, her current role, dictate her behavior. This is one of Amelia's problems. In the course of her training she'd learned to suppress herself, and perform. She'd lost touch with which parts of her were real and which parts were her performance as a doctor. She'd gotten lost. And now she was doing the same thing with the malpractice case.

Session Nineteen

Amelia and I had a phone session after my conference in San Antonio. I had a few hours before I had to catch my flight back, but by the time I landed, it would be too late for us to meet in my office. I sat in my hotel room with the curtains open. From my chair I looked out over the River Walk; tourists and locals walked the meandering sidewalks that line the river. I could see a brass quartet below, entertaining tourists who had gathered along the rails of a bridge that crosses the river. I dialed her number.

Amelia was at home; she said Jay was painting in the other room. She'd just been at another deposition.

It was the same cast of characters as last time. Our guy was an expert on cerebral palsy from the Dupont Institute in Delaware. It's the premier center in the United States and this guy had written a book published by Johns Hopkins. He was in his early fifties with little horn-rimmed glasses. He looked like a professor. Not slick at all. He reminded me of my ex-boyfriend's father, the family doctor in Iowa. We were huddled together before the deposition and Wally was practically giddy. I asked why and he said, "What are you, kidding? Look, he's Mr. Rogers. Who's going to want to see Mr. Rogers cross-examined? Not a juror in Tucson. Just wait."

After the expert was sworn in, Stacy's lawyer went through every one of the guy's achievements. Medical school in Colorado, his surgical residency and orthopedics fellowship. He'd worked at a bunch of children's hospitals in Canada and the United States. The lawyer asked why he'd moved around so much, maybe suggesting that our expert couldn't hold down a job. The expert said, "I was offered more money and better resources and my wife generously supported the move."

I was surprised by a few of the early questions. The lawyer asked if the expert and I knew each other, if we'd trained together or if he'd heard of me. If we'd ever spoken before or shared any cases. He asked if the expert had discussed the case with anyone else, or if there were any special compensation arrangements depending on the outcome of the case.

Eventually they got around to his current job. He'd cofounded a special institute in Delaware dedicated to the study of cerebral palsy. It was strange; they weren't looking at each other at all. Stacy's lawyer asked questions and took notes on a legal pad without even looking up. Then the lawyer asked if the expert had prepared a report and Mr. Rogers said yes.

The lawyer asked, "So even though you're a surgeon by training, and not an obstetrician, you feel comfortable commenting on the professional behavior of an obstetrician?"

Mr. Rogers didn't bat an eye. "My expertise is cerebral palsy, sir, including its causes."

"You've never delivered a baby?"

"Not since internship."

"How many did you deliver during your internship?"

"I assisted twice."

"And you don't do research on babies?"

"No."

There was a pause. The lawyers all scratched away on their pads.

"How many children with cerebral palsy have you treated?"

"Thousands."

"But your caseload has slowed down?"

"No."

"How many times do you testify every year?"

"Between ten and twenty times."

"Always for the defense in malpractice cases?"

"Usually."

"Of the last twenty cases, how often have you testified for the plaintiff and how often for the defense?"

"All for the defense." More pens on legal pads. There was a long pause. Stacy's lawyer looked over a list of questions he'd prepared.

"Is this your report?" Mr. Rogers had written a report about our case. He'd taken sixteen hours to go through all the medical records and then wrote a summary statement. The lawyer showed him the report and they spent some time going over details about how it was numbered and the dates. Then the lawyer asked the expert to walk him through the report.

The first three pages covered the nature of cerebral palsy, the next couple of pages went over our case, and then there was a final summary paragraph.

In the first section he covered developmental differences, typical and nontypical courses, and even how the disorder was discovered. He'd written that Dr. William Little first described cerebral palsy in the 1800s and had originally ascribed the cause of the ailment to birth injury. The expert said, "While we owe Dr. Little a great deal, he was incorrect about the cause of static encephalopathy, what we now refer to as cerebral palsy. Eventually, Dr. Sigmund Freud, who was a prominent neurologist before creating psychiatry, also investigated the causes of cerebral palsy but thought that the condition was due to prenatal events." It was pedantic until he said, "Researchers during the last thirty years have confirmed that Freud was right, most causes of cerebral palsy occur prior to the birthing process."

The lawyer said, "But not all?"

"Not all. Congenital malformations in the brain usually exist prior to the birthing process and aren't always detectable by physicians, even using the best technology." I felt lighter. He was saying that it wasn't my fault.

The remainder of that section of his report listed things Stacy herself might have done to cause the cerebral palsy. He said, "It's been shown that maternal alcohol use, cigarette smoking, malnutrition, and cocaine use can all contribute." Then he said that exposure to German measles or cytomegalovirus can cause brain injuries to the baby. Toxoplasmosis, which is caused by handling kitty litter, can also be the culprit.

Sitting there, I knew that Stacy hadn't been using alcohol or smoking or using cocaine. But the seed of doubt was planted. What if she hadn't told me the truth? What if she'd lied? I started to feel angry. Indignant. It was fun to feel self-righteous for a few minutes.

The expert continued, "Even if the mother followed an excellent prenatal routine, it is also possible that this birth defect could have been caused by a congenital abnormality we aren't familiar with yet, or through an unusual chemical exposure. We simply don't know."

Her lawyer said, "If you turn to the next section of the report, page four, you said that it is impossible to ascribe a cause to Miranda Paulsen's condition?"

Mr. Rogers answered, "Right."

Her lawyer smiled at him. "Then why the rush to deliver her when she saw the decelerations?"

"*I don't know. She was probably worried about other potential birth-related problems.*"

"*But not cerebral palsy? You're saying that when she finally did notice the decelerations and rushed to deliver the baby, she was worried about what exactly; what does a slowed heartbeat signal?*"

"*Probably oxygen deprivation.*"

"*I'm sorry, Doctor, I'm a little slow here. Doesn't oxygen deprivation cause cerebral palsy?*"

"*Studies of cerebral palsy show that birth injuries are responsible only about ten percent of the time. The rest of the time the culprit is in the developing brain. The prevalence rates of cerebral palsy in developing nations, where they don't use fetal monitoring, is the same as it is in northern Europe or the United States where they do, because monitoring the maternal or fetal heart rate doesn't help you prevent cerebral palsy. This is what I'm trying to tell you. Even if you have the best medical care in the world, you can't prevent cerebral palsy.*"

The lawyer wrote for a few minutes and then whispered in the calmest voice, "*I'm sure that what happens in other parts of the world is important, but in the interests of time, might you confine your speculations to Miranda Paulsen right now? We're all trying to get through the section of your report on Miranda. So yes or no, oxygen deprivation can cause cerebral palsy?*"

"*Yes.*"

"*Thank you. Now you said ten percent of the time birth injury is responsible, right?*"

"*I'm telling you that it's unlikely to have been asphyxia. About twenty-five percent of children are born with their umbilical cord wrapped around their necks, which causes mild asphyxia. They have cerebral palsy in only slightly greater numbers than babies born normally. My guess is that those late decelerations were the symptoms of a baby who was already sick.*"

"*Your guess?*"

"*My guess.*"

"*But you aren't certain, are you?*"

"*No.*"

"And you aren't an expert on birth injuries, obstetrics, or even pediatrics."

"Right."

"And even you, who testifies only for defendants, thinks it could have been asphyxia. You said that ten percent of the time it's a birth injury that causes cerebral palsy, right?"

"I doubt it."

There was a pause and I thought the deposition would be over when the lawyer asked, "Are you aware that the defendant is currently facing Driving Under the Influence charges?"

This time, Wally held out his arm and ordered the expert not to answer.

"Object! That's not cool, Leo."

"All right, I'm off it," Stacy's lawyer said, his hands up. The expert looked at me. That didn't bother me. For a few minutes, none of it bothered me. I felt inoculated. Light. For the first time it occurred to me that I really might not be responsible for Miranda's condition. No matter what I'd done, she might have had cerebral palsy anyway. It was fantastic.

I felt like celebrating with her, but her voice didn't sound elated now. She'd said the word *fantastic* with a low voice. It reminded me of a time on the beach when Alex and I were wading in the surf as the tide went out. We stood in one place and watched our feet appear to surge forward as the tide came in. I felt the illusion of movement, but we weren't moving.

"I gather you don't feel fantastic now?"

"I'm fine," she said, too quickly.

"What is it? I can't tell what you think about all this." Damned phone. Why did I agree to do this? I needed to look at her.

"I'm tired of this case. I'm tired of talking about it. He was very helpful; Wally and Michael both think we might win now. He's very credible." She exhaled during the last words—a sigh?

"But?"

"But nothing. He was very helpful."

"Are you still worried about losing the case anyway?"

"No."

"Are you worried about winning for the wrong reason?"

"No. I'm just tired. I need to go," she said.

"My guess is that you're realizing that winning this case won't make your feelings about what happened go away."

"I really need to go," she said. "Next Tuesday, in person, okay? I don't like the phone." The line went dead.

Session Twenty

A few days later, after I returned to Tucson, my little family was back in the throes of chaos. Terry's Camry had died, again. There were rumors about needing to replace the entire transmission. The estimate was in the thousands.

Driving one vehicle was an exercise in logistics. It reminded me of the puzzle involving sheep, wolves, and a single canoe that needs to ferry them back and forth across a river. Finally, things were settling down. We'd just finished a dinner of beans and rice. Alex was overtired; she had been awake with nightmares the night before and hadn't napped at preschool.

Dinner had been a culinary adventure. Alexandra is usually a neat eater, but not this time. I was clearing the table. It looked like a war zone. Here's where the tomato army ran into the beans, who must have been waiting in ambush behind the rice bowl. Long strips of lettuce were strewn across the table, beating a hasty retreat, no doubt. When Terry makes beans and rice there are little condiment bowls full of tomatoes and onions and chopped basil leaves. It's delicious. Alex had started demanding that we let her do things for herself; she had to start sometime. She'd been tired and impatient; upended bowls were the result.

As I moved from the table to the sink she slid around my legs, a walking hazard.

"Daddy. Daddy. Wrap me up like a burrito. Wrap me up like a burrito." And on and on. I'd already said that I would as soon as I was finished. The sleep deprivation was cranking her eagerness toward the edge of demanding. One more set of bowls to retrieve. The phone rang.

A male baritone voice. Familiar, but not. "Dr. Shapiro? I'm sorry to disturb you at your residence. I just wasn't sure how to reach you." Solicitor? Too familiar.

"Who's calling, please?"

The voice said, "I tried your cell phone, but it wasn't on and the paging operator said you weren't on call and wouldn't put me through. Oh, sorry. This is Jason Sells." Jason Sells. Jason Sells. Who is that? "Since you weren't on call I phoned a friend whose kid goes to school with yours. Alexandra Shapiro is your daughter, right?" *Who is this?* "My friend found your home number in the school directory. I know it must violate some psychologist rule, but this is an emergency." His voice was steady. The word *emergency* flowed out evenly. Not a syllable out of place. This is not a histrionic man. He said his name was Jason. Jay Sells. *Wait a minute. He's Amelia's husband.*

"What can I do for you, Jay?"

"She's gone."

"What do you mean, gone?"

"She's gone. Amelia told me she was meeting Lynn for lunch. That was seven or eight hours ago. I called Lynn's a while ago and her husband told me she's at a conference in Dublin. Lynn's been out of the country since Sunday."

It's happening.

"Where have you looked?"

"I've called her cell phone, she doesn't answer, of course. Honestly, Doc, I'm a little concerned."

"It's been eight hours?"

"I lost track of time. I was painting." I hadn't meant to imply that he should have called sooner, but my voice was rising involuntarily. *He sounds like the psychologist, I sound like the worried husband.*

"Do you have any idea where she might have gone?"

"I've tried the Y where she works out on Columbus, and I phoned Hugh and Elsie. I think I'm terrifying everyone I talk to."

"Tell me exactly what she said when she left."

Alexandra grabbed my leg. She growled. "Play with me! I want to be a burrito!" She started shouting. I couldn't hear what Jay was saying.

I yelled at Alex, "Leave me alone, I'm on the phone, you know better!" Too angry. Her eyes opened wide. Mortal wound. She's a sensitive kid.

"Jay, hold on." I covered the phone. "Alex, sweetheart, Daddy's on the phone." Calmly. Too late. She was already crying.

"But you said . . ." she sobbed, her head dropping. Terry appeared, picked her up. "It's not fair . . ." Alex continued.

"What's going on? Did she hurt herself?" Terry asked. Jay was saying something on the phone.

"I'm on the phone with a patient," I said to Terry. Stay calm.

"Do you want to take it in your office?"

I uncovered the phone. "Jay, tell me again. What exactly did she say?"

"Just that she was going to have lunch. Then she might pick up some groceries. Did I want anything from Wild Oats. But that was seven or eight hours ago. I just kept expecting . . . Wait a minute, I think I hear the garage door." The phone went silent. *Thank heavens.* I looked at Terry. She was holding Alex, who glowered at me. Then Jay was back. Energy filled his voice for the first time; he was speaking faster. "I could have sworn I heard it."

"She's not there?"

"No. False alarm."

"Have you called the police?"

"Yeah, as soon as I found out that Lynn was out of the country. They said six hours isn't enough time to consider someone a missing person, unless it's a child. They asked if we'd been fighting. We did have an argument this morning over the laundry, but this isn't like her. When I acknowledged the fight, the cop said I should call her friends. That's where they usually go. And then I should call back in the morning if she's still missing."

"Okay. Jay, hang tight. I'm going to make some calls. I'll phone you the minute I know anything."

"Thanks."

Terry was still standing there with Alex. "Rough one, huh? Look, if you can't put her down, I can."

"No. I'll do it. I just need a few minutes."

"Not too long though, it's almost eight o'clock. She's overtired."

"I am not!" Alex protested. She was doing the postcry gasp. Very dramatic.

I went into my office and shut the door. I called University Medical Center admitting. "This is Dr. Dan Shapiro, I'm on staff and need to know if one of my patients has been admitted." I waited while they looked her up. No. I did the same with Tucson Medical Center, Northwest Hospital, and St. Mary's. No. No. No.

What else can I do? I called Jay back and told him she wasn't in any of the hospitals. "Thank God," he said. I wasn't so sure it was a good thing. He told me he'd just phoned the police again but got the same sergeant who told him the same thing, but was irritated now. We hung up after promising to phone each other if anything new developed. I turned off my desk lamp and was walking out of my office when I looked outside.

It was bright. Another full moon. The hair on my arms stood on end. *Shit. It's really happening.*

I dialed 911.

"This is Dr. Dan Shapiro. I'm a psychologist on faculty at the medical school. I have an acutely suicidal patient on a path in the Catalina Mountains. I need the MAC team and paramedics to go up there immediately and bring her down. She's up on the saddle, Blackett's Ridge." Then I gave the 911 operator my cell phone number and told her to give it to the MAC team so that I could tell them how to get there. I hung up.

Alex was standing in my office. "I'm sorry," she said. When she's reluctant she mumbles. She's helped me realize that adolescence isn't a split-second change. Kids warm up to it. Terry was standing just outside my office door.

"Good girl," Terry said.

"I'm sorry too. I shouldn't have yelled at you, Alex."

"Wrap me up like a burrito?"

I heaved her up onto my shoulders and carried her, saying, "First I take the makings into the kitchen . . ."

Twenty minutes later I was sprawled on the floor in Alex's room. She'd already changed into pajamas. We were reading *The 500 Hats of Bartholomew Cubbins,* a Dr. Seuss. Our hero, Bart, had just been accused of not taking his hat off for the king. He'd been marched into the castle and down to the executioner. My cell phone rang.

"Dr. Shapiro? This is Mike Garvey with Pima County Sheriff's. I'm walking up toward the Phone Line Trail with Mark Berry from Fire and Rescue and Lisa Rodriguez, a paramedic. What exactly are we looking for and where?" I expected him to say he'd found her, but then I realized it was too early. Hang tight. Focus.

"Dr. Amelia Sorvino. She's a female physician, five foot six, brown hair, mid-thirties. She should be up on the saddle or at the juncture of Phone Line and the Blackett's Ridge trails."

"Does she carry a firearm?"

"No."

"She's suicidal?"

"Right."

"Needles?"

"She could have access to them, but I doubt she'd have one."

"Has she been dangerous to anyone other than herself recently?"

"No."

"If she's jumped, we won't find her tonight, you realize that."

"Right."

"All right, Dr. Shapiro. We'll use this number if we find anyone."

"I appreciate it."

So matter-of-fact. *If she's jumped.* The saddle has a view in all directions, and a drop-off of a few thousand feet. I swallowed and put down the cell phone. Our phone rang. I put down the book again. Alex said, *"Dad?"* while I ran into the living room and picked up.

"Is this Dan Shapiro?"

"Yes? Yes?"

"This is Lisa calling on behalf of Canyon Rocks, a four-star luxury home away from home. We're offering free weekends in our Palm Court or Desert Vista Towers. . . ." Her voice was ebullient. It said, *We are old friends finally reconnecting.* I hung up on her. Desert Vista Towers. I imagined a massive tower in the middle of the desert.

I walked back into the bedroom. Alex was barking orders into a play phone.

I wanted to get in my car and drive up to the Sabino Canyon parking lot. Maybe I'd wait there with my cell phone. Or go after her myself. I felt too frantic to be any use to Alexandra and Terry. But what would that accomplish? *Calm down.* When I was waiting for the results of biopsies, CT scans, and blood work that would tell me if I'd relapsed, I learned to stick to a routine to combat anxiety. *Stay near Alex.*

We brushed teeth. I held my hand on her forehead to take away the bad dreams. I gave her the stuffed purple dinosaur and her blanket. I've been wondering about her dinosaur. Perhaps twenty years from now a dictator will come to power, wearing a purple cape, and he'll sing "I love you, you love me, I'm taking over your military. . . ." I need to find her a new stuffed animal. My mind jumps around like this when I'm nervous. *Calm.*

We kissed and I turned off the light and sat next to her bed. Silver moonlight streamed in her window, illuminating my feet and my hands, including the one holding the cell phone. *This is dumb. What if the cell phone rings? It will wake her up.* When Alex's arms unfolded and fell open, the universal sign of the sleeping girl, I crept out.

I went into the kitchen. Terry had already washed and put away the dishes. I found her in our bedroom, lost in Armistead Maupin's latest novel. I slipped into bed and tried to read my new book. The season's new books were filled with stories of human hubris and natural disasters. *What's happening in the society that is tuning us all to this theme? Global warming?* In this book, hikers were lost on Everest in the midst of a snowstorm and things were looking grim. I kept reading the same lines over and over. I got out of bed, washed my face, and came back. Eventually I caught some momentum and the book carried me through the sad last words of lovers: one of them dying on a snowy ridge, the other, pregnant, a few continents away. They spoke by cell phone before he died and named their unborn child. It was a sniffle fest. What a stupid thing to be up on those mountains. How could anyone be so casual about their self-preservation? After fighting hard for my life all those years, I had a hard time empathizing. I'm angry. What's that about?

My cell phone rang.

"Dr. Shapiro?"

"Yes."

"This is Mike Garvey, we spoke earlier. We've got her."

I soared—up into the Catalina Mountains, around Blackett's Ridge a few times, stretched out my arms, and let the dry Tucson breeze wash over my naked body.

"The paramedic has given her the once-over. She's groggy and not very alert, but conscious enough to acknowledge taking a few Tylenol and downing some vodka, she couldn't say how much—but we have an empty bottle that looks to be roughly one liter. We've run some fluids. Our guess is that we'll get her down without too much trouble."

"Where was she?"

"She was lucky. We didn't see her on the way up. Lisa, our paramedic, spotted her a little off the trail when we were coming down. She was near the Blackett's Ridge trailhead, my guess is that she was drinking on her way up and wandered off the trail and got lost. She's really a doctor?"

"Yes."

"Takes all kinds. She have a specialty?"

"She's an obstetrician."

"I hope no one was waiting for her to do a delivery tonight."

"No."

"Where does she work?"

"Look, where are you going to bring her?"

"Usually we'd bring her to Kino. But you're on staff at UMC, right? If you think she'll have insurance we could get her to UMC emergency. She'll end up on Two East. You guys had beds earlier in the day."

"Can she talk to me?"

"Negative. She's pretty out of it, still."

"How soon do you think you'll be at UMC?"

"My guess is a few hours. We'll be taking it slow unless we get another call."

I thanked him. We hung up and I phoned Jay. He was matter-of-fact. There wasn't a trickle of emotion in his voice. He thanked me and said he'd try to meet the team at the emergency room. She'd probably want toiletries and he could help with the insurance forms.

Then I paged Scott Freeman, who directs the inpatient unit. He said he was on duty tonight and going in anyway. He'd make sure she was in good hands. When I clicked off, I was back in our bedroom. Terry looked at me. I wanted to tell her what had just happened—about the fear that had raged in my stomach for the last hour, and the relief—but it would violate Amelia's confidentiality. Terry put a hand in my hair and ruffled it.

"My turn to get cured, Shrink Boy," she said.

Hospitalization:
Session Twenty-one

There's a hallway near the cafeteria that leads to the inpatient unit. A heavy unmarked door is the only signal that there's a unit there. I pressed the button on the wall. A muffled voice came out of the speaker on the ceiling.

"Can I help you?"

"It's Dr. Shapiro."

"Okay." I pulled open the door and stepped onto the small unit. Off to my right was the common room that serves alternately as kitchen, dining room, and living room. Straight ahead was the group room, good for family meetings or group therapy. Behind me was the terrarium, where the staff have access to security cameras, charts, phones, and plenty of table space. A glass wall provides privacy for staff.

Farther back are the patient rooms, including a few padded rooms with observation windows. I stepped onto the unit and waved to Scott Freeman, who was carrying two charts toward a staff office in the back. Like me, he did part of his training in the Longwood area, in one of the Harvard residencies. He's bright and kind, with common sense and a healthy distrust of any bureaucracy that gets in the way of patient care. The patients, who can be hard to please when their freedom is limited, usually like him. Just as important, the psychiatry residents and nurses like him too.

Scott motioned to me and I walked back to join him.

"You slumming?" he asked me.

"Yeah, I heard the doughnuts were better down here."

"You heard wrong. Though I did once get court approval to lace a Pop-Tart with an antipsychotic."

"I'll have one of those. Make it two. How was Dr. Sorvino's night?"

"Rough. She was still sleeping when I last checked. When she hit the emergency room last night her tox screen showed she had a morphine derivative on board that she hadn't told the paramedics about. Not smart. Honestly, it wasn't that much. But they hit her with naloxone and then her night really got fun. She vomited a few times and was generally miserable."

Naloxone works by competing with opioids for the same receptors. Suddenly the patient goes from being anesthetized to screeching wakefulness. The side effects of suddenly withdrawing from opioids are nausea, vomiting, tachycardia, sweating, and even seizures.

Scott continued, "I think maybe they were pissed at her in the emergency room; she didn't need the naloxone, she could have slept it off."

It didn't surprise me that the staff reacted angrily to her suicide attempt. Staff in hospitals often cope with life on the front lines by telling ourselves that the tragedies we witness every day won't happen to us. When one of us comes through the system, we're terrified. And when it's volitional, like not wearing a seat belt or driving under the influence or ingesting opioids, it can provoke rage.

"I'm going to want to see her every day. Is that good with you?" I asked.

"That's great. The more the better. You want us to wake her up?"

"Nah. Let her sleep. I'll come back at lunchtime. I don't have anyone scheduled then."

"You're kind," he said, turning back to his routine.

I met Amelia in the inpatient unit conference room a few hours later. The walls are blue and gray. Natural light comes in through tinted mirrored windows that look out on a walkway between the hospital and the cancer center. There are heavy blue chairs on a tightly woven carpet. A phone, a faceless phone book, a Bible, and a box of tissues were strewn across a side table. She sat cross-legged in a chair.

If one were going to title her portrait, it would be *Hangover.* Her hair was dry and caked with dirt. Her lower lip was swollen and bloody. She'd awakened only a few minutes before and one of her eyes was crusty. If I'd met her on the street, I wouldn't have known her. I might have expected her to ask me for money.

"I didn't expect to see you again," she said.

"Even the best-laid plans . . ." I said, letting my voice fade out. I better watch my sarcasm. My frustration was leaking out. There was a pause, but she didn't seem to notice.

"I felt bad about not saying good-bye. I did. I just knew you'd never let me go."

She looked down and then slowly lifted her head. As her face came into the light, she looked gaunt. There were dark shadows beneath her cheekbones that I hadn't noticed before. She'd lost weight. How could I have missed the signs? And then I imagined her high up on Blackett's Ridge, leaping.

"What happened? Things were going well." My voice was urgent again. Calm down.

She rubbed her forehead and laughed a little. "You know Las Vegas? The way everyone there looks desperate? I feel it everywhere. Last night I drove by an old rusting Toyota hatchback, three unwashed kids sticking heads out of the windows, and I wanted to be one of those kids. Just sit in their torn backseat and watch the streetlights play across the roof.

"Maybe the dad, the guy driving the car, was a pawnshop owner, fat and lazy and with rancid breath. Maybe a drunk. I'd trade."

She touched her lip and ran a finger across it. Even though she looked exhausted there was a certainty to her language, a strength I hadn't seen recently. It's common among functional people who kill themselves. They don't do it in the midst of mind-numbing depression, they act when they start to come out of the depression, when energy and strength rush back, but before their anguish has subsided. There was fear there, too. She was surprised to be in the inpatient unit.

"I'm feeling better already. I appreciate that you put me in here, but I was just out of sorts last night. I'm ready to go home."

"Amelia?"

"Yes?"

"That won't be happening."

"Why not? I told you I was feeling better."

"Because we both know if you get out now you'll kill yourself. It's time to do some work." Her face grew harder.

"Hey, Dan."

"Yes?"

"Go away. I'm not talking to you today." She sounded suddenly enraged. "Really," she continued. "Leave me alone. For Christ's sake, leave me *alone.*"

"Okay," I muttered. "There's no rush."

As I waited for the aide to electronically release the door lock so that I could get off the unit, I felt my shoulders raising.

Anger. Anger at her. Anger at myself for not knowing what the hell to do to keep her alive. *You can't keep a patient alive if she doesn't want to be.* That is the credo of the field. No one can keep another human alive if they don't want to be.

But depression isn't cancer. Hopelessness shouldn't be terminal.

As I walked away from the unit I realized I liked Amelia. I liked her passion, her brilliance, her similarity to the women I'd respected my whole life. Instead of imagining her harming me or Alexandra, I couldn't stop the intrusive visions of her hiking up that ridge and leaping to her death.

I am a clinical psychologist. I believe in science. I believe in the clinical wisdom that has been passed down to me. But now that wisdom is like a man clinging to a guide rope that stops halfway down a well. Below all the words, there is just me and her. And now the rope dangles in the air and my hands are raw.

Psychology and psychiatry are filled with self-protective theory. If the patient doesn't get better, it's resistance, or they didn't do the pre-scribed homework. There were motivation problems. It's never our fault. Through training, the cascade of classes and conferences, nod-ding bearded faces and smartly dressed women, I've believed. All those applications and interviews, the sweating for grades and tests, what was it all for? To pull the mask off an entire field only to find dust and ether? I feel myself kneeling at the funeral of my profes-sional identity. I punched the elevator button. Amelia is going to kill herself and there's nothing I or this empty field can do.

In 1994, at McLean, after Rachel hanged herself, we had a service for her in a small chapel. We'd had over 100 inches of snow that winter and in April, Boston was still chilled. Professionals and patients took time away from therapy and seminars and paperwork to gather in the chapel. A few people stood up and talked about the horrible loss we'd suffered; how this sort of event scares all of us. One of the patients wanted to sing "We Shall Overcome," but a few clicked tongues and rolled eyes sat him back down.

Eventually, a few speeches too late, the service ended. I left the chapel and found myself walking next to the director of the day hospital, Dr. Beaumont, who suddenly muttered, "Well, treat enough suicidal people and guess what, eventually one of them kills herself." He was wearing only a sports coat, his hands were pressed into his pockets, his entire body leaned forward into the cold wind. He spoke his words to the ground, to me, or no one in particular. He turned his head in my direction. "Guess what? Some mental illnesses are terminal."

Dr. Beaumont was in his early sixties, bald with purple veins dotted beneath the wrinkles of his forehead and small red blotches on his cheeks. He was chewing the insides of his cheeks as if they offered his last sustenance. I could only think to say, "Oh." I wondered if he believed what he was saying.

When I called in at the end of the day, planning to come down to the unit and see her after my last patient, a nurse told me she was sleeping again. I was relieved. "Can you write a note for the night staff to make sure she's up at 7:00 tomorrow morning? I'm going to see her then."

"No prob," the voice said.

Hospitalization:
Session Twenty-two

The next morning we met and she greeted me as if nothing had happened. I'd reviewed her chart. She'd slept for twelve hours straight. She nodded at me when I stepped out of the staff station. She moved slowly. We went into the room and sat down. She ran her tongue along her lip. Her lip was still ugly, purple and black, and her hair hid beneath an Arizona baseball cap.

"The coffee on the unit is terrible. I'm used to stronger stuff." She yawned.

"Where should we start?"

"I've been thinking about that. You wanted to know how I got here? Should I start there?"

I shrugged.

She scratched an arm. Studied it for a moment.

"I feel like I did during residency. Beyond weary. I'm just sick of everything. Not burned out; scorched out. When I was a resident I was on call every fourth night, sometimes every third night. When I was on call I'd work twenty-four, sometimes thirty-two or even thirty-six hours in a row."

I remember one night, I'd been on in the morning and had been busy but it wasn't too bad. The nights before, Jay had had a cough that had kept me up, and I was just weary. Tired of working, tired of phone calls and pages and tired of the endless litany of patients. That night, it must have been 3 or 4 A.M., a woman was on the obstetrics floor. I still remember her wrists were these enormous fleshy things; she was in her forties, red hair and pale skin and horrible teeth, black near the gums. She smelled of cigarettes. And just as obese as you could be. Huge.

She'd just given birth that evening and slept until about 3. She'd had an episiotomy, you know, she was snipped from her vagina to her anus. She was in pain, but instead of saying anything, she just moaned. I wrote morphine for her and then went back to sleep in the call room and the nurses came and got me. "She's still moaning, she's still in pain." So I wrote for more. Same thing. Forty minutes later the nurse is back. I'd just fallen asleep.

I stood in her room, just one overhead fluorescent light on, in front of this mound of moaning pale flesh, thinking, I am so tired. That night I'd walked through a spill in the cafeteria and my sneakers squeaked and stuck to the floor. I smelled. She smelled. I'd been eating terribly, fast food—fried, starched, oily, toxic food. I felt greasy. And this whale of a woman wouldn't stop moaning, even after she had the morphine. But she wouldn't talk to me, she wouldn't tell me where she hurt. I needed her to tell me what was wrong. I kept asking her and stood there and she looked at me but just moaned. She wouldn't say a word. I was going to have to have her head scanned; did she have a major head bleed during the delivery? What I really thought was that she was a whiner. A scum-of-the-earth, boozing, drinking, smoking leech that had now managed to reproduce again when she probably had fourteen kids at home already. I'd never had thoughts like that before about a patient. Who was I to think these things? But I didn't care. I wanted out. I said, "If you can't tell me what's wrong I'm going to send you down to radiology and get your head scanned. I'm not giving you another drop of morphine." I shouted it at her.

Then I went out to write it up in her chart. I was doing the notes when the nurse who had awakened me came by and asked me what the plan was. I told her the patient hadn't spoken to me even though she was conscious and I was going to have her head scanned before I gave her any more opiates. She said, "Does she speak English?"

The patient had red hair. Her name was Bromberg or something like that. Not Mexican. Wrong. She was Mexican. We found a Spanish-speaking nurse. The patient had sprained her ankle getting into the bed.

I feel now like I did that night. Beyond tired. Beyond weary. And humiliated. You know, I would have crawled over that patient's head to get to a pillow and that's the way I am now. I'd crawl over you and anyone else to get out. Just be done. Have all of this over.

"Over, you mean kill yourself?"

"I don't care how it happens. The rest of the world doesn't feel this way. I can tell, it's like I'm fighting every moment to keep up appearances for everyone, when beneath it all I want to be gone."

Two days ago, before all the excitement, I went to have a bagel and a honey nut coffee at Einstein's on Swan and Sunrise. I was in line, the place is a zoo in the morning, when I saw this woman ahead of me in line, ordering.

She was my age, her hair was almost in a military cut. She was one of those gorgeous brunette women who look pretty even if you cut their hair using a bowl as a guide. She had huge blue eyes and thin leather bands on her wrists and a tattoo of a gecko on her upper arm. She was wearing military shorts, baggy, and they were patched and had been sloppily stitched.

She was ordering a Tasty Turkey on an everything bagel and she pointed at the basket of bagels behind the counter. She was laughing because she wanted a specific bagel and the kid in the overalls behind the counter couldn't tell which one she wanted and kept pointing at the wrong one in the bin. There were thousands of everything bagels in the bin. They were both laughing. She had her bare, long arm out pointing, her arm hanging in the air so gracefully, like an opened swan's wing, but there was authority there too. I'd never have the nerve to pick out a specific bagel. Because it's absurd. But she could. I think those of us in line behind her would have let her do anything. I was transfixed by her. I didn't even hear the little counter girl asking me what I wanted to order.

I was jealous. Not of her beauty, not even the grace. It was that she exuded wholeness. Everything she did said, "Here I am, world, here's all of me, take me or leave me." She knew who she was and anyone could see that. There were no secret parts. Nothing hidden. And I know that I will never be like her.

We sat for a few moments. She looked uncomfortable.

I said, "I'm missing how the Tasty Turkey ended you up in here?"

"She was all there, truly there. She was a living reminder of what I'm not. You've been hinting at it. I have a curtained-off place." She rubbed one of her wrists. It looked so small. Elegant little fingers wrapped around it. Like a girl.

She continued, "When I was a senior in college one of my friends told me I walked with my elbows touching my ribs as if I was scared. That's how he could tell it was me from across the dining center; I was the one with her elbows touching her ribs. So I practiced walking with my arms out swinging. If you look close you can tell they aren't relaxed. I force my arms to swing because it looks more confident. Isn't that crazy? I practiced walking up stairs and across a room, and rising and walking and carrying something with one arm. I wanted to walk like a doctor.

"I'm not alone, you know, just about every female doctor I know fakes confidence. Even some of the men. I don't think you'll get this. Women are more tuned in to how much vulnerability it takes to walk into a doctor's office. Maybe it's the experience of having a Pap and pelvic from adolescence on. We know what it feels like to be afraid and we want our doctors to be confident. Some of the women physicians burn the scared parts out of themselves. They become überdoktors. More masculine than the men. Colder. Angrier. More competitive. Others just wash out. They leave. And then there are the ones like me. We sew curtains and seal the parts of ourselves that are crumpled and afraid away from everyone. But it's always there. I've been scared as long as I can remember. The truth is that we're all scared. I wanted a Tasty Turkey. On an everything. But instead I got the salmon spread. I didn't want anyone to compare me to her."

"So the thing behind the curtain is what?"

"I don't know."

"Hang with it for a little longer. It's important. You said the woman ordering the bagel . . ."

"A Tasty Turkey."

"Right. The Tasty Turkey woman, you said she had wholeness."

Amelia looked frustrated; I wasn't getting something important. "Yeah. Everything about her said, this is who I am."

"But you don't do that?

"To the outside world I look confident. The difference is that

I can tell she really *is* what she looks like, and I'm a poser. I look confident and warm. But I'm not." She looked at me. "You're not getting this, are you?"

"I don't understand how the bagel or even the fatigue led you to want to kill yourself."

"Look, for a minute, imagine it was you. Could you do it? What if you had a blade in *your* hands?" Her voice elevated. "The sharpest blade you've ever held in your life. In front of you, on a gurney, is a healthy woman. Inside her belly is a healthy baby. A roomful of masked faces is staring at you. It's your job to make the incision. And you know damned well that even though we call it an incision, a word that sounds clinical and cold, the reality is that you're holding a sharp knife to someone else's body. You also know that your hands don't always obey you. You dropped your keys this morning and you remember that. What if you do that now? And you know there are better people in the room who should be doing this. You've been lying to so many people for so long and now you've gotten what you deserve. The right to slice up someone else's life and then live with the consequences forever because you didn't have the guts to admit to everyone that you couldn't hack it."

She paused, and then looked straight at me. "Can't you see? A doctor was all I was. I wanted to be a mom, too, but that's over. I can't have a child after what I did to Stacy. There's nothing else."

She crossed her arms in front of her. Her eyes slowly relaxed. Then she scratched her neck as if she were a bored bureaucrat. Her voice was normal. "Would you mind if we cut this short? The nurse said they stop serving breakfast in a few minutes and I haven't eaten much the last few days, and what little I did consume, well, let's just say I'm hungry."

"I'd like to continue this now."

"I'd like to leap off Blackett's Ridge. Neither of us is going to get everything we want this morning." The edge was back in her voice.

"Okay, I'll be back at the end of the day."

Walking to the elevators I felt restless and decided to take the stairs up to the seventh floor. I found the stairwell and started running upward; it felt good to exert myself. It was ironic that she was talking about her curtained-off parts, while still keeping me at a distance. But at least she was talking to me, at least she was trying.

Some suicidal folks are most at risk when they push everyone away, or hide from them, as Amelia had with me before this latest attempt. It was the only comfort I had.

When I saw her at six that evening, after the rest of my day was over, she looked better. She'd showered. There were still dark circles beneath her eyes, but her lip looked smaller already and she'd washed her hair. I felt better too. I'd seen a couple I treat, the woman is a physician, and we were making real strides. I was in a good mood. We walked into the conference room again but this time she sat closer. For a moment it felt surreal. We could have been anywhere—in my office, or she could have been one of my colleagues. She looked so suddenly normal, it didn't feel like we were sitting on an inpatient psychiatry ward.

"Well, I've learned a lot since we spoke this morning," she said.

"Tell me."

"Instead of sleeping like yesterday, I spent the day with the other patients. I've decided that it's best not to have a diagnosis that begins with *B*. Borderline. Bipolar Disorder. That's bad. *S* sounds aren't much better. Suicidal. Psychotic. Schizophrenic, substance abuse. If you have both an S and a B it's particularly bad."

"You pretty much have this psychiatry thing nailed down."

"I've also learned that Ativan will keep inside of tinfoil inside your bra because Debby saves them up and then takes them all at once. The staff don't know. And if you cut yourself on the forearm with a plastic butter knife you can prolong your stay on the unit even if you have bad insurance. Giorgio taught me that.

He's borderline and a drinker." She looked at me. Smiled. "Don't look so sorry for me, I belong here right now. I don't blame you for my being here, it's just that some of my colleagues *really* belong here.

"The routine here is dreadful. I had another history and phys-ical from a resident who was nervous because I'm on the faculty. And then the nurses asked me a million questions and the social worker did the same. He was particularly annoying. I think he's more accustomed to working with the seriously mentally ill because he kept asking me about insurance and my prior hospi-talizations. And the food, it's so overcooked. I asked Jay to bring me a salad for lunch and a few of the girls and I shared it.

"Poor Jay, it's killing him to see me in here. He keeps asking me why I'm here and I don't have a response." She rubbed her eyes.

"Maybe it's time to be honest with him?" I said, leaning for-ward. "Let him in?"

"I don't know what to say to him. Or anyone. My family back in Philly is really worried. Jay must have called them. I've had a bunch of phone calls, including one from Aunt Mary. She's eighty. She said this must have happened because I have *"lorcho,"* Italian for the evil eye. She said she wanted me to make a gesture with my hand every few minutes to ward off ill intent." She held up her hand and waved it. "The worst part is, I've been doing it."

I was going to bring the conversation back to Jay but she interrupted. "Something else occurred to me, too. Did you know that Debby is a cashier when she stays on her meds, and Allan, who's severely depressed now, volunteers at hospice? Lisa's a prostitute. At least half of the patients in here work at some-thing. Even these people can work.

"After you left this morning Lisa took off her top when one of the male aides came into the day room. She has beautiful breasts and I don't think they're fake. The aide just spun on his heels and told one of the nurses that Lisa was topless again. When the nurse came in she had to chase Lisa around the table. When they finally got a towel around her she dropped to the floor and wept in a nurse's arms. She just sat on the floor and let go. I was jealous. I feel like I've got this weight inside me I can't let out. Lisa just lets it all go. She's the one with the frizzy red hair."

She pointed toward the kitchen area, as if I could see Lisa through the wall.

"Look," she said, her voice slower, "sorry about this morning. I didn't mean to go off like that at the end. I don't know where the anger comes from. I feel angry at everyone right now." She stopped and thought for a moment. Then she said, "I've been thinking about the fraud business all day." I perked up.

People think that med school is rough, but for me it wasn't. There was a lot of studying, a lot of regurgitation. They teach you facts and the names of this and that and you parrot it back. Penn was pretty supportive, actually. It wasn't until my internship here that life turned to shit. Internship was hard, there were ninety-hour weeks, even more. The moment I remember the clearest happened during my OB rotation. We used to round together, go from room to room in the mornings, the entire team, two attendings, a younger guy who was a rising star in the department who'd done his residency here, and an old-school guy who'd been on the faculty for like thirty years, he'd even been the chair of the department for a while.

These two guys were a mutual admiration society, always pointing out the brilliance of the other one, Fric and Frac, and then the rest of us would trail behind them like a silent entourage. We looked like a bunch of waiters walking around in our little white jackets, and my job on the team was chief scut dog.

I was assigned a bunch of the patients and I had to know everything about them. On internship we rotated through many of the other services, but this was the obstetrics service, my department, so I needed to be on my toes. That was the only grade that really counted. Unless you're grossly incompetent it's hard to outright fail the rotations, as long as it isn't yours. But in obstetrics they know they're stuck with you for four years and they want to know you aren't going to embarrass them, or worse, get one of the attendings sued. There are babies' lives on the line, mothers; the stakes are high.

So I'm on rounds with the mutual admiration society, and they sit us down, interns first, me and this guy, and then the upperclass residents, three of them, and the two attendings, and they start playing Obstetrics Jeopardy. Only it isn't a game. They start with one of the interns and they say, "What's the definition of high blood pressure in a thirty-two-week mom? How often does it convert to preeclampsia?" Which I guess I should have known, but then they get into real obscure stuff. "Aside from fever, what are the common symptoms of septic thrombophlebitis?" "Look, I've only just started obstetrics, I don't know anything yet," I tell them. The younger attending said, "But you've known how to read for a while, right?"

I felt this fire in my belly. I wanted to leap across the table and gouge out his eyes with his penlight. It seems silly to even say it out loud, but I was practically crying. I was postcall, I'd been up for twenty-six hours straight at that point, which usually didn't bother me that much, but I felt emotional, almost premenstrual, even though I'd just finished my period. I felt totally disconnected to everything; my cycle was off, my sleep was screwed up, and I was talking to these people who had such different customs. When he said that bit about my knowing how to read I looked at the other residents but they acted as if it were normal. One of them even joked with me after, "I bet you'll never forget the symptoms of septic thrombophlebitis, huh?"

Where the hell was Dr. Kildare? Where was the cast of Chicago Hope *and* E.R., General Hospital, M*A*S*H*?

Here's what I wanted you to know. A few years later I did that to someone. When I was the chief resident, this cute girl came through, starting her residency, and I pimped her. She was from Berkeley. It's a good school, a good program. I knew she was good—she reminded me of myself. She had the same wholesomeness, you know? But I asked her hard questions, material I knew she had no way of knowing though the answers were obvious enough to everyone else. "How do we treat previas at sixteen weeks?"

I even gave her an ultrasound that showed blood on it, knowing full well she'd never seen one before, and asked her to tell me what she saw on it, in front of the entire team. She crumbled. It was subtle but I could tell. Her mouth hung open just a tiny bit and then she sniffled. There were no tears but I could tell she wanted to cry. And I didn't do anything to help her or take her off the hook.

That was rock bottom.

"So what do you make of that now?"

"What do you mean?"

"So how does this contribute to you feeling like a fraud?"

"I was pretending to be Ms. Caring with my patients, but behind closed doors I was assassinating innocents."

"So, in addition to wanting to murder yourself, can you think of anyone else you should be angry at for that?"

She thought for a second. Her voice was quieter, slower. "The mutual admiration society—but I knew there would be a few jerks, some great attendings and some jerks. I'm angry at those bastards for treating me like that. I was on my way to becoming a good doctor. They screwed me up, and then I went and turned into one of them." She looked at the window. The sun was still high even though it was six o'clock. Long jet trails streaked the sky.

"How long did it last? How many times did you do that to the trainees under you?"

"A few times before that, though that was the worst one."

"It's good for you to know who deserves your anger. Sometimes you assume you deserve it instead of other people. You may deserve your share, but let's give others their due."

She looked like she'd eaten something sour, I didn't know how to interpret her expression.

"What prevented you from telling me this? What's taken you so long?"

"I don't . . . wait a minute." She looked at the floor. "Just now, and for a while, I've had feelings about you that remind me of feelings I have about my father. I feel like a failure, like I need to prove something, and it makes me so tired."

"I remind you of him?"

"No. But I think I've been expecting you to treat me like my father treated me, that anything I did to help myself wouldn't be good enough. When I was telling you the story about the mutual admiration society, I thought you were going to assume it was all my fault."

"So you've been keeping me in the dark because you've been afraid that I'll think you're inadequate?"

"That's how I treat all authority, as if they are all just like my dad, waiting for me to screw up, expecting it."

"That's insightful. Nice work."

"You're telling me that so I won't treat you like my father?"

"No. It's nice work. Now that you know you can do something about it, separate me from him. Maybe it will help you hear me—help you to tell me what's in your heart as it happens."

She smiled weakly at the praise and nodded slowly.

"Tell me, how suicidal are you right now?"

"Do I have to?"

I waited.

She held up her hands in measurement and spread them as if she'd caught a medium-sized salmon. It was the first time we'd calmly discussed her willingness to kill herself.

Hospitalization:
Session Twenty-three

The next morning I drove Alexandra into school. She'd changed rooms, moved up to be with the three-year-olds. She stood tentatively at the window outside the door and I felt the familiar guilt; I should be spending more time with her. On the drive into work I felt something under me on the seat. A pacifier. Alexandra gave them up when she turned two, but they still turned up every now and then. I put it in my pocket.

When I got to the hospital I went in to see Amelia before starting my routine. She was waiting, eager to see me. She'd already showered and was wearing sweatpants and a sweatshirt. Her hair was up in a ponytail. She looked like a college student prepared for a long study session. We got back into the room and she said, "You look good, thinner, have you lost weight or did you do something to your hair?"

"Thank you," I said. "Where should we start?"

"I feel relieved that I told you I was avoiding you. That you're like my dad to me. It's like a door opened. I remembered something I wanted to tell you."

I did a rotation in the NICU when I was a resident, it's where we take care of the sickest infants and preemies. These days only pediatric residents do rotations on the neonatal intensive care units but when I went through residency, we got to work there too. Our NICU was a nice space. To get in there you have to go through the sink room. Everyone going into the NICU has to wash their hands for five minutes. The sinks are big and industrial looking. Ugly. But the sink room opens into a big airy space with natural light. The wallpaper had balloons and bears on it. There were rocking chairs everywhere and the windows overlook a courtyard.

Wendy was my first preemie. Her mom was only twenty-seven weeks along when she gave birth to her, but that's not too bad. We've rescued preemies at twenty-four, even twenty-three, weeks. As it happened my last day in obstetrics was a Saturday. She was born that day. I switched to the NICU that Monday so I helped deliver her, and then saw her on the unit.

Her mom had started bleeding on the Friday before and then she had contractions. We tried to slow her delivery but Wendy had other ideas.

She was coming. I assisted a senior resident with the delivery and then we gave her to the NICU team. She weighed a little better than a pound when she was born. She was the tiniest thing. She had black hair and her skin was transparent on her forehead. I could see blue veins that made a W. It was like her name was emblazoned on her forehead. We joked about it with the mom. Her skin was so smooth and healthy looking, darker in places than you'd expect, I just thought she looked great considering how early she was.

That Monday I looked forward to seeing her. Despite never stepping foot on the NICU I felt like I already knew someone there. When I first found her on the unit I was shocked. She was in an incubator and there were wires everywhere. We were monitoring her heart rate and respiration, mostly just her blood pressure and oxygen saturation. We were also feeding her through a tube in her mouth and she had IVs in her arms and legs and I think she even had a catheter in her umbilical stump. Her liver functions, her bilirubin, was screwy, of course, so she was under the bili lights too.

The moment I first saw her she was moving her arms and legs, little awkward movements, as if she wanted something. I just stood at her incubator and read her chart. She had multiple systems out of whack, her lungs kept filling with fluid, which is fairly predictable. There was some question about her cardiac function too, but I don't remember it exactly. She kept desatting, she wasn't getting enough oxygen, and she had some funky murmur. In fact, I don't think any part of her was normal. Her renal function and liver enzymes were off too.

I was assigned a number of babies to monitor and learn about, but she was the only one who'd just arrived, and none of the others were in crisis, so I justified to myself that it was okay if I spent most of my time focused on her. From then on, I did my phone calls and paperwork next to her incubator.

Her mom was freaked. She looked like she'd just stepped out of a Laundromat. Her fingers were cigarette yellow and her hair was always frizzy, held together with bandannas. She had another child at home. She was young and single, so she couldn't just stay at the hospital. She was always leaving to take her other child from school to her sister's and then coming back as soon as she could.

The attending on the NICU was a brilliant tactician with the preemies. He was a short guy with a gut. He never chatted about anything other than the babies. He really understood how tinkering with one system would impact the others, but he talked about Wendy as if she was a little machine, like a watch, that just needed to have its gears recut. He reminded me of an accountant. But she wasn't a watch. I swear she had the best personality. She was a real fighter. I could tell from the way she moved. She was fighting for her life. But she was so alone in that incubator. It was like a cage.

I tried to talk to her whenever I could, mostly when there wasn't anyone else around the incubator, and I sang to her too. I tried to be subtle about it but about a week into the rotation one of the older nurses came up to me when I was doing paperwork. She pointed at Wendy and said, "This one's got bad protoplasm, don't get too attached, you hear?"

And I put on my best professional game face and nodded, "Of course." And she smirked at me like, "Whatever."

I was only assigned to the NICU for a month but after eight days Wendy started going downhill. Everything was off. First her pressure destabilized and then she developed an infection and she just couldn't fight it off. I panicked, but the rest of the team acted like this was entirely normal. And then on rounds one of the fellows asked if anyone had spoken to the mom about how serious things were. I didn't understand at first, and then I got it. Wendy was dying. After rounds I stood next to her incubator and I wanted to take her out of there. I knew on some level that it was foolish to try but I wanted to hold Wendy outside of the incubator.

I just felt like she deserved one chance at real human connection. Maybe if she were touched a little more she'd have a reason to live. She'd spent her entire little life in there, with almost no human contact. So the next morning during rounds we were supposed to be going from infant to infant and only spending a few moments at each one, but Wendy was first and I hogged the team's time by explaining every little bit of Wendy's situation, hoping they might have some ideas. Then I sprang the idea of taking her out and holding her. The attending got right in my face and said, "You are a doctor, not a child. Your first task is to do no harm. This baby needs an opportunity to fight off the infection she has, not to have some emotional nut pulling her out of her one opportunity. You take that preemie out of that chamber and she'll die. Period. Do you understand, Dr. Sorvino?"

I nodded. Rooted to the spot.

I should have said that she was going to die anyway. That she deserved some human contact, she deserved to be stroked, held, sung to, and I was happy to do the job. But I didn't say anything. She was dead the next day. Her mother wasn't even there. After she died I opened the incubator, I gently unhooked everything and pulled her out of there. I took her to the window, cried, and I held her in my palms.

Tears gathered in her eyes; she tightened her cheeks as if to prevent herself from letting go.

She looked at me. "I think that was my last good cry. I can't believe I told you this." Her eyes were filled. Her lower lip began to quiver, and then her chin. She dropped over her knees; I saw a dark spot on her sneakers. And another. When she sat up her face was stained with long swaths of pink wetness. She was sobbing. She wiped her cheeks but to no avail. Through sobs she said, "Dan, that day I let Wendy stay in that incubator I traded something away. We all knew she was going to die. Even I knew it, and I'd only worked there for eight days. I should have pulled her out when she was alive." She took a deep breath.

From Wendy's death on, I never got that close to another preemie or her parents. I was Dr. Matter-of-Fact. I might have been worse than the attending. I buried myself in the data. Potassium levels, saturation, cardiac output. I learned all I could about saving preemies. I didn't actually learn that much, I wasn't there for that long. But I avoided speaking to the moms about anything other than our interventions. No one said anything either. In fact, the attending told me I was one of the most improved residents he'd ever had. He took me aside on the last day and said, "Becoming an intensivist is only for the very best physicians, most can't manage the complexity, pressure, or attention to detail. You've got what it takes." He wanted me to switch to peds and do an intensivist fellowship. The prick.

But it wasn't just the preemies. Wendy colored every experience I've had since then. I've withdrawn from all of my patients, not just the sick ones. I say the right things when the babies are born and can comfort a nervous mother, but it's not the same as throwing myself into their lives, truly being there for them like I was for Wendy. When things have gone badly because Mother Nature is a random bitch sometimes, I've said a few comforting words and gone about my day.

When new patients tell me they've heard I'm the kindest of all the obstetricians in town I cringe. Not only because there are amazing obstetricians here, but because I know that it's bullshit. They can knock all they want. There's no one home anymore.

Eventually she cleared her eyes, looked at me, and laughed. Then she was crying and gasping again. I stood up and moved next to her, rubbing her back slowly. She cried for a long time.

Eventually the tears slowed. Her breath was uneven, still not in her control. She took breaths in the middle of words. "I think maybe I needed this."

"Maybe you did."

"Can I see you tomorrow? I think I'm empty." She dabbed one eye with the corner of a tissue as if she'd only gotten something small in her eye.

"I think you've got a good heart and you've paved over it with the need to impress your father, with the desire to be the doctor the system taught you to be, and now to be the defendant your attorneys want you to be. And you're good at doing all of those things, trying to please all those people, but you've paid a price. Authenticity. Genuineness. Being Amelia first, the girl who walks awkwardly but has a good head on her shoulders. The girl with a heart big enough to put a blue hat on a dead child, and to almost pull a preemie out of her incubator so she could have a few moments of tenderness. You've got healing in your blood. If you will just be Amelia, you will be the best physician on the planet."

She nodded at me and the tears came harder.

"So this is your new job, Amelia. I want you to practice being totally Amelia everywhere. Okay?"

She nodded. Eventually her crying slowed. She sniffled, took a few deep breaths and then laughed and cried some more.

"I'm just going to sit here for a little while, alone, if that's okay," she said eventually. I stood, nodded, and was opening the door when she said softly from behind me, "Thanks."

I turned back.

"You know, for all of this." She waved her arm in front of her and laughed a little.

Hospitalization:
Session Twenty-four

W hen I checked my voice mail at the end of the day there was a message. Scott Freeman's voice. "Hey, Dan. It's Scott. Your patient says she has court-ordered community service tomorrow morning. She wants a pass for four hours; her husband faxed me the paperwork to prove it. Says she doesn't feel well enough to go home yet, but needs to do the community service. I'm inclined to believe her, she says she can take cabs. Give me a call."

It took most of the morning to connect with him, we exchanged voice mail a few more times, but when I got him he said he'd just come out of rounds and Amelia was improving.

Unlike the first days of her hospitalization, Scott said she'd acknowledged that she was still suicidal, but also appeared to be starting to focus on the future and seemed less evasive. What did I think about the community service? I told him I thought it would be fine. She was working in treatment with me, and she'd been honest about her lethality. Neither of us was ready for her to be released, but we both felt that if she went to the community service and came back immediately after, she'd be fine. Then I asked him if he knew that Debby was keeping Ativan in her bra. "Damn. We'd looked just about everywhere else for it. Thanks," he said.

If Amelia was going to use the community service as an excuse to get out, and then kill herself, I wanted her to have to face me first. The next morning, at 6:30, Dr. Sorvino was temporarily released from the inpatient unit. I met her at the door to the unit. It opened and she walked out. She was wearing khakis and a golf shirt. She looked like the casual professional.

"How are you feeling?" I asked.

"I'm good. Fine."

We walked a hundred feet or so and got into the main hallway. It was change of shift for the nursing staff and the hall was filled with nurses heading in to grab a quick bite from the cafeteria before ascending to their floors. Junior residents were there, too; some were getting off from the night before, others would continue to work through the rest of the day. There were lots of droopy eyes, ponytails full of split ends, and wrinkled lab coats. We'd gone a little way down the hall when a scruffy, lab-coated man of about twenty-five recognized Amelia and approached us. I could feel Amelia trying not to meet his eyes. She looked down and tried to appear rushed but he blocked our path. He pushed his tortoise rims up onto the bridge of his nose. He looked down like an adolescent son asking his mother for permission.

"Dr. Sorvino?" he asked.

Amelia looked up. We stopped in the middle of the hall.

"I'm glad I ran into you. Can I ask you a really quick question?"

Amelia looked at me and let out a tired laugh. The resident continued, "I've got a mother upstairs who's at thirty-six weeks with proteinuria, some edema, borderline, actually. Elevated pressure and nausea . . ."

Amelia swallowed. "Who's your attending? You should ask your attending, right now I'm not—"

"Dr. Kathy Reed. She's not in yet, and her cell phone died when we were talking. She'll be in soon, I just . . ."

"How old?"

"Thanks. She's thirty-nine. No. Sorry. She's forty."

An older man pushing his wife in a wheelchair asked me where the cafeteria was. I pointed.

"What's her BP?" Amelia asked. She had her arms folded in front of her. She lifted one hand and rested her chin on it—it was the slightest change in posture, but her look altered completely. She radiated authority. The resident continued,

"One forty-five over eighty-five. Her highest was one fifty over ninety-five a few hours ago."

"You've taken it a few times after rest, it's not just white coat, right?"

"Three times. Resting. And it's new. She was normal until this week."

"How big is she?"

"Premorbid moderate obesity."

"You said proteinuria?"

"Yeah. Three plus."

"How many times have you taken it?"

"Dipped three times over four hours. All of them at least two plus. She's had some rib pain too. This is classic preeclampsia, right?"

"Yeah. You're going to want to induce her. Mom and baby will both do better with baby on the outside now. Wait for Kathy to get in and see how she wants to handle the delivery."

"Cool." The resident suppressed a slight smile. "Thanks!" He headed for the stairs.

It was impressive, the way she rattled off criteria. She looked at me.

"What?" she asked.

"Nothing."

"That doesn't prove anything. Dr. Dan, even a psychologist could diagnose preeclampsia." She smiled at me.

We went through the double doors, weaving slowly through the staff coming in, and stood out in the circle watching the cars. It was a beautiful morning; the sky was painted with orange and pink, long cirrus framing the mountains to the north. *I had a rush of sudden anxiety: What if I don't ever see her again?* Her taxi approached, she got in, and waved at me as it pulled away.

That afternoon, when I stepped out of the staff station and onto the unit, she was sitting in the common room with another patient, a small woman in her mid-sixties with gray hair that reached out in every direction. They were chatting. Amelia saw me and waved as if we were old friends finding each other by accident.

She stood and came over to me. "That woman is a trip," she said as we walked into the group room. "She had a manic episode two nights ago and she literally lifted a cop off the ground. She talks a mile a minute and she's stronger than she looks."

I nodded. "Where should we start? How was the community service?"

"I spent the morning at the Pima Animal Control Shelter on Sweetwater Road, behind the highway. They gave me an orange jumper to wear, can you believe it? I'm a regular convict. No one out there had any idea of my profession. There were a lot of community service women out there. One of them was sentenced the same day I was; I think she stole someone's mail and tried to cash their checks. We were assigned to different parts of the pound. I was the waiting room sweeper and window cleaner. I thought I'd worry about being seen by someone I knew but I wasn't. I don't care anymore. I'm practicing what I've learned with you. This is who I am. I'm not pretending with anyone anymore."

The pound is a brick building with concrete floors and bars on the windows. There are a few reception windows in front. I swept up the waiting room for an hour before it opened and then people started gathering outside the door. They opened the place up at nine. A woman came in with her two kids, and an older guy. The older guy went straight to the reception window. He leaned into it and was filling out forms while talking with one of the receptionists.

"Yeah, she's just old is all," I heard him say. He was about fifty, I guessed, wearing blue industrial pants and work boots. He had a thin layer of beard. He hadn't shaved the last few days. His wallet was on a chain that attached to his belt loop. The bureaucrat asked him for a check for twenty-five dollars and he started filling it out.

He said, "Do I bring her in here or around back? She's in the truck." And there was a pause. And he said, "This isn't . . . well, it isn't easy is all."

The bureaucrat was filling out a form and pretended not to hear him, in that way clerks at government offices pretend you aren't there. He scratched the back of his neck and patted down his hair in back, even though it looked in place.

She said something I couldn't hear and then he asked her what the date was. Through the window I could see a thin dog sitting in the passenger seat of an old pickup, a greyhound. She leaned against the truck door and looked dignified.

I had to start mopping, so I grabbed my empty bucket and went back to the sinks. I didn't hear the rest of his conversation with the bureaucrat.

When I came back the man was gone. I looked out into the parking lot and he was sitting with the dog on the ground next to his truck. The dog was leaning against him. A few other people came in and I mopped around them, all the while watching the man out in the parking lot through the window on the door.

Eventually he stood up and carried the dog into the shelter. He stood outside the door for a moment, unable to open it with the dog in his arms. I put down my mop and was heading toward the door when someone else went out. The man managed to kick the door back open and stood, awkwardly, just inside the entrance. He looked toward the bureaucrat but she didn't look up. She acted like she didn't see him. But I did. He had the same look my father gets sometimes, when the world swirls together and he can't make out details. He put down the dog and looked around.

I thought about our conversations, about being myself. Acting genuine. I walked up to him and I hugged him. I didn't say anything to him. I just tilted my head and we embraced. And I took the dog's leash.

"You say your good-byes?" I asked him. He nodded. I told him to wait. And I crouched down and picked up the dog and carried her back to the kennels. I had no idea where I was going, and when my supervisor saw me she asked me what the hell I was doing and I told her we had to put the dog down. I don't remember everything she said to me; she was fairly abusive, actually, but one of the real employees came and together we took the dog back to the euthanasia station. I held the dog and she gave her an injection and I petted her while she died.

As I knelt over her I could smell the mutts and the cat food and the mold. I could feel the tremble as I petted the dog's brown fur. I heard other dogs barking. I felt like I was emerging, floating up after being under muddy water for a long time.

I went back out and gave the man the leash and collar. The waiting room was teeming by then. He thanked me and shook my hand with both of his. We could have been standing at UMC, in the Labor and Delivery waiting room, and he could have been a new father.

Tears filled her eyes again and she didn't flinch. They descended down her cheek and she didn't move to wipe them away. She laughed a little. And then cried more. Still as an oak. Then, when the tears had passed, she said, "I blame you for this. You've turned me into a ninny. I'm going to be the junior Olympic crying champion."

"It's a mark of health, you know. The ability to laugh and cry easily, especially if you can do both simultaneously. I think you're finding yourself, Dr. Amelia."

On the drive home I turned up the stereo and Counting Crows serenaded me. I opened the windows, sang, and beat my hands on the steering wheel along to "Rain King." It was an appropriate song. There were dark clouds over the Catalinas. Driving up Campbell toward River Road I could see a plume of showers falling in the foothills just ahead of me and to the east, the first monsoon of the summer. Every July the rains come. Most afternoons the sky blackens with clouds. The temperature can drop thirty or forty degrees in minutes. The Navajo say the monsoon clouds are male. They are angry and snap thunder, filling the desert with moisture.

I was passing Fort Lowell when the first heavy drops fell on the windshield and then the white snaps of water and mist filled the air. I tried to roll up the windows before getting damp but it was too late—the wind came up and in a moment my hair and face were wet. I turned down the music and listened to the melodic patter of water on the roof.

I pulled into the local pharmacy and ran in, wet and hunched over, as if that would magically protect me from getting wet. I headed back into the photo-developing section. A few minutes later the clerk was handing me photographs from our trip to Michigan when a man tapped me on the shoulder. "Dr. Shapiro?" he said. He looked familiar and then I smiled. Charlotte's dad. We greeted one another and he said, "Charlotte's here somewhere, I bet she'd love to see you."

I was eager to see her too. I started down the center aisle when he stopped me. He looked toward the ceiling. "I'm learning to listen for the sound of one crutch," he said. And then I heard it too. The light popping sound of a metal crutch on linoleum. I followed him toward the magazine section.

I wouldn't have recognized her. She already had the smallest black curls and they changed her face. She looked taller, older. Still skinny. I realized I'd only seen her when she was bald. Her face opened into a broad smile and then that familiar voice started. Singsong. She was wearing jeans so I couldn't see her prosthetic but if I hadn't known better, I would have thought she had a twisted ankle. She told me about school and her sister and her mother's impending birthday. And then, she stopped and nodded her head.

"And the most important news is, of course, Rommey. He's my mutt."

She grinned a toothy smile. I did too, and then was surprised to feel myself laughing. It was wonderful to be in her presence; I was a small part of her standing here so confidently. I felt like a coach, running into a talented star who had long since left my tutelage.

It gave me an idea.

The next morning, when I was opening my office, Scott Freeman was there. "Hey, I'm glad I ran into you, no phone tag. We've seen a real improvement in your patient. I'm ready to release her and wanted to check with you. She said she had a breakthrough in her sessions with you. Is that true?"

It was true that she felt more genuine to me and less depressed. She'd told me about the preemie and had finally connected her emotions with her experiences. She was on her way— still not done, but I felt she wasn't about to kill herself. On the other hand, I could never know that for sure.

"She's ready to go. I'll want to see her frequently, but she can leave." I sounded more confident than I felt, and sagged. Now I'd have to worry about her safety again. Late in the day when I checked my voice mail I had a message. It was Scott. "We released her. She's scheduled to see you tomorrow."

Session Twenty-five

We met the next day. She'd had a haircut. Her cheeks were rosy; she'd been outside recently. She settled into the love seat and ran her hands along its leather cushions. Her wrists looked small and delicate against the brown of the leather.

"It's nice to be back," she said. "I feel a little lost. It was strange—great but strange—to go home. In only a few days I got used to that unit. I got used to Lisa's little snores." She rubbed her hands together, as if to warm them. "I feel unsure of myself, more unsure than I thought I would."

"Reentry after an inpatient stay can feel surreal," I said.

"Yeah. And I don't know what to do with myself. How to pass my time. On the unit there's something happening every hour, group or meals or rounds. I kind of liked it."

"I have an idea I want to run by you."

"I'm all ears."

"I want you to go find Samantha, the baby whose life you saved when you were a resident. The one in the photograph in your office with the crimped umbilical cord."

She squinted at me, as if the lights had grown darker.

"Why?"

"You're going to have to trust me."

"How do you know it won't be just another reminder of everything I'm not anymore?"

"You've been a fraud the whole time, right? You've only just been exposed."

"I guess."

"Then you were a fraud when you delivered her."

"I guess."

"I want you to see Samantha in person. Find her."

"I think she's in northern California. I got a Christmas card from them a few years ago. It's that important? To go all the way up there?"

"Go there."

"I'll think about it."

Late that night, after Alexandra was down, Terry spread our fertility records out on the dining room table. As a nurse practitioner, Terry is familiar with the arcane structure of medical charts. She knows where to find the assorted scraps of information; she knows the abbreviations and how to interpret the tables and lab reports. I'd been back in my home office, trying to clean up a bit. I walked out and found that she'd made piles across the table and had a notebook open; she was tallying something.

"Wow," I said. "What's all this? You getting a jump on our taxes?" She didn't smile.

"I got our records from Linden so that we can mail them to Schoolcraft in Colorado. I'm trying to make sense of it. It looks like she lost, or misplaced, some of your sperm samples."

"How many?" I asked. We'd started with sixteen samples, stored in thin straws that were submerged in liquid nitrogen. We'd used two in Boston, and we thought we'd used eight with Linden.

"This lab sheet says there are only two left. There should be six." The samples were our last chance to have children biologically related to both of us.

"I don't understand," she continued.

I stood, silently, while she shuffled through papers. But I already knew she was right.

For the first time I had obvious evidence that while Linden was giving us the appearance of caring deeply, in private she was treating our biological hopes with indifference. It had been performance. Here was another example of a physician's callous disregard for the intensity of my experience. Her sloppiness reflected a deeper disregard for the seriousness of the situation from our side. And more, there were consequences. With only two vials left we had a slim chance at pregnancy.

I was clenching my fists. But had I any right? Linden was sloppy with her paperwork, is that really a reason to raise my fists? Standing in our dining room I felt that intensity in my chest, fight or flight, the fire of vulnerability.

"If we can't have another baby let's sue," I heard myself saying.

Terry looked at me. It's the same look she had when she discovered, just prior to us sitting down to dinner at her parents', that I'd forgotten to put a diaper on Alex. Oh, silly man.

She's right. Then I remembered the last mistake I made, letting Amelia come down from Blackett's Ridge on her own when she was drunk. With only a small turn of events, that could have ended in tragedy. The difference was that I really cared. Or did I? Was I too tired to have called the MAC team in the middle of the night? Is that why I didn't do it? Was I no different from Linden?

"Let's write her a letter." She interrupted my self-deprecation. "We'll tell her to change her paperwork and keep better track of people's samples," she nodded. "If she doesn't respond we'll pass it on to the board."

"When did you get so enlightened?"

There was a pause. "There's a lot you don't know." She stuck her tongue out. She was gathering up the medical records, putting them into folders and labeling them. She still had hope. She held up one piece of paper with her handwriting on it, "A summary." She said, "I'm almost done. Give me a few more minutes to finish it. Go from here." She shooed me away.

I went out on the porch. If I'd felt that Linden understood the emotional magnitude of what we were going through then I wouldn't have wanted to pummel her. But she'd plastered on a caring face, doling out empathy and meaningless hope, viewing herself as if she were a nun on a Feed the Hungry mission. I wanted an apology from her. An acknowledgment of the gravity of her mistake.

Terry came out on the porch. She had two envelopes, already stamped and addressed.

"This one goes to Linden at her new office, this one is a summary of our fertility history and your illness for Schoolcraft in Colorado. I'm putting them on top of your wallet; drop them in the mail tomorrow on your way in?"

I nodded.

Session Twenty-six

A week later there was a message on my machine. "I can't see you today. Sorry to do this at the last minute; there was a fare war, I got tickets cheap, and I'm going. I'm on my way to Arcata to find Samantha Arbetter. That kid I delivered. Think good thoughts."

The following Wednesday Amelia had that fatigued, competent look like so many of the physicians wandering the halls. She sat down and took a deep breath.

"I brought you something," she said. She reached into a backpack and pulled out a Freud action figure doll. She leaned over and put it next to the tissue box. He was five inches tall and wore a gray suit with a bow tie. She smiled.

I thanked her and for a moment we sat in silence, both smirking at Freud. Then she started.

I stopped at the Albertson's on the drive to the airport to get some snacks, a disposable camera in case I found Sam, and a few magazines. I like the puzzle magazines and I've been known to read a People *or two. Don't you dare sneer at me, Dr. Dan, you told me not to conceal anything from you, so now you have to hear the disgusting truth. Sometimes I read* People.

On the flight from Tucson to Los Angeles I sat next to a fifty-year-old woman. She was bubbly, and obviously starting vacation. We had the briefest of exchanges but she leaned forward and confided, as if we were part of the international sisterhood, that she was off to Hawaii to lounge on a beach and seduce the locals. She asked me if I was traveling on business or pleasure. I said business. She said, "Oh, what's your business?"

She was so exuberant. She seemed immune from everything. I leaned forward just like she had and whispered, "I'm an assassin." Then I lifted my eyebrows just like she had. She sat back in her chair and the rest of the trip was quiet.

After we landed I learned that United Airlines had canceled my flight from Los Angeles to San Francisco. There was a long wait in line for the one agent trying to reroute everyone. It felt like a sign that I shouldn't be doing this, that the cosmos wanted me to stay home. I spent four hours in Los Angeles. Eventually I got up to San Francisco and caught the last flight to Arcata, up on the coast, a few hours south of the Oregon border.

The flight attendant was so cheerful I wondered if she'd dropped Ecstasy before flying. "I would be honored to serve you Cran-Apple, apple, orange juice, cola, or Sierra Mist with a delicious oatmeal cookie or travel snack mix." And then "Hey, your seat cushion does float!

Woo-hoo!" She reminded me of Gene Wilder as Willie Wonka, smiling at Charlie at the end of the movie, a Cheshire cat grin, while she announced that if we dropped 20,000 feet we might have a chance at life if we clung to a foam cushion.

Once we cleared San Francisco and I could see the endless expanse of ocean, I lifted my plastic cup into the light streaming through the window and it cast large white halos across the cabin. For a second I had the sense of being powerful, strong. I tried not to think about it. I knew it would be fleeting.

The pilot came on a few minutes later and told us the airport in Arcata was fogged in. There was talk of diverting us inland to Redding. That would mean a four-hour drive back to Arcata or a long wait for the fog to lift. I put down the cup. It was my fault for enjoying that brief moment of levity with the cup. I knew something would kill the mood. But forty minutes later the pilot dropped us right through the gray mist and found the runway.

It was cool when we stepped down the stairs off the plane. Cool ocean air. I had that flash of hope again. Most of the other passengers were Humboldt State students. There were partial beards, dreadlocks, and ponytails. The smell of cigarettes and patchouli. I waited for my bags and envied the kids greeted by parents or lovers. I felt alone, but there was that vein of hope too.

I rented a car from a sixteen-year-old at Avis. If she'd been moving any slower she would have fallen right through the space-time continuum. I tried to be patient but I drummed the counter like a city dweller. It didn't endear me to her.

Once in the rental car I drove about fifteen minutes and checked into the old Arcata Hotel. It looks out on a grassy square filled with guitar players and stoners. The square has a little statue in the middle and kids lounged around and on it. The street out on the perimeter is surrounded by camping outfitters, pubs, used-book stores, and curio shops. Jay would have said it was too damned quaint. After checking into my room I missed him suddenly. It surprised me. I called him, but he wasn't home. I had the fleeting thought that he *was out with Rebecca, but I knew it was more likely that he was painting.*

Then I looked up Daphne's number in the thin phone book. There were only two Arbetters. It was late but I called anyway. I got her voice saying, "Hello, you've reached Daphne, Jack, and Sam. Leave a message." There was a barking dog in the background. I didn't actually want to talk to Daphne. It would have meant explaining everything.

I tried to sleep but I couldn't. The room opened onto the square and as soon as I started to fall asleep there were shouts, or the sound of breaking glass, or car horns. At some point during the night I think there was a fight. When I did sleep my dreams were tense. I had that nightmare again when I'm delivering my own mother but thankfully it stopped before it got to the point where I pull off the bloody cloth. That stuff you taught me, the dream rehearsal thing, is working—the dream still occurs but it's not as intense.

I awoke in the morning feeling heavy and still tired. And angry. Mostly at you for suggesting this. What the hell was I doing up there, in the middle of nowhere? Who the hell are you to waste what little hope I have left on a wild-goose chase? I even called your office in a rage but hung up when I heard your optimistic voice-mail message. Your soothing voice. I do like your voice.

I knew they couldn't have much money so they were probably sending Samantha to the local public school. I called the elementary schools and asked about her, claiming to be a nurse needing some school records but they chastised me and reminded me that they don't release records over the phone to anyone. I got angry at you again. How was I supposed to do this without interacting with Daphne and telling her everything? I tried calling her again, prepared to tell her if I had to, but they weren't home. Then I bummed around Arcata, buying more used CDs than I could carry home.

In the early afternoon I called Daphne again and got her husband. I casually asked to speak to Daphne and he just said, "She's over at Pacific Union, the school, Samantha's got soccer." A stroke of luck. Maybe the cosmic winds were changing. He was so trusting. I could have been any-one. So I looked up the school on the map, grabbed the disposable camera, and ran out to the rental car.

When I got there I could see a flock of small children on the fields. There were no stands; the parents just lined the side of the pitch. When I got closer I could see two games. I searched the faces for Daphne's, but didn't recognize any of them. I'd met her when she was pregnant. Her face was swollen then. I walked the sidelines slowly, just a woman out for a walk. When I found a woman who looked like her, I stood near her until she began shouting advice to the goalie, who looked a few years too old, so I walked on. What a waste of time. What the hell am I doing here? I'll never find her.

Then I saw Daphne. No mistake. On the other side of the field. I watched her for a long time. I couldn't tell which child was hers. Then she yelled to an awkward kid who had her hair in a bun. She was all limbs and elbows. When the flock of kids followed the ball to one side, she was on the other side. When the ball moved toward her, she moved away. She had no sense of the field or what she was doing. But she didn't seem frustrated like I would have been. She looked like she was just running randomly. At one point, one of her teammates was throwing the ball in, and all eyes were on that kid, except mine, I think, and I saw Samantha smile. My mother used to say, "She's got a smile as wide as a city bus," and that's what Samantha's face was like. All freckles and teeth. Like a kid used to life coming her way. I had the disposable camera and I snapped a few photographs of her.

I felt something as I looked at her; a chord resonated, like, "I did that." I brought her into the world. I saved her so she could do this and climb mountains and clean her room and fall in love and diet and run around on this jade green field. Goose bumps. Euphoria.

I was shaken out of my reverie when I felt a hand on my shoulder and a voice said, "Dr. Sorvino? Is that you? Oh my God, what are you doing here?" Close up, Daphne looked great. Trim and wholesome with no makeup; she was wearing a summer dress and was barefoot. She looked so much smaller than I remembered.

"Oh my God, Daphne?" I said.

"You remembered my name!" she said. That part was awful. I made up a story about considering moving to Arcata. Her eyes opened wide, incredulous. I went on about hearing that this was a good community and wanting to check out the schools. I'm not much of a liar. She started asking questions, like weren't things going well at the university and how was my family and where was I thinking of working, would I be in the local clinic and how many women she knew who were pregnant and would love me and on and on. She said, "Oh, you're checking out the schools, how old are your children?" With each new lie my smile wore thinner; my face felt fragile, like it would crumble at any second. Relief came when Samantha's game reached halftime. She bounced over.

Daphne said, "Sam, this is the first person who ever touched you. This is Dr. Sorvino. She brought you into the world." I felt euphoric again and hoped it didn't show in my face.

Samantha was quiet and then she said, "No way. You're from Tucson? What are you doing here?" It wasn't a real question because she said, "Mom, I've decided that losing sucks."

Daphne told her not to say "sucks" and Samantha said, "Okay, losing bites moth scum." And it was so funny. Daphne started laughing, and then I did too; it bubbled out of me, spontaneous laughter.

Dan, Samantha was so beautiful. Her eyes were huge with long lashes. I leaned over and got down at her level and smiled. "Good luck in the next half, Samantha." I held out my hand and she shook it. I did that. I was the difference between her standing on a soccer field and being in a little grave.

When the game started again I told Daphne I had to leave. I lied that my husband was waiting with a real estate broker. She invited us to dinner but I said I was leaving that night.

I caught the next flight back. And you know what? All my flights were on time.

She smiled. After a few moments she said, "I almost feel ready to do what I really need to do."

"Which is?"

"I have another phone call to make. I just can't bring myself to do it."

I nodded. "There's time," I told her. "There's time."

Session Twenty-seven

W e had a few canceled sessions. Amelia's family came into town, her mother and father and sisters' families. They were worried about her. The hospitalization had mobilized the Sorvino clan. She called and canceled, her hurried voice telling me about trips to the Desert Museum and the zoo.

Two weeks later Amelia returned. She looked great, well rested. She sat in the corner of the love seat and leaned into the arm of the seat, her head tilted, and smiled.

"You'll never guess who I had a quick lunch with a few days ago!"

I phoned and her husband answered. I almost hung up when he gruffly asked me why I was calling. I told him I wanted to speak with Stacy. When she picked up she asked me to hold on and she put her hand over the mouthpiece. I assumed she was telling her husband to back off. When she came back on I asked her if we could have lunch together soon. She said she couldn't talk now. She'd call me back. I didn't know what to say and we hung up. I realized after I put down the receiver that I should have asked her when. When would she call back?

A few days went by. Nothing. And then there was a message from her on the machine. I called her back and we agreed to meet at Beyond

Bread on Campbell. I couldn't read her response on the phone. I had no idea how she felt about it, or what she would do when she got there.

I didn't know how to dress. I wanted to look like I felt. Serious. Honest. Genuine. What clothing goes with those qualities? I decided on shorts and a T-shirt.

I arrived early. I bought a tuna sandwich and was surprised that I had an appetite. I was eating and watching the door when I remembered TROT. That girl named June, the one with the serious forehead, who put her arms up over her head. What if Miranda was that profoundly impaired?

She came in about ten minutes late, pushing Miranda in a stroller. She wore overalls and a softball T-shirt. Her hair was back. She looked different from the enthusiastic mother-to-be that I remembered. Older. As she walked in I reminded myself to be genuine. I focused on what you and I have been working on, that I should be authentic.

Stacy pushed Miranda up to the little table and we shook hands. Naturally, I looked in the stroller. Miranda had a lot of hair, red ringlets with bright blue eyes.

"She's beautiful," I told her.

"Thank you," Stacy said. "She was a demon in the car but I think she's better now."

Miranda was lying back in the stroller, holding a McDonald's toy in one hand, a bottle in the other. Her legs looked spindly. All of her looked smaller than most eleven-month-olds. She seemed content, though. She was making little noises and her eyes were at half-mast.

Stacy looked up toward the menu hanging about twenty feet away behind the counter. Beyond Bread is popular at lunchtime. There was a line, and no room for a stroller. I thought she might mutter, "This was a mistake," grab the stroller, and leave.

I said, "I'll watch her. You go order." She lingered a moment, unsure, and then said, "Okay. You need anything else?" I said no. And she went and got in line. She stood there behind a few college kids and watched me and Miranda while trying not to be obvious about it.

Miranda yawned a huge yawn, dropped the McDonald's toy, grabbed her bottle with both hands, and started drinking.

After she ordered, Stacy came back and sat down. "My husband didn't want me to meet with you. He's still pretty angry."

"I appreciate your meeting with me."

"He's an angry guy in general, though, you know?" *she confessed.* "He thinks you're meeting with us to gloat because your expert ripped our case apart. He thinks you're going to try to bully me into dropping the case. He called our lawyer, who told me not to meet with you."

"That's funny, my lawyer said the same thing."

"Really?" *She smiled.* "Is it okay with you if we don't talk about legal stuff?"

I nodded. "I'm not here to talk about the case."

"My friends didn't understand why I would meet with you. They've only heard me say bad things about you. I guess I still have a lot of questions and you're the only person who can answer them."

I felt a twinge but I nodded at her. Her name was called and she went to get her sandwich. She came back and sat down, unwrapped it, and took a few bites.

She said, "So, if you didn't want to talk about the case, why did you want to meet with me?" *She was looking down, eating her sandwich.*

I said, "I wanted to apologize in person."

She put her sandwich down and looked up.

I took a breath and launched in. "Stacy, I'm so sorry that I didn't deliver Miranda sooner. I was tired and didn't check the monitor strip as frequently as I should have. I didn't see the late decelerations. It's unlikely, but possible, that I caused Miranda's cerebral palsy, and no matter what the outcome of the case, we'll never know if I'm responsible or not. I'm also sorry that I didn't apologize sooner."

Stacy covered her mouth with her hands. She didn't say anything for a while. Her hand trembled and she started to cry but wiped her face quickly. "I promised myself I wouldn't do this."

"I'm sorry," *I said.*

"I used to think about you at night. Miranda had terrible feeding problems at the beginning. She wouldn't latch on to breast-feed and she kept losing weight. She'd cry and scream constantly and I used to sit with her in the middle of the night and feel so hopeless. I'd wonder what *happened. I still want to know. Why didn't you see the heart changes? What happened?"*

I hadn't expected the question. I said, "I was tired. I was sloppy. I watched the strip periodically but I missed the decelerations. I had the urge to do the C-section but I didn't listen to my instincts. I knew you wanted a vaginal delivery and I wanted that for you. I missed them."

She shook her head. We sat for a while. Then she pointed at the stroller. "She has spastic diplegia. The muscles in her legs flex at the wrong time and she can't balance as well as other children. Her neurologist thinks she might walk eventually, but it won't be for a while. She's not even crawling yet." We sat quietly for a moment and then she said, "I'm working on for-giveness. I really am. When I heard that you weren't working as a doctor anymore, I was sorry, but I was glad. I didn't want you to do this to any-one else. But then when I met other moms of children with CP they said it might not be your fault. The lawyers say that what you did was terrible, but the other moms were less certain. And then I felt badly for you."

I nodded. Then she said, "She's going to need physical therapy and she might need surgeries on her legs. Water therapy. Horse therapy. She might need special schools. I don't work anymore, we haven't found a day care that will take her, and my husband is doing construction and landscap-ing. Where's the money going to come from? We're using COBRA from my old firm for insurance but it's so expensive and it doesn't cover much."

"That's so scary."

"It is. On the other hand"—Stacy turned toward the stroller—"she's fantastic. She's not delayed verbally at all, she's already saying words, and I think she's going to have a sense of humor. She's very tick-lish and she has solid ideas about what she wants and doesn't want. She's strong. She's no pushover."

"She's like her mother."

"Yeah. She is."

For a while we were quiet. I finished my sandwich. She ate a little but then wrapped most of hers in a napkin and put it in a diaper bag.

She said, "I accept your apology. Coming here, doing this. Apologiz-ing. Takes guts. I admire that." She took a breath and then said, "I don't ever want to talk to you again, but I give you that. Guts."

"I understand."

"I'm not sure you do. I don't think you'll understand until you have children. But you're trying. Anyway. Good-bye." We both looked in the stroller. Miranda's eyes were almost closed. Stacy stood up, gathered her things, and pushed the stroller out.

I stayed there for a while. I just wanted to let my reaction emerge instead of rushing it. I felt okay. I'm not sure what I expected, maybe that she'd attack me or get enraged. She had attacked. But she was decent too. Honest. I felt okay afterward. I'm still sad and still angry that I might have caused this family so much grief and hardship. That still is . . . well, it's still upsetting. But I feel okay too. That I responded like a human. She said that I had guts. I haven't felt like a person with guts in a long time. I've felt pretty gutless. I'm proud that I apologized. I'm proud that I listened.

When I told the lawyers they flipped. They made me go over the entire conversation with them three times on the phone. They were enraged that I'd apologized, they felt that the case was locked up until I did that. They're in the process of trying to settle the case right now.

"It sounds like it went well," I said.

"It did go well. Thank you for encouraging me to do that. I didn't feel like a defendant, or a scared girl, or a timid medical student. I felt like a doctor being honest. I felt good inside my own skin."

Session Twenty-eight

A week later Amelia came for her session in shorts and a T-shirt. Her hair looked wet.

"I've been swimming quite a bit. I'm getting into great shape. My plan is to have buns of steel."

"It's good to have a purpose in life," I said. We laughed.

"Speaking of buns, you'll also be happy to know that Anton's rear is once again rousing a response."

"I'm happy to hear that."

Aside from that C-section, you know I haven't touched or been around a pregnant woman in months. On purpose. They remind me of everything that happened, everything I gave up. But they're hard to avoid; it turns out that they're everywhere.

Yesterday I went to the supermarket to do the big shopping. I found everything and got in line. I was staring at the tabloids, just bored, when I noticed that there was a pregnant girl in line behind me. She was Hispanic, a beautiful girl with big brown eyes. I don't know why but I asked her how far along she was. She said she was eight months along and smiled at me, one of those new-mother smiles, and then her face changed and she said, "He's kicking! He's kicking!" and she grabbed my hand and put it on her belly and I could feel the little foot.

"I feel it," I told her. I thought I'd recoil but I didn't. I felt natural.

"Do you? Do you feel it?" she asked me.

"I do." And she held my hand on her belly for a long time.

When I got out to the car I got my groceries into the trunk and sat down in the driver's seat and started bawling. The car must have been 120 degrees but it bubbled out of me. I could barely breathe. I finally went home, drove into my garage, and was unloading the groceries, when I smelled the most foul stench. It smelled like shit. And right away I knew that my mind wouldn't leave me alone. Even though I feel ready to come back, my mind is going to continue to torture me, like when I smelled those alcohol wipes at the bank, or that rancid smell in the nursery. I looked all over for the source of the smell—the bathrooms, the garage. I was frantic, nothing. Then I realized I was humming. This crazy hum. I was losing it.

I felt so defeated, and was trying to figure out what my mind was trying to tell me. What could the smell signify? Is my life shit? Is everything shit? I sat down on the floor in the kitchen, the refrigerator was open, the phone started ringing. And I couldn't move. I was stuck there. The smell was in my hair and my clothes, everywhere.

Then I decided I would just stick to my routines like you taught me. I'd keep doing the things I need to do. Put away the groceries. Bread, cheese, soup. Check the machine for voice mail. There were a couple, I wrote down the messages. Go get the mail. I went out to go down to the street to get the mail when I saw Mr. Amaniani, my next-door neighbor, huddled next to his citrus trees. The stench was even worse outside.

Then I noticed the huge bags. Mr. Amaniani had huge clumps of fertilizer in his hands and he was digging holes around the trees in the caliche, the hard soil, and putting in the fertilizer. Mr. Amaniani is a widower, in his sixties, a loner. His wife had an ovarian tumor and I helped her find an oncologist when she was first having troubles. The smell was terrible. He was wearing a mask. He pulled it down.

"The aroma is strong, eh?" he said to me, with a twinkle. "My apologies, I promise to share the grapefruit of my labors with your family when it ripens, it's too much for me. It looks like nothing, but this tree produces the most spectacular fruit. Isn't it amazing that something that nutritious starts as excrement?"

I started laughing. I was so relieved that the smell was real. "It's not so bad," I lied to him.

"If you want, you can stand here with me and wait for the fruit to come in. Or you can go get your mail. Feed your family. I'll stay here and when it's ready, I'll bring it over, how's that?"

I told him that sounded great.

I don't usually do this sort of thing, but it felt right. Two weeks later, Amelia and I made the long walk up to Blackett's Ridge. There was another monsoon the night before and the air was light; every detail in the mountains was clear: Finger Rock, the saddle, Bear Canyon. We started in the Sabino Canyon parking lot and walked that first flat mile toward Bear Canyon. Then we crossed the few brick bridges, stopped to watch the running water beneath them, and then started the ascent. We walked quietly. She led, confidently striding up the thin path. The ridge has three false peaks, three spots on the hike when you think you're at the top but aren't. She told me this while we rested after the switchbacks. "Apropos, huh?" she laughed, both of us breathless.

We walked on and eventually, after ninety minutes, we were there, unmistakably. Forty-five hundred feet. Surrounded by air and view, this way the Santa Catalinas unfolding and rising, that way the Thimble and its long rock walls, and to the south, Tucson expanding all the way to the Santa Rita peaks in the distance.

The cliff swallows were up there, diving through the air with teasing swoops. She quickly pulled Miranda's heart rate strip out of her pocket and set it on the ground. She took out a lighter and had trouble getting a flame.

"Wouldn't you know it? The lighter is childproof," she said, concentrating.

It took a little while to get it going, but then there was the thinnest thread of smoke rising off a corner.

She was hunched over the strip, holding her hands to protect the flame when she looked up at me. She smiled. I could smell creosote, and a hint of jasmine. The monitor strip burned quickly, and then she stood, hugged me quickly, and we started walking back down.

Postscript

It's been a year since that heart tone strip burned. The number of physicians in my caseload has tripled. Dr. Sorvino and I have continued meeting, but most of our work is in the past.

The case was settled six weeks after their conversation. Stacy got $250,000, all of it paid by the malpractice carrier. Amelia returned to work two weeks after that. She works half-time now and sees about a third of the patients she once did. Patients still fight to get in to see her. She and Jay were in marital therapy briefly; they are doing well now and are contemplating parenthood. She still has the occasional nightmare and practices medicine more defensively than she'd like, but both are slowly improving. She describes herself as "mostly happy" but completely authentic.

Three months after the hike up Blackett's Ridge, Terry and I went to Colorado for a few weeks. On his first attempt, our new physician was successful.

Terry is carrying a girl.